KIDS AT WORK

Kids at Work

Latinx Families Selling Food
on the Streets of Los Angeles

Emir Estrada

NEW YORK UNIVERSITY PRESS
New York

NEW YORK UNIVERSITY PRESS
New York
www.nyupress.org
© 2019 by New York University
All rights reserved

A previous version of chapter 5 was published as Emir Estrada and Pierrette Hondagneu-Sotelo, "Living the Third Shift: Latina Adolescent Street Vendors in Los Angeles," in *Immigrant Women Workers in the Neoliberal Age*, edited by Nilda Flores-González, Anna Romina Guevarra, Maura Toro-Morn, and Grace Chang (Urbana: University of Illinois Press, 2013), 144–63.

Library of Congress Cataloging-in-Publication Data
Names: Estrada, Emir, author.
Title: Kids at work : Latinx families selling food on the streets of Los Angeles / Emir Estrada.
Description: New York : New York University Press, [2019] | Series: Latina/o sociology series | Includes bibliographical references and index.
Identifiers: LCCN 2018037664 | ISBN 9781479811519 (cl : alk. paper) | ISBN 9781479873708 (pb : alk. paper)
Subjects: LCSH: Street-food vendors—California—Los Angeles—Case studies. | Child labor—California—Los Angeles—Case studies. | Latin Americans—California— Los Angeles—Social conditions. | Hispanic American families—California—Los Angeles— Social conditions. | Immigrant families—California—Los Angeles. | Children of illegal aliens— California—Los Angeles.
Classification: LCC HF5459.U6 E88 2019 | DDC 331.3/18—dc23
LC record available at https://lccn.loc.gov/2018037664

New York University Press books are printed on acid-free paper, and their binding materials are chosen for strength and durability. We strive to use environmentally responsible suppliers and materials to the greatest extent possible in publishing our books.
Manufactured in the United States of America
10 9 8 7 6 5 4 3 2 1
Also available as an ebook

To the two most important mujeres *in my life:*

Para la Maestra Leonor Estrada Rivas
Por ser una madre, maestra, y mujer ejemplar

Para mi hija Xitlali
Porque es bello ser tu mamá

CONTENTS

Introduction: Working with *la Familia*   1

1. "If I Don't Help Them, Who Will?": The Working Life   23

2. Street Vending in Los Angeles: A Cultural
   Economic Innovation   43

3. Working Side by Side: Intergenerational Family Dynamics   64

4. Making a Living Together: Communal Family Obligation
   Code and Economic Empathy   83

5. "I Get Mad and I Tell Them, 'Guys Could Clean, Too!'"   99

6. Street Violence: "I Don't Put Up a Fight Anymore"   116

7. "My Parents Want Me to Be Something in Life, Like a
   Lawyer or a Hero"   129

   Conclusion: "So, Are You Saying Children Should Work?"   147

   Acknowledgments   161

   Notes   165

   Bibliography   183

   Index   195

   About the Author   207

Introduction

Working with la Familia

Martha's alarm rings at six o'clock every morning. During the week, she wakes up early in order to make it to her private Catholic high school on time, but every Saturday and Sunday, she wakes up at dawn to sell corn on the cob, cut-up fruit, churros, and shaved ice, commonly known in Spanish as *raspados*. Martha, now eighteen years old, began street vending with her undocumented parents when she was seven. At first, she and her younger sister Sofia sold food outside their local church with their mother. Later, when Martha turned thirteen, she and her sister started street vending by themselves. I met Martha during the summer of 2008 while she was street vending at a park. By then she had been street vending for eleven years, five of which were on her own. I bought and ate a diced mango on a stick that Martha cut—with great agility—in a way that resembled a flower in bloom dressed with lemon juice and sprinkled with powdered chili and salt. As I nibbled on the mango, I told Martha about my study and she agreed to an interview for the following Friday after school. The interview took place in the backyard of her parents' house. After the interview, she challenged me to street vend with her so that I could get a real sense of her life, and so I did.[1]

The first time I went street vending with Martha, the weather forecast had promised a typical sunny summer day in Southern California. I arrived at her house at six o'clock in the morning. Martha's mother, Lourdes, greeted me at the door, and the warmth from a large pot of freshly steamed corn permeated the house with an earthy aroma. Lourdes told me that Martha and Sofia had helped strip off the leaves from the ear of corn the night before. They had also placed the corn inside the large pot, ready for Lourdes as she turned on the stove early the next morning before the day of street vending. While Lourdes continued explaining their evening routine, she offered me a cup of coffee. I enjoyed the coffee and Lourdes's story while we waited for her daughters to wake up and get dressed. When Martha exited her bedroom, I was sitting on a tall stool near the stove drinking my coffee. She glanced at me with her intimidating side look and said with a smirk, "Is that what you are wearing?" Holding my mug with my two hands, I discreetly scanned myself, noticing my sandals, blue jeans, and a spaghetti strap turquoise blouse. "You're gonna get burned, girl," she exclaimed. She was right—that day I got the worst sunburn of my life, and I actually think Martha enjoyed telling me "I told you so" at the end of the day. In contrast, Martha dressed appropriately with a flannel shirt, blue jeans, tennis shoes, and a Dodger hat that protected her from the sun and kept her long wavy black hair in a ponytail off her face and away from the food she will sell. Her younger sister Sofia wore something similar.

For the next hour, I saw the entire family prepare for their long day of street vending work. Both Martha and Sofia took turns carrying crates full of mangos, boxes of canned soda, small bags of peanuts that they bagged the night before, and several plastic milk containers now full of colorful concentrated syrups for the raspados. Meanwhile, Martha's father, Javier, hooked a small trailer onto the truck containing three street vending carts: one for him, another for Martha, and the last one for Sofia.[2] This has been a typical weekend morning routine for Martha and Sofia since they were little girls.

Linger around the streets of Los Angeles and Boyle Heights and you will notice, as I did, that many children like Martha and Sofia are vending with their immigrant parents. These children are full-time students, but they are also economic co-contributors in the household. They relax, play, and socialize when business is slow, but for the most part, they are busy charging customers, taking food orders, heating up tortillas, running errands to the store, and translating for parents. I also saw them do work at home at different times of the day and night, as they cut, bag, sort, and cook the food they will later sell. For example, fourteen-year-old Leticia is in charge of making seven types of sauces, sixteen-year-old Sofia bags peanuts and the churros she makes at home, and twelve-year-old Salvador cooks goat meat in his backyard while his mother and sister Norma make the sauces and dice onions in the kitchen.

The role of child street vendors in the United States remains largely uninvestigated. The children of immigrants experience additional adult responsibilities that are often taken for granted or are rendered invisible. For example, children of immigrants play key roles in their families' social integration into their adopted communities. We know how children serve as cultural and language *brokers* for their parents.[3] Scholars have also demonstrated the collective agency of undocumented immigrant youth to organize for their legal and social rights.[4] What these scholars have missed, however, is the quiet, quotidian economic agency of the children of undocumented immigrants, who, through their work with *la familia*, are helping their families achieve economic incorporation, and simultaneously improving their own economic futures and life chances.

This phenomenon is not unique to street vending families in Los Angeles. As we zoom out to other Latinx occupations, we can see that Latinx children and adolescents working alongside their immigrant parents in informal sector occupations are both ubiquitous and seemingly invisible. We see this pattern not only in street vending, but also paid domestic work, gardening, garment production, and seasonal farm work.[5] All of these occupations are part of the informal sector of unregulated or semi-regulated income-generating jobs. In this book, I use "informal sector" and "informal economy" interchangeably, and I define this concept as "all income-earning activities that are not regulated by the state in social environments where similar activities are regulated."[6] In this sector, these children and their work experiences remain invisible in the already invisible occupation of their parents.

In *Kids at Work*, I bring the stories of these children to light. This is the first book to look at the participation of child street vendors in the United States. The children portrayed in this book are the children of undocumented Latinx immigrants who are relegated to street vending because their parents lack opportunities to work in the formal sector of the economy. On the streets of Los Angeles, California, they help their parents prepare and sell ethnic food from México and Central America, such as pozole, pupusas, tamales, champurrado, tacos, and tejuino (a corn-based drink).

Shedding light on the experiences of children in this occupation highlights the complexities and nuances of family relations when children become economic co-contributors. This book is primarily based on the point of view of street vending children, and it is complemented by my interviews with their parents. I spent three years with various

Figure I.1. Family working together.

street vending families and conducted formal sit-down interviews with children and their parents separately. To be candid, gaining their trust was not easy. At first, parents thought I was a health inspector, a police officer, or a social worker; some even thought I was their competition trying to steal their recipes in order to open my own street vending stand. I conducted a total of sixty-six interviews with the youth and their parents. I recruited the children and their families while they worked on the street. After I spent time with one family, moreover, they usually referred me to friends who also sold food on the street with their children.

This snowball method of recruitment was very effective for meeting new families, but it was still difficult to gain their trust after the initial introduction was made. When I first met the families, I told them about my study while I purchased and ate their food. I also told them about my experience working as a young girl, and sometimes that helped gain their trust. One mother told me that she agreed to an interview only because I ate her food. She assured me that a police officer or a health inspector would not have eaten the food she and her daughter sold.[7]

The children I interviewed were between the ages of ten and eighteen. I also interviewed fifteen mothers and three fathers. In addition to interviewing parents and children who work together, I have also included a small comparative sample of five street vending families whose children are not involved in the street vending business.

Most of the time, I spent with families or on my own conducting field observations at two different street vending sites I call La Cumbrita and El Callejón, in Boyle Heights, a small neighborhood in Los Angeles

Table I.1. Descriptive Table of Participants

Study Sample (*n*=66)

Sample Characteristics	Youth	Parents	Youth Comparison Group	Parents Comparison Group	TOTAL YOUTH SAMPLE
	n=38	*n*=18	*n*=5	*n*=5	*n*=43
Age					
10–13	10	---	1	---	11
14–15	5	---	2	---	7
16–17	10	---	2	---	12
18	10	---	---	---	10
19–23	3	---	---	---	3
36–39	---	8	---	---	---
40–49	---	9	---	4	---
50–52	---	1	---	1	---
Gender					
Female	27	15	5	3	32
Male	11	3	0	2	11
Nationality					
México	31	16	5	5	36
El Salvador	3	2	---	---	3
Guatemala	3	---	---	---	3
Honduras	1	---	---	---	1
Citizenship Status					
Undocumented	10	15	0	3	10
U.S. Citizens	28	1	5	---	33
Legal Residents	---	2	---	2	---

Figure I.2. Sociologist in the field: Dr. Estrada
helping the families during her fieldwork.

where 95 percent of the population is Latinx.[8] I conducted observations
in three different arenas of social life: (1) the work site while children
worked alongside their parents or on their own; (2) at various social
events; and (3) in their homes. At first, I blended in with the customers
and stood along the sidewalk eating food from paper plates or comfortably sat on a folding chair in front of a small television provided by one
of the street vendors. Later, I helped the families by running errands
to the store. I also cut fruit and assisted customers while the children
took bathroom breaks or socialized with their cousins and friends. Some
families also street vended outside these two sites. For example, a few
families sold their food at local parks, near freeway entrances, and outside churches. I also conducted observations in these locations. I shadowed five families for two months at a time in many social settings.

Because I spent time in these two street vending sites for three years,
I kept in touch with the children and their families at different times and

saw little kids turn into young teenagers and some teenagers turn into adults. This gave me opportunities to see how their involvement in the family business shifted and evolved over time. For disclosure, the interview data I present in this book are from the time the interview took place. All of the quotes are presented in English, but I tried to maintain their original tone and voice when possible. The quotes translated from Spanish to English are in their original form in the endnotes of each chapter.

Why Focus on Child Vendors?

I began this study with a personal interest in the subject of children and work. As a young girl, I worked with my parents in both México and the United States. I saw working with my family as something normal and as my responsibility to help my parents. When I lived in México, during my formative years, I worked at a small, family-owned grocery store, or *tienda de abarrotes*. While I helped my mother run the store as she taught at a local academy, my father worked as a parking attendant in Los Angeles, California. Later, when I turned seventeen, my father unexpectedly passed away from a stroke. My mother, along with my brothers and me, decided to move to the United States due to our financial dependence on my father's remittances. Ironically, my father earned more as a parking attendant in the United States than my mother did as a teacher in México. Once in the United States, I also worked with my mother temporarily when she cleaned houses before she landed steady employment at a factory, where she worked for almost eighteen years. Aside from working with my mother, I always held other jobs, and sold my own artwork to help cover some of the household costs as well as my own educational expenses.[9]

Furthermore, when I was a college student at Long Beach City College and later at the University of California, Los Angeles (UCLA), I became interested in topics related to immigrant families. Yet my story was conspicuously absent from the many books assigned in my sociology and Chicana/o studies courses. Some readings, however, did stand out as important correctives to this oversight. *Doméstica*, by Pierrette Hondagneu-Sotelo, allowed me to see the experiences of women like my mother who worked in informal low-wage work.[10] Later, the work by

Marjorie F. Orellana on the role of children of immigrants as language brokers began to highlight the contributions of children in immigrant families as translators.[11] Reading their scholarship made me feel as if I also had a place in academia. I fantasized about the day that I too would also share the story of children who work with *la familia* just like I did.

Now I have a Ph.D. in sociology from the University of Southern California and I teach courses on immigration at Arizona State University in the School of Human Evolution and Social Change. I have spent my educational career studying Latinx families with a specific focus on children and their role in the family, including their economic role. My profession as a university professor also allows me to meet students from diverse socioeconomic classes and racial and ethnic backgrounds; I enjoy learning about their childhood experiences when I teach about children and work. During these lessons, I learn that many of my students have worked when they were young. Some worked as babysitters, tutors, and lifeguards, and some interned with their professional parents. For example, in one of my classes, when I asked my students to share about their work experience growing up, James, a White male student from the Midwest, shared how he worked at his family's farm and how he now owns his own business and helps provide for his dying mother.[12] Holding back tears, he confided with the class that after his mother was diagnosed with cancer, he took on more responsibilities related to the household expenses. Although this was difficult for him, it was most difficult for his mom because she had been accustomed to being the one who cared for her son and not the other way around. James left class early that day, almost immediately after sharing his experience with the class.

Jordan told us that he worked as a lifeguard when he was younger. Jordan recognized that the connections he had with his coaches helped him land this fun and well-remunerated summer job. Similarly, Kathy was very proud of the work she did at a law firm. She too found this job through a personal recommendation from her father. Yet not all students in my classes had these same types of social networks.

Other students cleaned houses with their parents, did farm work, worked in family-owned businesses, helped maintain manicured lawns with their fathers, and sold merchandise at local swap meets; others, such as the children interviewed for this book, sold food and other goods on the streets. These were typically the experiences of my Latinx students. One semester, my student César, who is visually impaired, stood up to share his experience working as a little kid. He told us that he grew up selling mops and brooms with his parents. From a young age, he learned how to sell. He is now married, has children of his own, and is furthering his education at Arizona State. As he works toward his degree, he continues to sell mops and brooms to help support his family.

My student Isabel, who had recently graduated high school, told the class that she used to clean houses with her mother prior to moving for college. She told us about a time she bumped into her classmate one day she and her mother were cleaning a house in the nice side of town. Isabel and her mother were each carrying a bucket full of cleaning supplies when Isabel's classmate dashed out of her house with her friends. It was a beautiful sunny Saturday morning, Isabel remembered. A nice day to enjoy out with her friends, but she had to work with her mother instead. "She didn't even recognize me," she murmured. "I mean, it's great that she didn't"—Isabel laughed and so did the class—"but I felt so embarrassed," she continued in a low voice, "to know that I was my classmate's maid and she didn't even recognize me." The class's laughter quickly came to a stop as people recognized the seriousness in Isabel's voice. Later, Isabel shared with me that she was one of just two Latinas in her Advanced Placement history class, and throughout high school she continued helping her mother. She graduated from high school with honors and wants to become a professor one day. Another student, Reina, waited for me after class to tell me that she used to street vend with her mom and was planning on studying law after finishing her bachelor's degree. I usually hear these types of stories from my Latinx students, many of whom grew up poor. I assume that they feel comfortable with me because I am also Latina, but perhaps it is the fact that I am open about my childhood work experience when I teach on this subject.

These may seem like polar examples of childhood work. To some degree they are. However, when we list on the whiteboard lessons from their work, the lists from these two groups are very similar. Students say that they learn time management skills and the value of the dollar, and some say that work keeps them out of trouble. A major difference comes when I ask students what they do with their earnings. Students in my first category usually worked to have extra spending money, while the students in the second category usually worked to help with the family household expenses. Another difference is deeply rooted in the nature of the work they do. Often, students in the second category do not define the work they do as "real" work; rather, they see it as helping the family. Others, such as Isabel and Reina, see it as stigmatized work that they seldom chose to talk about in public, especially not in a school setting where they take a subordinate class position among their more affluent classmates.

I highlight these personal classroom observations because they mirror the literature that points to one type of work experience as normative in the United States while the other is not.[13] It is more acceptable when children work to gain experience and earn a little bit of pocket money and less so when they do it to help with the family's economic survival. In the United States, the association of children and work has been paradoxical since the turn of the twentieth century. Sociologist Viviana Zelizer analyzed the transformation of childhood that took place in the United States between 1870 and 1930.[14] She used the term *useful child* to refer to the nineteenth-century child who actively contributed to the family's economic survival through labor.[15] She notes the emergence in the twentieth century of the productively "useless" yet emotionally "priceless" child.[16] The dominant view is that school and work are antithetical spheres. The notion of childhood that prevails in most postindustrial societies is that children must be educated, "developed," and "raised."[17] You might recall my student James and his mother, and how uncomfortable she felt receiving financial help from her son, even though he was already a young adult. In fact, children's protected, sacred status defines modernity, an era characteristic of order and structure and a movement away from tradition.[18] As one scholar has observed, "The dissociation of childhood from the performance of valued work is considered a yardstick of modernity."[19]

However, divergent meanings of childhood also coexist in a given time period and in the same location.[20] Academic researchers confirm this observation. Antonella Invernizzi found that in Andean rural communities in Peru, the "work done by children is much valued and seen as a means of taking an active part in family and community life."[21] In contrast, the middle classes in the urban regions "see the child's daily life as being geared exclusively to education and play."[22] Similar to what

Invernizzi found in Peru, anthropologist Tobias Hecht distinguishes between two ways of experiencing childhood in northeastern Brazil. He refers to children who do not work as having "nurtured childhoods" of protected freedom and play. In contrast, poor children, who are expected to work from an early age and contribute to the production and income of the household, experience "nurturing childhoods."[23] Nurturing childhoods are common in developing nations like Brazil, Peru, and México, but they are supposed to be anomalies in postindustrial societies such as the United States,[24] where children are still defined as "emotionally priceless" and a child is expected to have a nurtured childhood.[25] Today, the general consensus is that in the United States, children and teens require parental protection and economic support, and if children do work, the normative view is that it should be for their own pocket money or savings and not to help support the family.[26] What happens, however, when many of us cannot meet these normative childhood standards?

The reality is that these normative childhood standards have been difficult to uphold for struggling American families as well. History shows us that in times of economic crisis, American children also work with *la familia*. The Great Depression of 1929 is a quintessential example of this paradox. Sociologist Glen H. Elder Jr. shows that despite the social expectation that American fathers should be the sole breadwinners, extreme unemployment rates during the Great Depression made it difficult for most men to uphold this role. This reality often had repercussions for the rest of the family, as wives and children worked outside the home to help make ends meet. In his book *Children of the Great Depression,* Elder sheds light on how American children juggled school and part-time jobs such as "newspaper carrier, baby sitter, janitorial assistance, store clerk, and delivery agent."[27] The wages for these types of work were low, but the extra earnings helped supplement the family income.[28] Since then, some children in the United States have continued to do work outside the home.

There are classic examples everywhere you look. For example, Shirley Temple, Elizabeth Taylor, Drew Barrymore, the Jacksons, and Selena Gomez are iconic celebrities of different generations, but they are also popular examples of child workers. Today, major television networks such as the Disney Channel, Nickelodeon, Sprout, and PBS provide entertainment not only for children, but almost strictly by children as the main actors, whereas adults merely appear in the periphery of certain shows.[29]

As a polar opposite, we can also find other not so visible examples of child workers. The literature on the ethnic economy has shed light on the experience of children in businesses owned by ethnic minorities. The majority of these studies have focused on the role of children in Korean and Chinese family-owned businesses in the formal economy, such as restaurants, Laundromats, and liquor stores.[30] In contrast to Korean and Chinese immigrants that have high rates of business ownership and are hailed as entrepreneurially oriented groups, other immigrant groups, such as Mexicans, exhibit low levels of entrepreneurship in the United States.[31]

Self-employment has been an important avenue for the economic advancement of immigrant groups such as Cubans and Koreans and has been a key factor in the educational success of the second generation.[32] Current studies reveal that family-owned businesses can serve as springboards for the children of Mexican immigrants as they have for Koreans and for immigrants in the past—including Italians, Jews, Asian Indians, and Middle Easterners.[33] However, as sociologist Zulema Valdez points out in her book *The New Entrepreneurs*, it is not at all clear whether ethnic entrepreneurship among disadvantaged Mexican-origin immigrant parents provides a similar prospect of economic mobility and success among their second-generation children.

When compared to the Chinese and Korean children of quintessential ethnic entrepreneurs, the Latinx children in this study are at a disadvantage because their parents are more likely to experience a negative reception within the larger society and a vulnerable social location associated with lower levels of education, undocumented status, low English language proficiency and high poverty rates. Operating under these intersecting disadvantages, many first-generation Latinx immigrants and some of their children have turned to street vending as an economic strategy. The Latinx children in this study are intricately involved in their families' street vending businesses, performing work on the street that has been deemed inappropriate or dangerous for most children. According to Loukaitou-Sideris and Ehrenfeucht's study on the use of Los Angeles sidewalks, "children were common participants in sidewalk activities, but their presence became an indicator of disorder and neglect, which allowed the state to intervene in their care."[34] The common opinion was, and is still today, that the streets are not the proper place for children. However, the children in this study work in these highly visible spaces and are exposed to customers, urban traffic, and government officials, such as the police, health inspectors, and social workers, and they sometimes confront anti-immigrant xenophobia and racism. So, what can we learn from street vending Latinx families?

Mutually Supportive Children and Parents

I invite the reader to understand the children in this book and their family work dynamics beyond static idealized notions of what childhood and families—specifically, immigrant families—should be. This study challenges the dualistic view of children as *economically useful* or *emotionally priceless* or as experiencing "nurturing" or "nurtured" childhoods. The childhood period of the children in this book is fluid, situational, and context-based. The children in this book are in the intersection of these two polarized forms of childhood ideals and are mutually protective and supportive. The children's role in the family shifts depending on gender, age, need within the family, and the needs of children themselves. These families remind us that childhood is socially and culturally constructed and its definition continues to vary not only over time and geographical location, but also within one time and in one geographical location.[35]

Childhood is not static; it is constantly challenged, renegotiated, and transformed as structural, economic, and familial needs also change. Let us recall my classroom experience once more, where in one time and place, my students shared with each other different types of childhood work experiences. Should I have said to my students that one childhood upbringing was better than the other? Of course not. Rather, this exercise helps us understand how an intersectionality perspective is useful to seeing how different aspects of our identities, such as our race, class, and gender, can take greater or lesser salience in different contexts, situations, activities, relationships, and even stages of our lives.

For the last thirty years, intersectionality theory has helped us understand the life chances of people who are disadvantaged by race, class, and gender.[36] Before 1980, the experiences of women of color were misrepresented, marginalized, and often ignored in the feminist literature dominated by highly educated White women.[37] Similarly, in studies of race, women of color were just as marginalized since "men of color stood as the universal racial subject."[38] Intersectionality has also proven useful in the analyses of other systems of domination such as sexuality, immigration status, and racialization of first- and second-generation immigrant children and adolescents.[39]

The children in this book experience compounded disadvantages stemming from their parents' marginalized social location. First, classic intersection—race, class, and gender—added to unauthorized status, informal enterprise, and the stigma associated with street vending, presents parents with many challenges as they seek to raise a family in the United States. Second, vending children experience their own set of hardships associated with race, class, and gender, in addition to unpaid or low-wage family labor, informal work, stigma, and limited childhood freedom and safety. Last, the experience of children in this study highlights their own agency, resilience, and self-made resources in the context of street vending work in Los Angeles. Street vending children cannot be boxed in as *emotionally priceless* children as Zelizer once noticed, but their childhood is not defined as "nurturing" as Hecht observed with working-class children in Brazil.[40]

The experience of child street vendors bridges intersectionality theory, social capital theory, and the socialization of childhood and brings to light the hidden resources that are overshadowed by segmented assimilation theory, the leading theory that has been used to understand the experience of post-1965 immigrants and their children.[41]

Segmented assimilation theory builds on classic assimilation theory, which emerged in the early 1940s. Classical assimilation theory, developed by sociologists in the Chicago School, was once seen as forward-thinking because it challenged the racist ideologies in the eugenics movement, which portrayed race as deterministic and biologically fixed.[42] Eurocentric in nature, assimilation theory advanced a progressive idea that European immigrants who were at one point not considered White could become part of the American mainstream. This theory was myopic about the life chances of immigrants who came from non-European countries. Segmented assimilation theory, first developed by Alejandro Portes and Min Zhou, was groundbreaking because it provided a theoretical framework to explain the incorporation experience of immigrants of color, especially those from Latin America, Asia, and the Caribbean.[43]

Segmented assimilation theory brought a much-needed analysis to the context of reception, such as the U.S. racism against immigrants of color, and the level of co-ethnic ties in the receiving country. Portes and Zhou also highlight the importance of the changing structure of the economy. For example, they contrast the factory and industrial jobs once available for European immigrants, which offered ladders for upward mobility, to the growing service economy, which does not offer a living wage or job security. The assumption is that informal sector jobs are always exploitive. However, a new body of literature has shown how seemingly impoverished jobs can be viable platforms of social mobility.[44]

Measuring "upward" or "downward" mobility is beyond the scope of this research.[45] This study shows the processes by which children and parents who work together as street vendors develop strategies that buffer against downward mobility. This research challenges the top-down or parent-to-child acculturation model consistent with normative American beliefs of how children should be socialized. Children are normally thought to be dependent, socialized recipients of "cultural capital" from their parents.[46] In the immigration literature, as Barrie Thorne and Marjorie Faulstich Orellana have indicated, children are often framed as dependent "luggage," or something that parents simply bring with them.[47] Children are not viewed as full social actors and continue to be relegated to separate spheres of family and school that are largely excluded from paid work. This top-down, passive model is also present in segmented assimilation theory, which is problematic because it overlooks the resources that exist in working-class Latinx families, especially those resources that come from children.

This study looks at the role of the family and children in the context of family and work and sheds light on these hidden resources. These hidden resources shine through when we use an intersectionality approach to understand the lives and experiences of child street vendors in Los Angeles.[48] Rather than framing the work that child street vendors are doing as an indicator of deficiency or pathology, though, my analysis reveals that these young ethnic entrepreneurs play a key role in their families' economic integration into the United States. Their work enables them to help provide food, clothes, and shelter to all of their family members, while it also enables them to pay for their own school supplies and in some cases their tuition-based, private Catholic education.

My goal is to highlight the agency of the children and parents who made this book possible by sharing their life stories with me at the micro level, while also zooming out to see how the narratives of these street vending families fit into a larger narrative about immigration, incorporation, and race relations in the United States. Instead of asking, Why do these families choose to street vend?, I ask the following questions: (1) What social conditions did these families encounter in the United States that enabled or constrained them to do so? (2) What role do children play in the street vending family business? (3) Does children's work in the family alter parent-child relations in the household? (4) How do immigrant families navigate integration into the United States when their work places them so publicly and visibly in opposition to the country's laws and their social expectations?

We can think that street vending and child labor are anachronistic and that those are economic strategies that were supposed to disappear with modernization. However, their existence points to social problems that have systematically failed these immigrant families. The fact that a preindustrial form of economic family organization has emerged in our postindustrial Los Angeles makes this study so interesting. School, work, and play are not antithetical spheres for working-class children from México and Central America whose parents immigrated in the late 1980s and early 1990s and have remained undocumented and in the shadows of the U.S. economy. The children in this book *must* take an active role in family reproduction activities because their own labor contributions are what make it possible for their families to survive the structural economic and employment barriers they face in the lower sector of the economy.

The children interviewed for this book are a small sample of the 5.1 million children under age eighteen—both U.S. citizens and noncitizens— who are growing up with at least one undocumented parent.[49] They are the Latinx youth who are growing up in households where parents have less or no access to jobs that are safe, unionized, and offering a living wage. The Mexican-origin workforce was once overrepresented in agricultural work, but today it is predominately an urban population.[50] In this urban context, a great number of Latinxs are highly concentrated in occupations such as construction laborers, cement masons, roofers, dishwashers, painters, janitors, gardeners, and sewing operators. Latinas work as packagers, graders and sorters of agricultural products, maids, housekeeping cleaners, and sewing machine operators.[51] For these reasons, it seems unfathomable that even though Latinx people constitute a significant portion of the U.S. labor force, they are also a group with a high unemployment rate. According to the Bureau of Labor Statistics, the Latinx unemployment rate in 2010 was 12.8 percent, falling to 5.8 percent in 2016. Nonetheless, Latinx unemployment remains above its pre-recession minimum of 5.0 percent of 2006.

Many new immigrants from México and Central America are relegated to working in the informal sector of the economy or in low-wage jobs because they are undocumented, educationally disadvantaged, do not speak English, and lack the skills needed to find employment in the formal sector.[52] *Los Angeles Times* reporter Hector Becerra notes, "In the hierarchy of immigrant occupations, street vending is near the bottom. It is for those who can't find work at a factory or in construction or who think that maybe they'll do better working for themselves."[53] Increasingly, more undocumented immigrants are turning to street vending. According to a 2016 report, there are over fifty thousand street vendors in the Los Angeles area—a number that grew exponentially since 1990, when the street vending population was estimated at six thousand.[54]

Roadmap of the Book

Chapter 1, "'If I Don't Help Them, Who Will?': The Working Life," provides the readers with a clear sense of what is physically involved in this line of work for children and parents. In this chapter, I describe what children do on a typical day, what kinds of jobs children do, how old they are when they start working, and how these different tasks are initiated. I identified three different work patterns for working children: (1) vacation work, (2) weekends only, and (3) school nights and weekends. Some children of street vendors also opt out of street vending altogether. In this chapter, we see that children are nurtured by their parents and also nurture their parents. Children's voices and desires for material goods, combined with the structural circumstances that push the families to street vend, inform the ongoing sociological debate on structure and agency through the children's perspective.

Chapter 2, "Street Vending in Los Angeles: A Cultural Economic Innovation," situates the study historically in the context of U.S. and Mexican migration and traces the formation of the street vending economy in urban centers in México and in U.S. cities such as Los Angeles and New York. This chapter demonstrates that street vending across the borders is linked to macro structural forces and is not solely derivative of a Latinx cultural practice. This chapter also highlights the historical precedent of street vending in the United States, as opposed to portraying the work as a direct cultural transplant from Latin America. The Latinx street vendors in Los Angeles immigrated to a society where street vending had been an economic strategy since the early nineteenth century. In New York, ethnic groups such as Jews, Italians, and Greeks dominated street vending, and in Los Angeles, Chinese men sold vegetables on the streets. Vendors in the nineteenth century in New York and Los Angeles also experienced great opposition from community members, businessmen, and government. They also experienced discrimination based on their economic activity, ethnicity, and immigration status. This chapter also notes that as a result of political turmoil, organized collective action, and the rise of a foodie culture based on "authenticity," attitudes toward street vendors are becoming more sympathetic and respectful, leading to the decriminalization of street vending across the state of California.

Chapter 3, "Working Side by Side: Intergenerational Family Dynamics," uncovers the parent-child relations that result when children work alongside their disadvantaged immigrant parents as street vendors, and the ways children understand their social location and that of their parents in this context. This chapter challenges segmented assimilation theory by looking at parent-child work relations. Unlike the parents in this study, all of the children I interviewed speak English and are familiar with American culture and technology, and the majority of the children are also U.S. citizens. These are resources unique to the children and I call these *American generational resources* (AGR). I argue that children in street vending families share power in the household because they contribute to their families' income, and they are involved in business negotiations and decision-making processes. These children and youth speak English and enjoy legal status while most of their parents remain undocumented and are Spanish monolinguals. Segmented assimilation theory contends that this power imbalance in favor of the children could result in *dissonant acculturation.* Contrary to what segmented assimilation theory would predict, parents' authority over their children is not diminished as a result of children's faster acculturation. Rather, parents who work with their children have more control over them because they spend more time with them. In addition, children's AGRs are valued resources by their parents and are frequently useful for the family street vending business.

Chapter 4, "Making a Living Together: Communal Family Obligation Code and Economic Empathy," shows the resiliency that results when children experience their parents' position of oppression, which helps prevent an authority shift in favor of the children. Consequently, the children respect their parents' work efforts and report feeling closer to their parents. As a result of working together, children become keenly aware of the financial household and street vending obligations. I call this *economic empathy* and argue that this level of empathy is born when families develop a *communal family obligation code.* This chapter covers different forms of tensions between children and their parents and how children engage in *family bartering* with their parents. These street vending children are conflicted between their responsibility to help their parents and their desire to enjoy a "normal" childhood. Overall, though, I saw that economic empathy can serve to buffer against dissonant acculturation.

Chapter 5, "'I Get Mad and I Tell Them, "Guys Could Clean Too!",'" underlines how gender shapes the way this study's girls and boys experience this occupation and how the children and the families create gendered expectations as well as strategies for protection. While both boys and girls work alongside their parents on the street, my fieldwork revealed that the daughters of Mexican and Central American street vendors in Los Angeles are more active in street vending with the family than the sons. How do we explain this paradox? A gendered analysis helps explain why girls are compelled into street vending, while boys are allowed to withdraw or minimize their participation. This chapter extends the feminist literature on intersectionality by exploring the world of Latinx teenage street vendors. The analysis in this chapter takes into account gendered expectations not only resulting from the familiar intersecting relations of race, class, and gender, but also as a consequence of age as well as of the inequality of nations that gives rise to particular patterns of international labor migration.

Chapter 6, "Street Violence: 'I Don't Put Up a Fight Anymore,'" turns a familiar story of gendered labor on its head. This chapter adds greater complexity to our notions of male-centered spaces. In this context, women challenge gendered expectations and find the street to be a space of empowerment. The freedom of male privilege leaves men/boys more vulnerable to street violence while vending on the streets of Los Angeles. The presence of women of all ages serves to protect men against violence from other men. As a consequence, families develop gendered strategies to protect sons, which differ from the strategies to protect daughters. The findings challenge the belief that the street is more dangerous for females and more appropriate for males.

Chapter 7, "'My Parents Want Me to Be Something in Life, Like a Lawyer or a Hero,'" shows that all of the parents in this study want their children to go to school and become professionals. The parents use street vending work as a scaring mechanism and motivation to push their children to excel in school as elements of immigrant bargaining. None of the youth want to be street vendors for the rest of their lives. They talked about their educational aspirations in a social justice framework, explaining that their academic goals were motivated by their street vending experience and the inequalities they and their parents experience on the street. Children and parents alike said that work provided valuable lessons and skills that could be used in school, and I observed how work allowed them to create social networks that increased their social capital. I show how their educational and occupational trajectory is shaped by a *collectivist immigrant bargain* framework. Street vending also provides valuable material and educational resources for students, most of which remain invisible.

The book's conclusion, "'So, Are You Saying Children Should Work?,'" tackles an important and controversial question rooted in our normative and privileged notions of childhood life. Should children work to help support the family? In answering this question, the conclusion shows how the social construction of childhood defined as a period of freedom and play has been cemented in the minds of many people for almost a century. Even the families in this book struggled to see their family work arrangement as "normal" and fully acceptable by others. This chapter returns to the initial queries about childhood, family work relations, intergenerational family dynamics, and ethnic entrepreneurship, and asks more questions for future research, keeping as a core analysis the role of children as economic contributors in the family beyond the street vending occupation. *Kids at Work*, in a way, also tells the story of many more first-generation college students of diverse racial backgrounds who did not have a "normal" childhood because they too had to work to help the family.

Next, we will see, from the children's point of view how they decided to work with *la familia*.

1

"If I Don't Help Them, Who Will?"

The Working Life

At the age of fourteen, Joaquín identified an opportunity to earn extra money at his school to help his family. Joaquín's mom was a sewing operator at a clothing factory in Pico Rivera and his father worked as a handyman. They provided for him and his two younger siblings, but as the oldest son, he wanted to help. Although he knew that school policy prohibited him from selling his wares at school, he did it anyway. With his extra backpack full of merchandise, Joaquín would spend recess with his customers, some of whom were also teachers. Joaquín remembered one day when a security guard at his school signaled for him to come over as he was dropping off books at his locker and picking up his "second" backpack. Joaquín's friends looked at him with concern, but Joaquín walked over with confidence as he clutched his second backpack. At the end of the long hallway of metal lockers and blue-and-white checkered tile floor, the tall, muscular security guard waited for him with two dollars in hand. Joaquín took the money and, in exchange, gave him two small bags of chips and routinely asked whether he wanted Tapatio hot sauce.

Eighteen-year-old Joaquín laughed when he told me this suspenseful story in the living room of his house to explain his first experience vending food. His mother, Rosa, quietly shook her head and tried to control her laughter while she washed dishes in the kitchen. When Joaquín decided to sell chips, his parents were not street vendors, but one day he simply came up with the idea and told his mom, "Quisiera vender papas en la escuela" (I would like to sell chips at school)—and so he did. Joaquín opted to sell chips at school after seeing the demand for these types of snacks. He recalled, "A lot of people jumped the iron fence to go to the liquor stores" to buy chips because it was

Figure 1.1. Boy making juice.

against school policy to sell chips and sodas inside the school premises. With enthusiasm Joaquín elaborated:

> It got to the point where I had to take two backpacks full of chips because I was making money in high school. They already knew me. Every time I was at school, I was either doing my work or selling during my free time. They would come and they would ask me, "Do you have chips?" Teachers would ask me, too. The security guards used to buy my stuff. We had security in the halls to make sure we didn't do graffiti. They would always see me with my bag and they would buy chips too.

Little did Joaquín know that just one year later, circumstances would push him and his family to seek street vending as a financial alternative when his mother was fired from her job of fifteen years. Rosa had become ill over the years, and finally her employer decided to let her go, citing her undocumented status as a reason. She was fired with neither medical coverage nor severance pay. After Rosa lost her job, her husband became the only breadwinner. Again, Joaquín realized that his family was in need of help, and he chose to street vend with his uncles. Joaquín explained, "I went with my uncles one Saturday and I started vending. I helped them and noticed I made money. I said, I want to do this, and the first thing my uncle asked was if I was embarrassed." Later, Rosa joined her son and together they sold fresh orange, carrot, and beet juice on Saturdays and Sundays at a busy business district in Los Angeles.

Joaquín continued going to high school while street vending and graduated on time. When I met him, he was a freshman at a state university in California, where he was double majoring in sociology and criminology. Sadly, Rosa did not see her son graduate from college. Two years after Rosa and her son started street vending, she was diagnosed with cancer and passed away while I was still conducting my study.

Figure 1.2. Girl making juice.

Joaquín's story exemplifies the structural realities that motivate children to enact their agency in order to find economic solutions to help their parents. While it is well-documented why first-generation immigrants enter street vending, we know less about how and why children like Joaquín get involved in the family street vending business and what role they play in it.[1]

Street vending and family-pooled income strategies requiring that children work *are* common practices in countries like México.[2] A good deal of research on child labor and street vending has been conducted in "developing countries" in Africa, Asia, and Latin America.[3] However, these economic strategies are not uncommon in the United States.[4] What explains this? Some commentators might assume that the children of immigrants engage in street vending in Los Angeles as a cultural holdover from México, their parents' country. I argue that cultural explanations alone cannot explain why children and youth work as street vendors with their immigrant parents in East Los Angeles.

Structural Forces: "If I Don't Help Them, Who Will?"

Joaquín's story is also not unique among the children who shared their stories with me. All of the children in this study cited their parents' lack of legal status and lack of access to formal sector work as the reason why they needed to help make ends meet. For example, Norma, who had just turned eighteen, and her younger brother Salvador, age twelve, faced an important decision to make when their father, Pedro, lost his job soon after they immigrated from México, where they had been living with their mother. Pedro left his wife and two children in México for ten years; in 2009 he used most of his savings to pay a smuggler to bring his family to Boyle Heights, California, where he used to share an apartment with other immigrants from his hometown.

Essentially, this family experienced profound ambivalence. On the one hand, they rejoiced at being together again after a long period of separation, and on the other hand, they faced the harsh economic reality of unemployment. Salvador was only two years old when his father immigrated to the United States; his father-son interactions mostly entailed weekly phone conversations and periodic gifts on his birthday. Norma has more vivid memories of her father before he left, but she too was having a difficult time adjusting to their new family arrangement in the United States.[5] Before he brought his family to the United States, Pedro consistently sent remittances, and both Norma and her little brother Salvador focused entirely on their schoolwork.[6] With his family now in Los Angeles, Norma's father had to find a way to make money fast, but he was unable to find stable employment. When Norma's father had the idea to sell tacos de barbacoa (goat meat), he first asked his children whether they would help. Norma explained,

> My father asked us if we would agree to sell tacos de barbacoa on the street and he also asked if we could help him because they were not going to be able to do this on their own, and we said yes.

This is a typical conversation between parents and children when entering this occupation for the first time. This was unknown territory for all. Parents recognized that children's help was important, and so was their opinion. After seeing the financial needs at home, moreover, the children made a conscientious and mature decision to help.

When I interviewed Norma and her family, they had been selling tacos de barbacoa in front of a junkyard for almost a year. The truck served as an improvised store tent, and a blue tarp stretched from the truck onto a hook Salvador helped screw on the wall. Salvador and his father were in charge of setting up their stand with two large folding tables, chairs for customers, and the skillet to heat up the meat and tortillas. Norma was almost always in charge of heating up the tortillas, while her mother and sometimes her father prepared the tacos and served a traditional birria broth in a separate cup (birria is a spicy stew made from goat meat). Salvador or one of the parents typically handled the cash transactions. During my time with this family, I saw Salvador inside the truck many times taking breaks and playing with his new portable video game, but after my interview with him, I discovered that he did most of his share of the work at home, the night before they street vend. Salvador told me that he is the one in charge of cooking the goat meat in the backyard of their house. When Salvador told me how he cooked the goat meat by himself, I could see a spark of pride, though he seldom looked up when he talked. At the young age of twelve, he had already become a master chef and was excellent at seasoning this traditional dish from their native town in Jalisco. Children like Salvador allowed me to see that there is more to street vending than the actual street work. Much of the work these kids do takes place off the streets because children are involved in many aspects of behind-the-scenes prep work. For example, while Salvador prepares and cooks the goat meat for several hours, Norma chops onions and cilantro inside their kitchen.

While children typically got involved in street vending work after their parents lost their jobs, soon they realized the importance of their work and family contribution. In many cases, refusing to help meant not being able to pay the rent, buy groceries, or even afford their own personal wants and desires such as toys, clothes, and technological gadgets.[7] During my interview with fourteen-year-old Karen, she explained that she had convinced her mother to go back to street vending after she lost her iPod, a gadget that stored digital songs and pictures. In Karen's case, there was no urgent need to street vend, but simply a desire to replace a very expensive toy that cost about $200. Her mother, Olga, recounted, "Entonces ella y yo volvimos a vender porque ella ahorita quiere un iPod" (So she and I started vending again because she now wants an iPod.) Karen understood that it is not just a matter of replacing an expensive gadget; rather, she must literally work to get a new one.[8]

Other children felt that they were the only help their parents had. Flor, who is getting ready to celebrate her *quinceañera* (fifteenth birthday), works with her mother on Saturdays. They sell cosmetics and snacks for pedestrians at a busy commercial area in Los Angeles. When I asked Flor why she helped her mother, she replied, "Si no les ayudo yo, quién?" (If I don't help them, who will?) Children knew that street vending required extra help. Flor highlighted the importance of her work with a taken-for-granted example. She told me, "Sometimes I cover the stand while my mom goes to the bathroom." This was important help, especially when vendors worked for long stretches at a time. As a researcher standing among street venders for hours at a time, even I was called on to help watch over a stand when someone had to run to the restroom at nearby restaurants.

Structural forces such as undocumented status and limited work for parents created opportunities for children to enter this occupation. However, children constantly highlighted their own agency in the process. Many rationalized their participation in street vending work with individual characteristics that, according to them, made them more apt for this type of work.

Which Children Choose to Street Vend in Los Angeles

Independent of structural forces, children in my study told me that their decision to street vend was their own. As a researcher, I was constantly aware of my position and wondered whether their responses were ex post facto rationalizations, and I remained unsure whether this was something they felt compelled to tell me. This is ultimately left for the reader to judge. The degree of their agency or free will was made more compelling when I learned that out of the thirty-eight children interviewed, twenty-four had siblings living at home who did not work with the family regularly or at all. Individual characteristics such as an outgoing personality or having people skills were often cited as good traits for street vendors. The children frequently defined themselves in opposition to their nonworking siblings who were too shy to do this type of work.

Fourteen-year-old Leticia, for example, had two brothers who stayed home while she worked with her mother. Leticia has a bubbly personality and seemed to be happy all the time. Her smile and laughter were very contagious. Their customers and I had a difficult time keeping a straight face when in the company of Leticia and her mom. While they constantly made fun of politicians, regular customers, and themselves, I had to be careful and stay on the periphery; otherwise I would also be fair game for teasing. According to Leticia, both of her brothers lacked her outgoing personality and were simply too shy. She was right. A few times, I saw her brothers quickly stop by their stand only to drop off merchandise for the business, such as tortillas, cheese, or vegetables. Other times, they simply stopped by to pick up food to eat. Leticia did not mind that her brothers did not work with them. Yet she justified her brothers' lack of help:

> The thing with my brothers is that they are very shy. They are not very social like me. I'm loud and talkative. They are calm and they say that I'm crazy. I guess I get it from my mom. She is always talking and always

meets new people and I'm like that too. My brothers are shy. They don't like to meet new people. I guess they are scared. When they come [to the street vending stand] they talk to people, but they just stand looking around like, "What do I do next?" and I'm just, like, "Well, come here, carry this and carry that."

Similarly, Kenya said her older sister Erica simply lacked people skills to street vend. Unlike her, she did not have the personality needed to sell and handle rude customers. Kenya did clarify that Erica will help her mom as a last resort and only if no one else can help her:

Erica has gone [street vending] before, too. Whenever, like, I can't go or my older sister couldn't go. But she is like, "I just don't like it. I can't stand it there." She is like, "I can't sell like you guys do." She doesn't have people skills or anything. She is very nice, but she won't go.

Sometimes children like Erica had siblings who were willing to work and thus shielded them from street vending responsibilities, but not from household work. While Erica could sometimes get away with not street vending, she often stayed home and helped with the household chores. There was certainly a gender dynamic at play, since girls who opted not to street vend—unlike boys—could not opt out of household work (see chapter 5). It is important to underscore that the girls in these families are doing critical housework and social reproductive labor. Although most of the sociology of family and work, as well as feminist literature, assumes that this work is carried out by adult women, here it is daughters who are carrying a big load, often in addition to the street vending.[9]

When I interviewed the parents, they reiterated that only those children who wanted to help did so because it was an optional activity for children. José described his children's willingness to help:

It's work without being work. It's helping the family, but in a different way because it's optional. . . . Well, we always ask our kids if they want to come with me and if they say yes, I bring them. It's like when we go to the park. If you say, do you want to go to the park, and they say let's go, then we go. [Author's translation]

José's children were interviewed separately and both echoed his views about street vending. When I asked his fourteen-year-old daughter Chayo whether she had to street vend with her father, she thoughtfully replied, "No, I don't have to come." Both Chayo and her younger brother Juan did not feel obligated to help their father, but both knew that not helping also meant missing out on the family business earnings of twenty dollars each. Juan, who is about to turn ten, said, "I like helping my family and all because I want them to do me a birthday party. . . . That's why I'm trying to earn money to do it myself."

For some children, the decision to help was, as José stated earlier, like deciding to go to the park. Linda and Susana, two sisters who sold pupusas with their parents, agreed to help in a very nonchalant manner as well. Linda explained, "One day my mother just told us if we wanted to come and sell. We were like, 'Sure, we don't have anything else good to do.'" According to Susana, she and her sister used to "take turns" going with their mother when they sold pupusas door-to-door before they sold at La Cumbrita, one of the street vending sites where I conducted observations. Negotiations over who would help street vend were often done among siblings themselves. While some rationalize being better fit for the job, others exchanged household work obligations with sisters who could stay home to clean, cook, and care for younger siblings. Those who were stuck or opted for street vending work were not shielded from the stigma associated with street vending and what seemed to be "the worst part of their job."

Cultural Stereotypes: "They Tell Me That I'm Right Here . . . Like a Mexican Person Selling in the Streets"

Street vending marked the children in this study as foreign and undocumented even though the majority of them were born in the United States and had never traveled to México, the place they had been told to go back countless times. One thing was certain—street vending served as an immigrant shadow for these children. Sociologist Jody Agius Vallejo found that an immigrant shadow is even present among established middle-class Mexican professionals.[10] Similarly, sociologist Tomás R. Jiménez argues that due to a constant immigrant replenishment from Latin America, second- and third-generation children of immigrants are seen as forever foreign.[11] The youth in this study also experienced this "othering" while street vending. Their English language skills and even their own U.S. citizenship did not shield them from being labeled with an epithet such as "wetback," to underline the racialized connotations of the job. Take the case of eighteen-year-old Veronica, who started selling cups of sliced fruit on the streets of Los Angeles with her mother when she was twelve. She recalled the teasing she had endured from school friends this way:

> They used to tell me, "You sell in the streets? Aren't you embarrassed? People look at you and you have to tell them to buy your stuff!" So they were making fun of me, and they tell me that I'm right here in the street, like a Mexican person selling in the streets. People tell me, "Ha! You're a wetback!" . . . I wanted to cry because they were making fun of me, but then I got over it.

To be selling on the street is to be "like a Mexican person." It marks one publicly as marginal, backward, subordinate, and inferior. Another girl also said that she imagined that people who saw her selling on the street probably saw her as "a Mexican," when in fact, she identified as "Hispanic," a U.S.-born U.S. citizen. She thought people would be surprised to learn she was born in the United States. This distinction and the street vendor youths' contestation suggest the contours of widely circulating notions of racial hierarchy and immigrant inferiority.

The children were bewildered when random people told them to go "back to México." These young vendors were proud of their Latinx heritage, and they did not accept derogatory cultural depictions of Mexicans and Latinx attached to them simply for the work they performed.[12] Accordingly, the children I interviewed described their peers who did not work as "lazy" and "spoiled." When asked what her friends do, Chayo, who had just turned fourteen but spoke with the security of a much older person, assessed, "Nothing. They have their parents, but their parents work for them. Like, they get money either way. They don't have to do anything." Her ten-year-old brother Andrés disparagingly claimed that his friends were always "outside eating chips and they are all fat. . . . They just, like, always play around and eat junk food all the time." And Edgar disdainfully said of his Catholic school peers, "They don't even work. They are lazy." Not working was associated with slothfulness, junk food, and being fat.

Familiar and widely circulating racializations of Mexicans as lazy, illegal, and illegitimate were challenged by narratives that allowed the street vendor kids to position themselves as more authentically Mexican or Latinx than their nonworking peers. The street vendor kids said that their nonworking peers had lots of idle time. They reasoned that with all this idle time, their peers were more likely to get in trouble and turn to drugs, stealing, and gangs. Take the examples of the following three girls:

> Street vending gets you tired, but you have, like, time to do it. And you're not doing dumb stuff over there, seeing TV, sitting down, doing drugs, *tú sabes* [you know], not doing bad. . . . Like my cousin, he got into jail like three times already because he's, like, stealing and doing drugs and he's a gangster. I don't want to be like him. (Nadya, age thirteen)

> My neighbor just sleeps, smokes drugs, and then, like, he goes and eats and he doesn't even help his parents. And I feel bad for his parents because one of them *no puede caminar* [cannot walk]. . . . Like, if it was me, I have to help my parents. (Veronica, age eighteen)

> *Es mejor que estés trabajando que te cachen robando.* [It's better to work than be caught stealing.] I mean, that's the way I see it. I ain't stealing. (Martha, age eighteen)

Across the board, the children rejected traditional stereotypes of this profession. They countered the stigma by taking pride in this "cultural" activity that made them better Mexicans in the United States as it helped them develop a strong work ethic and kept them away from gangs and drugs. For street vending children, meanings of culture did not remain stagnant; rather, the children transformed and readapted cultural meanings through their work experience with their parents.

The children defined themselves as hardworking compared to their friends. For example, Leticia said that none of her friends could handle the work that she did with her mother. One night, Leticia's friends had a sleepover and witnessed all the work that Leticia and her family had to do the night before they went street vending. This was not a typical slumber party that entailed nail painting and boy talk. Leticia took her friends to downtown Los Angeles, where they bought the majority of their food in bulk. Once home, she diligently put away the food and made sure to separate the food for their street vending business in one refrigerator, and in another fridge, the food for the house. Later, Leticia began boiling water in different pots for the different types of salsas that she made. In one pot, she boiled tomatillo and dried chiles, in another she boiled red tomatoes with jalapeños, and so on. Leticia did not count the vegetables before putting them in the pot, as someone would while meticulously following a recipe. She cooked with confidence and skill, as if she were one of the kids depicted in the cooking show *MasterChef Junior*. In total, she made about eight different types of sauces to accompany the food they sold. Her friends were overwhelmed just by seeing all the work she had to do and confessed they could not handle even part of it. During our interview, Leticia shared that story with pride:

> Most of my friends have stepdads and their moms are always home. They mostly help around the house. One time my friends slept over for a weekend and they said they can't handle it and they don't know how I do it.

The children told me that they stood out among their friends. While some school friends who knew of their street vending work naively made fun of them, others regarded their work with admiration and respect. For example, Joaquín told me that his friends at first made fun of him, but later he gained their respect once his schoolmates saw how the fruit of his labor materialized.

> At the beginning a lot of them made fun of me, but they started seeing that I made money. They would ask me, "How come you have money?" I guess they thought I was doing something wrong, and I tell them I always liked to make money and I found ways to make money by making good things.

The list of things children disliked about street vending was long: waking up early, dealing with rude customers, running and hiding from the cops, getting tired, and so forth. However, as Joaquín put it in a very mature and matter-of-fact way, "I think I have lived my childhood and I

Time	Monday	Tuesday	Wednesday	Thursday	Friday	Saturday	Sunday
5:00 AM							
6:00							
7:00	School	School	School	School	School		
8:00						work	
9:00						at	
10:00						down-town	
11:00							
12:00							
1:00 PM							
2:00							
3:00	after	after	after				
4:00	school	school	school				
5:00	program	program	PROGRAM				
6:00							
7:00	Park						
8:00	SV	sell	A	A	A		
9:00	10 or	open					
10:00							
11:00							
12:00							
Income	$	$	$	$	$	$ 46.00	$ 45.00
From sales							

Figure 1.3. Handwritten work schedule of Adriana (age thirteen).

think it's time to face the real world." While children enacted their own agency, they also recognized that they had very limited options. Not helping would not only hurt their parents, but it would ultimately hurt them directly as well.

When Do Children Work?

Vacation Work

The children filled out a time schedule showing me what a typical week in their life looked like. One student jokingly said on her last day of school, "My vacation time has ended." By this she meant that she worked more during the summer than she did during the school year. Others echoed this sentiment. When I looked at Leticia's schedule, I was amazed by the number of hours she worked with her mom. She worked over forty-five hours per week. Immediately she clarified, "It's 'cause I'm on vacation. I have more time now." These young street vendors were ubiquitous on the streets of Los Angeles during vacation periods. In fact, I met most of the children in this book during summer and winter breaks.

Their street vending schedule was fluid and ever changing, but one thing was for sure: summer was a very busy time. Most children in

Time	Monday	Tuesday	Wednesday	Thursday	Friday	Saturday	Sunday
5:00 AM							
6:00					school		
7:00	School						
8:00						sell with	
9:00						mom	
10:00							
11:00							
12:00				→			
1:00 PM							—→
2:00							
3:00							
4:00					↙		
5:00							
6:00	↓					↓	
7:00	helped				sell @		
8:00	home .				park		
9:00							
10:00							
11:00							
12:00							
Income	$	$	$	$	$ 12.	$3	$ 2.
From sales							

Total hours at work:

Figure 1.4. Handwritten work schedule of Josefina (age seventeen).

the Los Angeles Unified School District are out of school during the summer. Budget cuts have greatly affected summer classes available to students in the Los Angeles area.[13] Lack of summer classes means that more children are now idle at home, often watching television or playing in the street with their friends. This is seldom the case with child street vendors, though. In fact, summer is the busiest time of the year for the children and youth who work with their parents as street vendors. The summer days, with temperatures reaching the high nineties, are the best season to sell raspados, cut-up fruit, aguas frescas (fruit-flavored water), elotes (corn on the cob), and tejuino. Since they do not have school responsibilities, they are able to street vend during the day and stay late at night without having to worry about assignments due the next day or getting up early to go to class.

Weekends Only

Other children worked only during the weekend, but their weekdays were packed with household and childcare work. Take the case of

Josefina as an example. My interview with Josefina started at sunset on the front porch of their small apartment, at around 6:00 p.m. Since she is the oldest, she is often left in charge of her little siblings. This was the case when I met her for our interview. Shortly after I arrived at Josefina's house, her mom and stepfather drove out to do the laundry and she was left in charge of her fourteen-year-old sister Elsa, her five-year-old brother José, and her four-year-old brother Juan. During our three-hour interview, I was able to see how much work and responsibilities Josefina had on her plate. She makes sure her siblings eat, do their homework, and take a shower before they go to sleep. She also does behavior management. For example, her little brothers José and Juan interrupted the interview with a constant opening and slamming of the heavy iron front door. After a while, this banging noise became part of the background soundtrack that included cars passing by, children playing, neighbors blasting loud music, dogs barking, and a TV playing in the living room. The kids wanted attention from their sister and from me. Josefina constantly scolded them to stop, but my presence inspired extra curiosity that kept them peeking out the door.

An hour into the interview, we decided to move to the kitchen table, where there was light, because I had started using my phone light to read my interview questions. We passed through the living room, which was converted into a second bedroom with a queen-size bed, an armoire, and a large plasma television. Josefina's younger sister and brothers lay on the bed watching *iCarly*, a TV show on the Nickelodeon channel. A curtain divided the kitchen from the improvised bedroom. Once in the kitchen, I sat on a chair by a small round table topped with a variety of food, including pan dulce (Mexican sweet bread), fruit, a box of small bags of chips, homemade salsa, and chiles curtidos (pickled jalapeños).

As in most of the houses I visited, the street vending merchandise was visible and stored around various living spaces. Josefina pointed at the few boxes of sodas and Gatorade bottles stacked next to the table and underneath it to explain what they sold on the weekend. In addition, she explained that she and her mother also sell hot dogs at a neighborhood park where large crowds join for friendly soccer games in the afternoon.

As we continued with our interview, Josefina's five-year-old brother approached her for help with his kindergarten homework. We stopped the interview several times to help him with his homework. This involved reading the instructions, correcting what he had already done, and looking for crayons to complete the assignment. After the interview, I went to the street where her parents were street vending until midnight. Josefina still had to give her brothers and herself a bath, put them to bed, and finish her own school assignments.

Josefina's street vending responsibilities have changed over time. She used to work more during the summer, but lately it has been more beneficial for her to stay home and care for her little siblings. She explained,

> Well, I used to go more often during the summer. But now I have to stay home, so sometimes my mom goes by herself, but I mean, I have to do my homework. . . . [Also] I don't want my brothers bugging my mom. So I keep them here at the house. . . . I keep my sister and my brothers here and I make sure they take a shower. I also put them to sleep because they don't like sleeping early, but I make sure they go to sleep, and sometimes I clean the house.

In addition, Josefina is on top of her academic work and tries to protect her study time as best as family and street vending responsibilities permit. As a senior in high school, Josefina is busy preparing a graduation portfolio that includes a personal statement, a résumé, sample essays from previous classes, and more. Josefina gets as much work done as she can while she is at school and in her after-school program, but when she gets home, it is time to help her mother with the household responsibilities while her mother goes to street vend. Josefina explained,

> Mostly the days that I would go help my mom is just Fridays, Saturdays, and Sundays. If we go on Fridays, which is rare, but I'll go because I don't have school on Saturday. But I'll go help her Fridays in the afternoon. Then Saturdays I help her the whole morning until, let's say, like five in the afternoon. And Sundays the same thing, like 5:00 a.m. to 5:30 p.m.

The children I interviewed had various work arrangements with parents. In addition to the type of street vending business, age, gender, and family composition helped determine when kids worked and how they helped. Others such as Josefina also worked during the week, but did so at home. Josefina seldom helped her mother with the street vending business during the week because her mother's business required no preparation at home. Her mother sold chips, Gatorade, juices, candy, and hot dogs at night. Since Josefina had younger siblings, it made more sense for her to stay home and watch over them. In contrast, Leticia, who did not have younger siblings, worked during the week on the street, preparing food, charging customers, arranging the merchandise, and running errands for her mother.

School Nights and Weekends

In addition to helping over the weekend, other children also helped during the week after school. The story of Mercedes and her two daughters, Adriana (age sixteen) and Norma (age fourteen) comes to mind. Mercedes is a single mother and to support her two daughters sells tamales early in the morning before her daughters go to school. She also sells chips, sodas, and an assortment of candy outside Norma's school immediately after classes let out.

Mercedes's workday starts very early. She sells tamales at four o'clock in the morning outside a factory in downtown Los Angeles while her two daughters are still sleeping. One early morning, I accompanied Mercedes as she prepared for and then went to work. I met her at her house at dawn; it was dark but the streetlights allowed me to see her loading into her small car a thermos with champurrado. She also loaded a jug of freshly squeezed orange juice, a small folding table, and an ice chest full of about sixty tamales. When I asked Mercedes whether her daughters helped, she explained that every night they gather around the kitchen table to *embarrar la masa* (spread the corn-based dough before adding the filling). Mercedes and her daughters form an assembly line where the youngest daughter takes the corn leaves drenched in a bucket of water and places them on the table, while Mercedes and her oldest daughter spread the masa, add the meat and mole (sauce), and fold the tamales inside a large pot. Time flies by quickly since they have a small television in their kitchen where they watch their favorite *novela* (soap opera).

I decided to follow Mercedes in my own car since her small car could not fit all of her merchandise plus an extra passenger. Mercedes parked on the street immediately in front of the small side entrance of the sewing factory, and then she instructed me to park behind her. She strategically used her car and my car as a shield to hide from the authorities. She placed her small folding table as close to the car as she could in order to not block the sidewalk. On the light post she placed a small 13" x 10" cardboard sign with the word "tamales" advertising her food. Mercedes diligently sold to new and regular customers. She usually makes about sixty to a hundred tamales per day. On that morning, since she did not sell all of the tamales she and her daughters had prepared the night before, she moved to a different spot at 6:30 a.m. after the factory closed the door. I helped her move down the street directly in front of a bus stop. Mercedes planned to get customers who were exiting the bus. She finally finished selling all of the tamales by 7:00 a.m., just in time to move her car because street parking is enforced at that time. After we loaded the car with the empty wares, an empty crate, and the table, Mercedes headed home at 7:15 to then drive her two daughters to their different schools. By this time, both of her daughters were up and ready for school. As soon as Mercedes parked in front of their apartment, the girls ran out, helped take the table and the empty containers out of the car, and went to school.

Meanwhile, I began my interview with her sister and next-door neighbor Carolina. When Mercedes returned around 9:00 a.m., she looked exhausted, so she took a nap. Mercedes slept during my two-hour interview with Carolina. After my interview, Mercedes got up and started getting ready to go street vend outside her daughter's middle school, where her youngest daughter will help. I met Mercedes and Carolina at the middle school at 2:00 p.m. after I also took a nap inside my car parked in the parking lot of a fast-food restaurant near their house. When I arrived, they were setting up their merchandise. I offered to help arrange the candy since she was busy with the first wave of hungry kids leaving the school. Mercedes thanked me for offering, but said that her daughter would help her. "I always try to leave some work for my daughter," she explained. When her daughter came out of school, she placed her backpack behind the stand and started hanging candy on a string with clothespins.

Mercedes's actions were significant to me because her decision to include her daughter in her sales represented more than needing her help. Mercedes left work for her daughter on purpose to teach her how to earn money. Instilling a work ethic in her daughters was one of the main reasons for getting them involved in the family business.

The Work Kids Do

This chapter illuminates the experiences of street vending children and their parents who experience multiple disadvantages. Children such as Joaquín, Norma, and Salvador reveal how their decisions to street vend were constrained by their parents' limited employment opportunities. Over and over, children cited their parents' job misfortunes as the catalyst to street vending. While lack of formal education, poor English language skills, and lack of legal residency status placed their parents at a structural disadvantage, the children in this study and their families found in these structural constraints an opportunity for self-employment through a collective family work effort.

The children highlight their agency and decision making when it comes to deciding to street vend and help their family make ends meet. Children are not thrilled that they have to work. Who can blame them? After all, street vending is hard work. However, most children showed a high level of maturity when explaining how they decided to help their parents. Through my conversations with these young entrepreneurs, they revealed that their motives extended beyond familial obligations. Their decision to street vend was also a solution to obtain expensive consumer items their parents alone could not afford. For example, wanting to replace a lost iPod, as in the case of Karen, is not a matter of simply asking for a new one; rather, children realize that they must literally work to get a new one. In the process of their work, children learned to see their work as unique and different from other children at their schools and in their neighborhoods. Instead of seeing their work as cultural baggage, they created a higher morality that sees them as strong, hardworking, good sons and daughters, and not lazy, delinquent, and a burden for their parents.

Street vending as a family enterprise is more than a cultural legacy from México (and more generally Latin America) that is induced by structural labor market constraints encountered by Latinx immigrants who face racial discrimination and are denied legal authorization to work in the United States. Street vending is an innovative form of self-employment, one that has created a market out of growing concentrations of co-ethnics, and now foodie tourists. We cannot explain the work of children in family business street vending as "either/or," that is, as due exclusively to cultural factors or exclusively to structural factors. The line between culture and structure is not always so neat and definitive. For example, family household economies and the resources of poverty are structurally induced. In the United States, and in immigrant barrios such as East Los Angeles, hundreds of thousands of Mexican immigrant families—many of them without access to legal authorization to work—have migrated and settled. Faced with saturated labor markets and poor job options, many of them have chosen to devise incomes of ingenuity, responding to the structural constraints they encounter in East Los Angeles with cultural resources and practices that are common in their country of origin. Street vending is a cultural and economic resource with which they were familiar, and which they employ to counter structural limitations they face in U.S. labor markets.

In the next chapter, we will see how structural and cultural factors are intertwined in history and place settings. The cultural factors that are important in explaining the popularization of street vending in East Los Angeles include the tradition of working-class communities buying and eating traditional prepared foods on the streets and around the plazas in México and other Latin American countries and the systematic exclusion of Latinx immigrants from jobs that offer a living wage.

Street Vending in Los Angeles

A Cultural Economic Innovation

In front of the hundred-year-old abandoned Jewish synagogue in Boyle Heights, an array of about eighty street vendors from México and Central America are reviving this urban landscape with elaborate food stands where they sell food from their country of origin.[1] On selected nights, local immigrants and foodies can enjoy authentic food from Latin America such as tamales and pozole from México and pupusas from El Salvador and Guatemala. Some also sell American junk food such as hot dogs, hamburgers, and chips. This snapshot captures the ongoing historical demographic transformation of Boyle Heights, a community wedged between downtown Los Angeles's iconic buildings, with factories for nineteenth-century immigrants on one side and the storied neighborhood of East Los Angeles on the other.[2] But before the synagogue, East Los Angeles was the home and property of a few wealthy Mexican families in the nineteenth century, most of whom lost the majority of their land along with their political and economic power after the signing of the Treaty of Guadalupe Hidalgo, which ended the U.S.-Mexican War in 1848. Since its foundation in 1781, East Los Angeles has been a predominately Mexican community, when California was still Mexican territory.[3]

According to historian Ricardo Romo, there was relatively little social and economic change from its foundation up to the U.S. conquest in 1848. A year later, as a result of the Gold Rush in 1849, Anglos, Chinese, Japanese, Jews, Germans, and African Americans made Los Angeles their new home, while Mexicans became a disenfranchised minority. In the early twentieth century the Los Angeles population grew exponentially, and by 1930 it was already a large metropolis.[4] However, low wages and poor living conditions dissuaded Anglos from settling in this barrio.[5] These same factors attracted new immigrants from México and former Mexican agricultural workers who did not return to México during their off-season in the winter. By 1929, East Los Angeles had already gained national fame as the largest "Mexican barrio."[6] Meanwhile, the established Jewish population in Boyle Heights plummeted after World War II due to out-migration, leaving behind structural reminders of their time in Boyle Heights, such as stores, temples, and even street names.[7] The fame of a "Mexican barrio" continues to this day—Latinx residents constitute 95 percent of the nearly 100,000 people in Boyle Heights. Yet East Los Angeles has remained a segregated Latinx community characterized by poor living conditions, with a median income of $35,000, high crime rates, low levels of education, and very few jobs. This is in part due to deindustrialization, White flight, and the influx of new immigrants from Latin America.[8]

As has been the case so often in American history, immigrants are playing a key role in reviving public life in many American cities. In Los Angeles, and in Boyle Heights in particular, street vendors are at the forefront of this trend. In 2008 cultural geographer Lorena Muñoz observed how sidewalk peddlers in immigrant neighborhoods utilize nostalgia for familiar foods and memory of place to construct what she called new "urban cultural landscapes."[9] Others, like historian Mike Davis, have credited vendors with transforming "dead urban spaces into convivial social places," blending traditions from the *mestizaje* of the Spanish plaza and the Meso-American *mercado*.[10] Sociologist Sharon Zukin credits street vendors with bringing authenticity and life to urban places through authentic cultural food.[11]

Boyle Heights, like other such neighborhoods in and around Los Angeles, features a large concentration of street vendors peddling traditional Latin American foods and other items. While many residents welcome these vendors for their products and convenience, others view them with resentment or hostility. Many academics see that these negative reactions reflect deep issues of culture and identity. In his 2004 study, activist and law professor Greg Kettles claimed that opponents of sidewalk vending reject the practice because "it signifies the rise of another culture that threatens the status of their own."[12] This analysis seems particularly applicable to a neighborhood like Boyle Heights that has experienced such a thorough ethnic transformation. Others, such as Loukaitou-Sideris and Ehrenfeucht, have seen culture clashes extend

Figure 2.1. Family making and selling huaraches.

beyond ethnicity, claiming that the street vendors represent a "Third World imagery" at odds with the First World expectations of more affluent residents.[13] Furthermore, as the specter of gentrification looms over Boyle Heights, street vendors are either romanticized as an aspect of exotic ethnic authenticity or demonized as an unacceptable vestige of a disreputable past.

Today, street vendors in the Los Angeles area navigate a complex terrain informed by a volatile political context. With the new pervasiveness of Latinx immigrant street vending, we see its embrace not only by Latinx immigrant consumers, but also by a variety of people seeking "authentic" food. Yet vendors—and immigrants and allies writ large—tread dangerously due to rampant xenophobia and hostility. Take the case of twenty-four-year-old Benjamin Ramirez, better known as the "elote man." On July 16, 2017, Benjamin recorded and uploaded a video that depicts an Argentinean metal musician, Carlos Hakas, violently overthrowing Benjamin's food cart in Hollywood.[14] In less than a week, the original Facebook video went viral with over 3.5 million views. Gustavo Arellano, a famous columnist for the *OC Weekly*, opened his post with the following sentence: "It hasn't even been a full day, yet seemingly every food lover, Southern Californian and Mexican in the United States knows about a video that depicted some loser violently overturning the food cart of Benjamin Ramirez in Hollywood."[15] As a testament to the presence of allies and solidarity with and for immigrants, though, the online community responded with positivism and support. A variety of GoFundMe pages opened up to raise money for Benjamin and his family, some raising up to $20,000. Cartoonist Lalo Alcaraz created a cartoon that depicted a giant corn shooting from the sky straight toward Hakas, who runs in fear. The caption states, "The Corn Gods are not pleased when immigrants hurt immigrants." Furthermore, social media commentators showered Benjamin with support. One YouTube commentator said, "If I saw this happening I'd run up and slap that mother fucker. Eloteros are always welcome in Hispanic neighborhoods."

Benjamin is one example of the complex daily realities of street vendors in Los Angeles. While many residents, particularly recent arrivals and foodies of different nationalities, see food carts as a comforting familiarity offering authentic experiences, others, including Latinx community members, see the carts as part of a Latinx "invasion" and a cultural and linguistic *reconquista*.[16] One of the most emblematic evocations of a *reconquista* through street vending gained national and international attention during the 2016 U.S. presidential election when Marco Gutierrez, founder of the group Latinos for Trump, equated taco trucks to Mexican culture. Gutierrez relied on cultural explanations to garner support for his candidate's agenda. Gutierrez famously said on an MSNBC interview, "My culture is a very dominant culture, and it's causing problems. If you don't do something about it, you're going to have a taco truck on every corner." His call to action was actually in support of Trump's plan to deport undocumented Mexican immigrants in the United States. Gutierrez's statement came a day after Trump delivered a campaign speech in Phoenix, Arizona, on August 13, 2016. In his speech,

Figure 2.2. Family working together and the author in the field.

Trump singled out immigrants from México and warned them about their stay in this country. Trump announced that undocumented Mexicans were living in the United States on borrowed time, and if elected, he would "break the cycle of amnesty and illegal immigration." This is a threat that his administration has promised to uphold, as we have seen with horrific results so far.

As an unintended consequence, the election of Trump in November 2016 motivated the city of Los Angeles, an immigrant sanctuary city, to decriminalize street vending in order to protect its most vulnerable and visible population from deportation.[17] As early as December 2016, the *Los Angeles Times* printed an article with the following opening: "Here's one small silver lining to the election of Donald Trump: It has forced Los

Angeles City Council members to get moving on the long-stalled pro-posal to legalize and regulate street vending." For decades, peddlers have been trying to legalize street vending in Los Angeles, "the only major American city where it is against the law to sell food and merchandise on the sidewalk."[18] The city council is expected to have a new street vending ordinance in place that offers street vendors an opportunity to apply and receive a street vending permit.[19] Almost two years after Los Angeles decriminalized street vending, California governor Jerry Brown signed SB 946, a bill introduced by Senator Ricardo Lara that expanded the decriminalization of street vendors statewide.[20]

As much as street vending is a visible and familiar part of urban Latin America, my research found that in Los Angeles, it is by and large *not* a cultural transplant from México or Central America. Street vend-ing is informed by cultural legacies from México, shaped by struc-tural forces and constraints, and innovated by creative, working-class Mexican immigrants who are striving to make a living for themselves and their families in Los Angeles. My study aligns with a newer body of scholarship that shines attention on the role of human agency in the informal economy while acknowledging the importance of cultural and structural forces. This "actor-oriented perspective" acknowledges historical and macro-structural forces, but focuses analysis on human agency, culture, and social interaction in street vending in contempo-rary U.S. cities.[21]

Street Vending Here, There, and Everywhere

The Latinx street vendors in this study immigrated to a society where street vending was already an economic strategy for other ethnic groups in American cities such as New York and Los Angeles since the early nineteenth century.[22] In New York, ethnic groups such as Jews, Ital-ians, and Greeks once peddled their wares on the streets. Instead of the tacos and tamales of today's sidewalk stands they sold oysters, hot corn, pickles, knishes, and sausages, and most recently kabobs. In fact, many travelers today would argue that no trip to the Big Apple is complete without eating a hot dog from a sidewalk vendor. Clearly, street vending is neither new nor unique to Latin American immigrant neighborhoods in North America.

In nineteenth-century Los Angeles, street vending was often done by Chinese men.[23] Asian immigrants sold vegetables in Los Angeles and were opposed by middle-class Americans, civic authorities, and merchants. The local anti-vending sentiment against Chinese peddlers was fueled by a nationwide xenophobia that also produced a vast array of exclusionary anti-immigrant laws such as the 1882 Chinese Exclusion Act, the 1907 Gentlemen's Agreement, and the 1924 Immigration Act, which collectively established a system of racial quotas that excluded labor immigration from Asia.[24] This anti-Asian sentiment at the federal level was felt at the local level as well. In Los Angeles, the first anti–street vending ordinance was passed in 1910, making it illegal for Chinese people to sell produce on the street.[25]

Street vending was not a popular economic strategy for Mexicans during the early twentieth century. Rather, Mexicans in particular were recruited to work in the Southwest in agriculture. The U.S. industrial expansion and the anti-Asian sentiment that developed in the United States during this time provided work opportunities for Mexican immigrants in agriculture, mining, and the construction and maintenance of the railroads.[26] Instead of recruiting menial labor from Asia, U.S. employers turned to México as the new supplier of workers. In fact, U.S. capitalists fought arduously to prevent federal restrictions on immigration from México. Thus "when the Immigration Act of 1924 was passed . . . immigrants from México and other parts of Latin America were exempted."[27] These recruitment efforts continued from 1900 to 1929 as the United States aggressively recruited Mexican workers through U.S. *enganchadores* (labor recruiters) who sought to recruit Mexican workers to build the railroad line that was extending into the West.

In 1942 the United States once again recruited workers form México through the Bracero Program, a binational agreement between the United States and México.[28] The program was initially intended to last only five years, but was extended several times, finally ending in 1964.[29] The economic boom during World War II offered employment opportunities to Mexican immigrants. According to Kettles, street vending in the 1940s was less prevalent due to the new jobs available in the manufacturing sector.[30]

Three years later, and for the very first time, Mexican immigration was subject to numerical restrictions beginning in 1965. Despite these restrictions, networks had been established and there was a built-in demand for Mexican workers. On the one hand, agricultural growers were dependent on cheap labor from México, and on the other hand, U.S. citizens did not want to work in racialized immigrant jobs. The built-in demand, social networks, and new immigration restrictions on México resulted in an increase of undocumented Mexican workers.[31] Although many undocumented immigrants were still able to find work, the 1986 Immigration Reform and Control Act (IRCA) enacted more stringent hiring restrictions for undocumented immigrants. This legislation was the result of an unprecedented compromise between the two sides of the immigration debate. On the one hand, the legislation increased the budget of the Immigration and Naturalization Service (INS) and imposed sanctions on employers who knowingly hired undocumented workers. On the other hand, it provided amnesty to 2.3 million undocumented Mexicans. IRCA started a new era of restricted immigration policies and the militarization of the U.S.-México border. Ultimately, the exclusion of formal sector employment gave rise to informal sector strategies.

In the 1970s and 1980s, street vendors became familiar sights in various Latinx immigrant-receiving neighborhoods in California, including Los Angeles, Huntington Park, San Gabriel, South Gate, and Pacoima. This time, Latinx immigrants were at the forefront of this economic activity.[32] This reflected the immigration influx of undocumented immigrants from México and Central America, who had limited access to jobs and legal status. By 1991, there were an estimated six thousand street vendors in Los Angeles.[33] In 1992 the majority (two-thirds) of the vendors were Mexican and the rest were Central American.[34] Today, scholars estimate that there are over fifty thousand street vendors in Los Angeles, and as this study will show, many of them are children and teenagers.[35] However, the diversity of street vending and vendors continues to grow. According to Los Angeles Times reporter Tiffany Hsu, African Americans are also turning to temporarily street vending amid the weak economy.[36] In addition, Asian American "night markets" in Pasadena, Los Angeles, and Orange County have become very popular.[37] As these night markets offer street vendors opportunities to sell a variety of Asian dishes in a designated vending location, it also provides authentic Asian food options to foodies.

Latinx street vendors have always experienced hostility in Los Angeles due to the city's ordinance that prohibits sidewalk vending, but it likely has to do as much with the economic climate as it does with the cultural transformations the United States is currently experiencing. In their 2001 study, Nora Hamilton and Norma Stoltz Chinchilla noted an increased hostility toward Latinx vendors during the recession in the early 1990s. While I collected data, moreover, I also witnessed increased concerted hostility from the police and health departments in 2008 during the global economic crisis and the collapse of the U.S. housing market.

This type of hostility was evident to me from the first day I went to the streets of Los Angeles in search of street vending families to interview in 2008. On a sunny summer afternoon, I ventured to Olvera Street, an iconic Mexican cultural landmark, hoping to find street vendors for my study. I parked my car in one of the lots across Olvera Street. I took a deep breath and marveled at the history of this landmark known as "the birthplace of Los Angeles," now reminiscent of an old Mexican marketplace. The music, architecture, colonial-style church, colorful walls, cloth awnings at storefronts that protected the various merchandise, and the abundant potted plants nicely positioned along the corridors, balconies, and stairways gave me a sense of traveling through time and space to an imagined quaint town in México. This was in fact the feeling this space was meant to evoke, since Christine Sterling, a privileged White woman, dedicated her life to turning Olvera Street into an "exotic," "Spanish-Mexican romance" destination she had dreamt about since childhood.[38] William D. Estrada states that since its foundation in the midst of the Great Depression in the 1930s, the theme for Olvera Street was an "'old Mexico,' pitting a timeless, homogeneous Spanish-Mexican culture against industrialization, immigration, urban decay and modernity itself."[39] This timeless, small-town feel is juxtaposed with the fast-paced traffic that runs through the two major arteries that encapsulate this narrow corridor.

As I made my way to Olvera Street, I immediately saw signs of street vendors. People ate corn on a stick, churros, hot dogs, and raspados. Only a street vendor could sell this kind of food, I thought. In my mind this added a layer of authenticity to a place where being Mexican or Latinx was safe and even celebrated. As I kept walking toward

Olvera Street, my thoughts were interrupted by a big commotion, with women screaming and running. A Latina woman in her mid-forties wearing shorts, a plain T-shirt, and an apron walked away from Olvera Street screaming profanity in Spanish while she pushed an improvised homemade hot dog cart. In a loud voice she complained about the "pinches policías" (damn cops) while her young daughter silently followed her, rolling a large ice chest full of half-melted ice, sodas, water, and juice. On that day, the cops were not allowing vendors near this street. The young girl walked toward the parking lot where I had parked. She hid her ice chest behind the parked cars and later joined her mother and a group of female vendors who had also been pushed out of Olvera Street.

Suddenly, three other girls came out of hiding, joined their mothers, and tucked their merchandise away behind the parked cars. I walked toward the group and asked whether they were okay. What happened? I asked, expressing sympathy. Only one woman replied, "Pues aquí nomás trabajando y la policía que no nos deja." (Well, we are here trying to work, but the police are not letting us.) The other women looked away, annoyed at my presence and my questions. While I did not take offense, I felt uncomfortable prying. The young girls seemed comfortable with the situation, as if this was not their first encounter with police altercations. They talked amongst themselves the way girls usually do during recess at school. When I mustered the courage to ask for an interview, they politely declined. Throughout my research, this was not the first time I was rejected. Gaining the trust of the families that I interviewed took time. The girls told me to go to the plaza and that I was sure to find someone to interview there. After three hours at the plaza, I conducted two interviews and then decided to leave. On my way out, I saw them again still trying to go back to the plaza to sell their bacon-wrapped hot dogs and drinks. "A intentarlo otra vez?" (Giving it another try?), I asked. "Pues sí, mija" (Well, yes, my dear), she replied with a tone of resignation. I left Olvera Street that day reflecting how the same people and culture can be celebrated, commodified, and systematically rejected in one place and time. This was a theme that I continued to see throughout my time in the field.

When I conducted this study, street vending in Los Angeles was a criminalized activity, punished by fines of up to $1,000 or jail time.[40]

Figure 2.3. The author observing children and parents at work.

While I did not see these women receive a citation or get arrested on that summer afternoon, later in my study I did witness many of the families fined unreasonably large amounts of money merely for selling goods on the street. One family also said that their son had been arrested. I too experienced running and hiding from the cops during my field observations.

During my time in the field, street vending continued to be an illegal activity enforced by the Los Angeles Health Department (LAHD) and Los Angeles Police Department (LAPD).[41] Street vending was considered a misdemeanor.[42] However, when the LAHD and the LAPD joined forces and conducted sweeps together, the punishment was usually more serious and could result in six months in jail and confiscation of merchandise and wares. According to the California law in place, "health inspectors can impound any food, equipment or utensil that is suspected of being unsanitary or in such disrepair that food could become contaminated."[43] According to *Los Angeles Times* reporter Emily Alpert Reyes, most of

Figure 2.4. Fourteen-year-old girl getting a citation for street vending.

the time, police officers confiscate street vending goods without giving vendors receipts, as they are supposed to do by law.[44] More than 1,200 arrests related to street vending were reported in 2014, and in 2016 the city of Los Angeles collected $9,880 in fines.[45] I also witnessed many of the family members I interviewed receiving citations while street vending for other reasons not directly connected to vending (e.g., blocking the sidewalk or the street). Scholars argue that the criminalization of street vending has been in place since the turn of the twentieth century, as the city became more Anglicized,[46] but as my present-day research shows, allies and enemies alike come in all different types. Since then, vendors have fought an uphill battle for the right to vend legally on the streets that they have called home for decades. Finally, and long after the families for this book were interviewed, on September 20, 2018, street vendors won a major victory with the signing of SB 946, which will prohibit the criminal punishment of vendors across the state.[47]

In México, the home country from which the majority of my respondents immigrated, street vending also developed as a result of economic hardship and lopsided development strategies pursued by the state that can be traced back to the early 1900s. During this time, the Mexican government under the administration of Lázaro Cárdenas (1934–1940) implemented a program of land redistribution called *ejidos*, or acres of land confiscated from hacienda owners and given to landless peasants, some of whom previously worked for the hacienda owner. The *campesinos* or *ejidatarios* did not own the *ejido*, but it was theirs for as long as they could cultivate the land. If they did not cultivate the land for more than two years, the *ejido* could be taken away. *Campesinos* had to borrow money from the hacienda owner to be able to cultivate the land, which often resulted in debt peonage. Some *campesinos* moved to urban cities to earn money through informal work, including street vending. In Tijuana and México City, for example, many indigenous female street vendors migrated from poor rural regions of southwestern México. These women are stereotypically referred to as *las Marías*.[48] This type of internal migration and the development of the informal sector was a social phenomenon in México and was often seen as an urban problem by middle-class Mexican political leaders.

Some of these cultural representations of *las Marías* have spilled over to the United States and permeated the local imaginary of this Latinx subgroup. While I never saw any of the people I interviewed dressed in traditional Mixteca attire, geographer Lorena Muñoz did notice that some of her respondents "dressed up" for work in indigenous attire and called this their work uniform.[49] Yet understanding street vending solely through a cultural lens is problematic because it places the burden on the individual and their culture and ignores larger social structures that both constrain and enable the existence of this occupation over time. Problems arise when culture is the *only* explanation to understand why Latinxs sell merchandise in the United States. Rather, I argue that street vending is a cultural tradition, as well as an economic response to structural economic exclusions of people disadvantaged by class, race, and immigration status. Street vendors resort to the production and sale of cultural food from their home country, which they cater to consumers seeking "authentic" Mexican food and established communities that have immigrated and settled in barrios such as Boyle Heights.

The practice of street vending is learned, adjusted, and shared among Latinx immigrants, and so is the food that is sold. Nilda and Leticia's story below points to larger social structures both in the sending and receiving countries that help explain why immigrants resort to street vending and how children are seamlessly incorporated into this informal occupation. Through narratives of other vendors in my study, this chapter demonstrates that street vending is not a cultural transplant, but rather a cultural economic innovation for street vendors who are at the intersection of multiple forms of inequalities magnified by anti-immigrant policies post-1965 that paved the way for an increasing informal market among Latinx immigrants.

Nilda and Leticia

Like most of the people I interviewed for this book, Nilda did not immigrate to the United States hoping to become a street vendor. In fact, at the age of twenty-two, in an effort to escape her street vending destiny, Nilda decided to leave México City and immigrate to the United States. She left behind her mother and siblings, all of whom made a living selling quesadillas and carnitas (pork meat) on the streets. Nilda was the only one in her family who refused to sell items on the street; in fact, she was ashamed of it and avoided any type of association with her street vending mother and siblings. When I interviewed Nilda on the porch of her East Los Angeles home, she told me,

> I was the only one [in my family] who did not sell quesadillas or anything. How was I supposed to do that work if I was going to high school? Oh no! And then it was a poor neighborhood and they [people in my neighborhood] would tell me, "Your mom is the one that sells pork meat?" because she would make them very tasty. I would answer, "No! No, my mom is at the park." I would never say that my mom sold there. And on Saturdays when it was my turn to help her, I wouldn't do it.[50]

Little did she know that in Boyle Heights, Nilda's home since she immigrated to the United States in 1991, she would be known as the *reina de las quesadillas* (queen of the quesadillas).

I first met Nilda and her fourteen-year-old daughter Leticia one cool Friday evening at La Cumbrita, an unremarkable commercial street surrounded by two parking lots just off a main avenue in Boyle Heights.

This street stands in direct contrast to the "old Mexico" feel consumed in Olvera Street. In La Cumbrita, you can find multiple bus stops, a low-cost supermarket, a 99-cent store, clothing shops, a taco restaurant, and a bank. However, every Friday, Saturday, and Sunday, when the sun starts to set at around 7:00 p.m., the street transforms into an open market place, or *mercado*, and you are sure to find a conglomerate of about sixty street vendors among them. Nilda and Leticia's elaborate stand includes a skillet, two large folding tables adorned with a colorful tablecloth, and a variety of toppings for their food. La Cumbrita attracts local customers as well as tourists looking for "authentic" Mexican food.[51] These tourists and foodies come from all over the city, and some even visit from out of state. During my field observations in March 2010, I met a Los Angeles marathon runner from New York who sought out Nilda's stand after reading about her food on a foodie's blog. He wanted to taste her famous pambazos, a Mexican snack, or *antojito*, made with white bread dipped in a red guajillo pepper sauce and filled with chorizo. This dish and Leticia's sesame seed and peanut hot sauce earned them the first West Coast Vendy Award, a popular street food contest modeled after one on the East Coast.

Observers once believed that street vending—and all forms of informal, unregulated, income-generating activity—would fade away with modernization, but today street vending and informal economic activity are generally recognized as constitutive elements of advanced global capitalism.[52] In fact, cosmopolitan urbanites and "foodies" are now tracking down the best "authentic" immigrant street food in New York City and Los Angeles, and both cities have now celebrated the Vendy Awards for the tastiest street food.[53] Formal and informal sectors of the economy are linked and include industrial informality such as home-based piecework or assembly and informal vending, which traditionally provides the basic consumption needs of the working poor.[54]

Nilda and Leticia are proud of the food they make and sell on the streets of Boyle Heights, but that is not the American Dream that Nilda had hoped for when she made the decision to immigrate to the United States. Once in the United States, in her early twenties, she landed a job at a bar as a waitress. She was paid less than the minimum wage, but was happy not to be street vending for a living. While she worked at the bar, she met her husband, and together they had three children.

At the time of our interview, her oldest son was sixteen years old and her twins, Leticia and Luís, were fourteen years old. Soon after Nilda got married, she joined her husband's food truck business. Their business flourished in the mid-1990s, but after six years of marriage, Nilda divorced her husband when she caught him cheating. Nilda continued selling food after her divorce, but this time, on the street with neither a truck nor a vending permit. Fourteen-year-old Leticia recalled street vending with her mother when she was just a little girl. When I asked Leticia how old she was when she started street vending, she jokingly told me that she started street vending from her stroller. While her comment sparked laughter, it actually did resemble the reality of most female street vendors in Los Angeles who start their street vending endeavors from their own baby's stroller. More than once I saw women of all ages sell bottled water, sodas, chips, tamales, and an assortment of candy out of their strollers. The stroller is practical because food can easily be transported, yet conveniently covered with a blanket and kept from the sight of police officers.

While Leticia saw these early street vending moments as fun park outings, Nilda still resisted the idea of street vending. Like many women who immigrated in the 1990s, Nilda encountered a gendered labor market in the United States that offered undocumented immigrant women low-wage labor opportunities in sectors such as domestic, garment, and hotel housekeeping work.[55] Unlike earlier waves of immigrants who benefited from industrialization, post-1990 Latinx immigrants from México and Central America entered a society with an hourglass economy consisting of professional jobs on top and service and unskilled labor on the bottom.[56] However, among her limited work options, she preferred to street vend and keep her kids close to her. While she loathed the idea of street vending, she realized that street vending gave her the flexibility she needed to take care of her kids as a single mother. Studies show that it is precisely that flexible nature of the job that is appealing about street vending for women with young children.[57] Scholars studying street vending have observed how street vending mothers in the United States bring their children to work with them as a daycare strategy.[58] This is a compelling reason, since finding adequate childcare is often an extra constraint relegated to working mothers, including those who have professional jobs and are privileged by race and class.[59]

Nilda later started helping an established street vending family from Jalisco. Soon thereafter, she opened her own stand, where she sold a variety of *antojitos mexicanos* such as quesadillas, sopes, gorditas, tamales, fried tacos, and more, depending on the time of year. Nilda repeatedly made it clear that she never wanted to become a street vendor like her mother, but by a twist of fate, she ended up doing just that in the United States. Meanwhile, back in México, Nilda's mother no longer street vends, and all of her siblings have graduated from university and have professional careers. They often send Nilda remittances from México when she struggles to make ends meet or simply needs help paying a bill. This was a surprise to me, since remittances often flow from the United States to México and not the other way around. During our interview, Nilda's eyes could not hide a sense of deep sorrow—masked by her humor and sarcasm—when she talked about her siblings' educational accomplishments back in México. Nilda recalled, "My mom was surprised and told me, 'Look, the only one who never wanted to help me is the one that street vends in the United States.'"[60]

A Cultural Hangover or Cultural Economic Innovation?

It is no surprise that Nilda was embarrassed to sell merchandise on the street while in México. In México, street vending has always been a part of the culinary landscape, but despite its long-standing tradition, it continues to be semi-regulated and a stigmatized occupation. In the 1980s, when México was embroiled in a severe economic crisis, street vending expanded widely. Street vendors represented an urban problem because they created competition with established businesses and because they portrayed the "worst image of México."[61] To middle- and upper-class Mexicans, street vendors were antithetical to their modern views of Mexican culture and public aesthetics. Some scholars argue that for *las Marías*, indigenous women in Tijuana, street vending is not an economic strategy to combat unemployment but rather a "way of life."[62] In other words, street vending was seen as traditional and a "cultural choice" and not as an economic strategy to combat structural barriers such as unemployment.[63] The stigma associated with these cultural representations of vendors in México has permeated the popular imaginary and even mestizo vendors try to disassociate from these cultural associations.

Nilda's good friend Lorena, for example, remembered defining herself in opposition to *las Marías*. Forty-five-year-old Lorena grew up in a family where everyone was a street vendor. "We like this business," she told me. Unlike Nilda, Lorena loved to street vend. Her favorite thing to sell as a young girl growing up in México City was newspapers. Lorena was a proud street vendor in México, but she made sure to distance herself from *las Marías*. *Las Marías* stand out from Mexican vendors like Lorena because they dress in typical indigenous attire characterized by long colorful skirts, sandals, and *trenzas* (braided hair). At a very young age, Lorena knew she was not that "type" of street vendor and even dressed up like them to mock them. But even if she dressed like them, she identified as a light-skinned Mexican from the city, and explicitly not dark-skinned and not from rural parts of México. During my interview with Lorena, she narrated her street vending experience in México in the following manner:

> I had a rivalry with the Marías. They would say, "*Patroncita*, would you buy gum from me?" And I would make fun of them. I was about thirteen or fourteen years old and I told my mom, "Mom, make me a dress like theirs [indigenous]." And she made it for me and then I had long hair and she braided it. I felt very Chiapaneca, but white. . . . I was not ashamed of selling. I was not embarrassed to sell my newspapers.[64]

Lorena used imagery of indigenous vendors, including their form of speech, their dress, and their hairstyles, to define herself in opposition to them. When she dressed up like them, she felt Chiapaneca, like a person from the southern Mexican state of Chiapas. She referenced this state due to its high concentration of indigenous peoples and their notoriety, bringing to light what sociologist Sylvia Zamora calls *racial remittances*, or the "movement of racial discourses and stereotypes across national borders."[65] Nilda and Lorena's pre-migration and street vending experiences, including Lorena's depiction of *las Marías*, shed light on the class and cultural heterogeneity of street vendors in México. However, unlike Nilda and Lorena, the rest of the parents I interviewed for this study had no prior experience with street vending in México.

The rest of the adult vendors I interviewed for this book learned how to street vend after being in the United States for a few years. For them,

street vending was not a cultural transplant, but rather a cultural economic innovation that helped them escape dead-end jobs relegated to
undocumented immigrants in the United States. The most poignant example of this is forty-three-year-old Isidro, who decided to sell raspados
after living in the United States for eighteen years. Isidro immigrated to
the United States when he was twenty-one. He immigrated from Puebla,
México, hoping to study in the United States. He imagined that once
in the United States he could work and go to school, an opportunity
he did not have when he lived in México with his single mom. Those
dreams were shattered once in the United States. He lived with his older
brother and with other young men from his town, who discouraged him
from going to school. "Aquí tienes que tener papeles para estudiar" (You
need papers to study here), they told him. Later, Isidro found out that
he could go to school even if he was undocumented, and so he enrolled
in English classes at a local high school. He told me, "No pos cuando
me dijeron que sí podía, empecé a ir a la escuela. Y ya estudié poquito
inglés." (When they told me I could, I started going to school. I studied
a little bit of English.) While he was in school, he also worked in the
garment industry and made twenty cents per garment. This payment
arrangement required him to work overtime to cover his part of the rent
and food. Since he could not keep up with school and work, he stopped
going to school. Later he worked as a carpet installer. By this time, he
was married and had his first daughter, and his income was not enough
to cover his basic family expenses. His monthly rent alone was $1,025.

In 1994 Proposition 187, a state initiative that would prohibit undocumented immigrants from using non-emergency healthcare, public education, and other services in the state of California, passed. It was not
until 1999 that this proposition was ruled unconstitutional by a federal
district court. Threatened by an uncertain future between 1994 and 1999,
Isidro decided to return to México, but lasted there only one year.

> Supposedly I was going to leave because of the 187 proposition. This made
> me feel that undocumented people were not wanted here and I said, "I have
> nothing left here to do. Let's go!" They don't want us, they don't give us pa-
> pers. It's not because we don't want to work. Work is what we always do. If
> they don't want us, then we leave. And we left, but things were not the same.
> I was already used to living in the U.S. Well, things are just not the same.[66]

He only lasted one year in México and paid a smuggler $400 to cross the border again in 2000 before the terrorist attack of September 11, 2001, when border enforcement tightened dramatically.

After his return, Isidro found what would become his last job in the formal sector. He worked at a furniture store for a little over four years and made $200 per week. He saved enough to bring his wife and daughter and again struggled to make ends meet with such a low salary. Despite his productivity and various requests to his boss, Isidro was unsuccessful at getting a pay increase at his job. One day he finally decided to quit his job, and on that same day he asked a friend to teach him to street vend. "Pos ahora sí vengo para que me enseñes a los raspados" (I am here so you can teach me how to make raspados), Isidro told his friend. Isidro learned what he needed to buy for his new business, how he should prepare the raspados, and what streets he should avoid. "Mi compadre me dijo, 'Asegúrate de irte por acá. Cuidado con las pandillas, que aquí hay cholos." (My compadre said to me, "Make sure you go this way. Be careful with the gangs because there are gang members here.") Isidro soon learned that street vending was more complex than just learning how to make the food, reminding us that no work is "unskilled."[67] Finding an area to sell and learning how to avoid the police and the local gang members were just as important. However, he also saw the fruit of his labor materialize soon. On his first day street vending he made $90, whereas he had made $200 per week at the furniture store.

Other vendors who did not have established networks in street vending had to learn on their own. For example, forty-eight-year-old Héctor and his wife, Alejandra, who are originally from Puebla, did not street vend prior to coming to the United States. Once in Los Angeles, though, Héctor and Alejandra started selling tamales on Sundays outside a church. In addition to not having prior street vending experience, they also did not know how to make any type of street vending food. They both confessed not knowing how to make tamales when they initially started street vending. During my interview with Héctor, he elaborated on these challenges:

> It was a bit difficult because we did not know how to make the tamales and we would burn them, or undercook them, or they were too spicy. Well, she then made different ones and we tasted them and that is how we

decided on the right flavor. And with the clients, well, some liked them and some did not. We made a mole and they did not like it. Now we have three moles that customers do like.[68]

Héctor and Alejandra did not bring authentic Poblano country cooking skills with them. They had to learn in California how to cook typical Mexican foods like tamales. To begin, they tried different ways of making them, as well as different sauces and ingredients until they learned to make the ones that customers liked.

While some had to learn how to make food and how to sell on the streets of Los Angeles, others like fifty-two-year-old Olga from El Salvador decided to hire help. For Olga and her daughter, street vending was a temporary resource to meet a specific need. She never liked making food, she confessed. "Toman mucho tiempo para hacer" (They take too much time to make), she told me. Rather, she decided to hire her *comadre*, who is a great cook. During our interview, she said, "Yo vendo las pupusas. No las hago yo porque no las puedo hacer." (I sell pupusas. I do not make them because I don't know how.) Olga's husband worked full-time in construction and she street vended when there was a need for extra money. From chapter 1, you might recall how she and her daughter went back to street vending after the daughter had lost her iPod and needed to earn money to buy a new one.

All except two of the parents I interviewed, Nilda and Lorena, had to learn how to street vend once they were in the United States because they never did so prior to immigrating. Even those who had some experience required learning what dangerous areas to avoid. The stories of the families I interviewed demonstrate that street vending, although a common activity in places like México, is not a cultural inheritance, but rather a cultural economic innovation born out of need and ingenuity. In the next chapter, I show how children's American generational resources are changing the way families do street vending and the role of children in this informal occupation.

3

Working Side by Side

Intergenerational Family Dynamics

Customers are like, "I can't believe you are helping your dad.
And you know English!" I mean, even most of the people are
like, "Oh my God! I can't believe you know English!" And I
am like, "Dude, I was born here, what is wrong with you?"
—Martha, street vendor, age eighteen

Throughout this book, child street vendors have challenged the problematic, stereotypical profile of Latinx street vendors propagated in the media and in academic journals as being Spanish monolinguals and undocumented immigrants.[1] On a broader spectrum, they also challenge stereotypes of Latinx youth as downwardly mobile, delinquent, and lazy.[2] On the contrary, street vending children have what I call American generational resources (AGRs) because unlike their parents, the majority were born in the United States, attend school, all speak English, and are astutely familiar with American culture and technology. The last two are a result of their faster acculturation to the United States. Consequently, their AGRs play a significant part in the families' survival and economic integration. These children are not merely "language brokers" for their families in the way some previous work on immigrant children has documented.[3]

In studies of Mexican and Central American immigrant children in Los Angeles, Orellana documented children engaged in translating for parents and taking care of younger siblings.[4] The work of street vending children is also a form of resilient agency through which children earn themselves shared power within the family. They play an even more centrally integrated role within the family. The children of immigrants help the family with social adaptation by serving as translators and mediators between schoolteachers, doctors, and lawyers.[5] Vikki Katz shows that

Latinx children in Los Angeles are also *media brokers* for their immigrant parents.[6] These families depend on their children to use old media—telephones, U.S. mail, and more—as well as new media that include the Internet and cellular technologies to integrate into the new society.

"They Don't Have to Work Like I Do, You Know. Their Parents Are Rich"

Within minutes into Martha's interview, she broke down in tears. With every tear, her eye makeup began to smear all over her face as she started talking about her street vending experience. "I hate it!" she repeated as she tried to control her tears. We decided to stop the interview for a few minutes while she went inside to wash her face; she walked back ten minutes later. Her face was now makeup-free and her hair was pulled back in a ponytail. She sat down again and decided to continue her story. "Well, I started going with my dad since I was little, like seven or eight. Sometimes I would go with my mom. But doing it alone? . . . Probably when I was fourteen or so." Like most children in this book, Martha began to street vend when her father lost his job. She and her sister had attended an all-girls Catholic school and when her father lost his job, they all decided to street vend in order to keep up with their lifestyle, which included their house mortgage, car payments, and private school tuition of $630 per month.

Martha could not help but compare her life with that of her wealthy classmates. "They don't have to work like I do, you know. Their parents are rich. They own restaurants and they are little *fresitas*," sobbed Martha. She used the term *fresitas*, which literally means strawberries, but in Spanish refers to children who come from money and are spoiled by their parents. Martha was conflicted with her longing for a "normal" childhood, free of work, and her obligations to her family. The stigma attached to street vending placed a lot of weight on her shoulders. It was not so much that she did not want to work at all; rather, street vending work was her issue. Martha kept her street vending life a secret from her schoolmates. This meant that she never even had friends over to the house. Her reluctance to talk about her family and what they do for a living caused tensions among her friends and made her very angry. Some even accused her parents of dealing drugs. How else could they afford an expensive tuition, nice clothes, and an expensive truck? Martha recalled a conversation when one of her classmates questioned her dad's line of work:

> C: What does your dad work on?
> M: Why are you asking me this? Since when do you ask me this? You know I don't answer this.
> C: What, is he a drug dealer?
> M: What the fuck! You're stupid. Seriously.
> C: So how come you don't tell us?
> M: Why do you care? It doesn't matter. You're getting to know me, not my family, so don't worry about them.

Martha relived this conversation during our interview in the form of a dramatic monologue, going so far as to switch voices and mannerisms to capture the arrogance of her classmate. I was also able to see her deep frustration and anger. Martha's interaction with wealthier class members had made her dislike her own family's business even more. Yet, despite Martha's disdain for street vending, she could see clear benefits from her work. As the interview progressed, she concluded, "So it is a better-paying job, but it is hard work."

Martha's tone had changed an hour into our interview. Her eyes were wide open, she was very animated in her stories, and she leaned forward to almost express pride in the work that she did. She exemplified a paradox of shame and pride in her street vending experience:[7]

> If we don't really work, we don't have everything we wanted. . . . We are a big family. I mean, like, if my dad was working on a simple job getting 700 bucks, like, come on. And especially because we added these two rooms, so it's, like, I sleep in the master room. And then my dad wants to get me my truck. And that is why, honestly, like, I don't mind working because I know that in a sense I get anything I want. Anything I ask for, if I do ask for it, I could get it. My dad also tells us, "Yeah, I thank you guys for helping me." He would always tell me, "Yeah, instead of your brother helping me you guys are helping me," you know.

Martha carefully acknowledged the various material benefits of her work. She pointed at the two new room additions to their house, visible through the backyard where we were sitting. With a sense of pride, she also highlighted that she slept in the master bedroom, the biggest bedroom in the house, and that she even had her own private bathroom. Martha got even more excited when she detailed the kind of truck she was going to get: "I want a Chevrolet, but the Blazer. The two-door one. I like big trucks." Martha also recognized that she could not acquire all of these material goods without helping the family business. She even highlighted that her dad could not earn what they do as a family if he worked at a "simple job getting 700 bucks."

Furthermore, Martha's mother reinforced these ideas. She constantly reminded them how important their help was for the family. Martha's mother, who was interviewed separately, confided in me compelling details of their household:

> As they grew up, my husband asked them for help and they said yes. First, they saw it as a game, but now it is harder on them. But they know, as I tell them, this is the way we can pay for all that we need. Because my two oldest daughters are in a private school. We enrolled them in a private school to try to protect them from the dangers of public schools. This [street vending] is the way we get the money for all that they need.[8]

The work contribution of children, in addition to bringing direct financial benefits for all family members, also created the space for family negotiations in which children had bargaining power, decision-making input within the household, and purchasing power. Through the daily demands of work, they had earned themselves shared power within the family. Martha and her sister also earned mobility opportunities, in part by their own labor, since their work had enabled them to attend a private Catholic school that offered them a safer environment.

The sociology of immigration illuminates some of the familial behavior transitions that occur as a result of immigration. Scholars have drawn attention to gender realignments that occur in spousal relations. When men are unable to be sole economic supporters, women seek employment outside the home. As a result, men's authority in the house is often diminished, and inversely, these earnings give women agency and power within the household.[9] Migration also provokes consequences that affect all family members, not only spouses. What happens when children are also economic co-contributors? Like the women in previous household studies, the street vending children in this study are also economic contributors, and their work supplements the low earnings of their parents in the United States.

During my time in the field, I saw that children were very influential in key family decisions. They had a say in how money was spent, and in the family business their opinion was also valued. For example, eighteen-year-old Veronica convinced her father to street vend full-time and actually quit his back-breaking job as a driver. Veronica was a full-time community college student when I interviewed her, and she also sold tejuino with her family. She did this part-time on the weekend and sometimes after school. Veronica was tired of seeing her parents suffer at their jobs. Her dad constantly endured back pain and her mother "always used to come, like, all stressed" from her job at the factory. Since Veronica's father knew how to make tejuino, she encouraged her parents to leave their jobs after showing them her calculations that revealed that they would make more money selling this specialized drink. Veronica felt responsible and somewhat vulnerable after her parents followed up on her proposal because the money they made from selling tejuino became their only source of income. One summer afternoon, she expressed her fears when I spoke with her at the side of the road:

> I was scared because what if we didn't make that much money and I had already told my dad that it's better that we work here because we could make more money. But no, I have seen the difference and, yeah, my father was even happy. He was like, . . . "It was good that you told me . . . that it's better right here [selling tejuino] than over there [previous job]."

The youth in this study were business-savvy risk takers, and constantly had ideas on how to increase revenues. Studies regarding street vending families in developing countries have noted the role of the patriarchal father who would "order them to get out of the house and sell merchandise he would bring home."[10] In these household studies, the children are portrayed as disenfranchised and obligated to obey their father. However, the children in this study were an important part of the decision-making processes involved in street vending because they had unique resources that their parents respected and valued. Some of these resources resulted from the children's faster acculturation to the United States.

American Generational Resources

The children in this study have acculturated faster than their immigrant parents. They speak English and are very familiar with American culture and technology, and most are also U.S. citizens. Both the children and their parents see these American generational resources—language ability, citizenship, cultural knowledge, and familiarity with technology—as invaluable for the family and the family business. According to segmented assimilation theory, however, when children of immigrants acculturate faster than the parents, the result is downward mobility, also known as *dissonant acculturation*.[11] In theory, of course, this all makes sense. Lack of harmony between parents and children means that there are greater disagreements in their values, and according to the theory, it also means that children have an advantage over parents. How? Well, speaking English is an empowering asset. Studies have shown that English proficiency can have a significant and enduring impact on later socioeconomic status and integration into U.S. society.[12]

But in a family context, it also means that children can control situations and even withhold information from parents.[13] For example, according to segmented assimilation theory, children often serve as interpreters at teacher conferences and misinform their parents about their school progress or lack of progress. Proponents of the theory also assert that parents lose authority to discipline their children. This power shift in the household is a source of concern because lack of parental control can lead children to adopt deviant behavior from their community peers, including gang members.[14] If we use segmented assimilation theory to understand the experience of street vending children, we could believe that they are on a path to dissonant acculturation. After all, they have acculturated to the United States faster than their parents, and, if you recall from chapter 1, most street vending children interact with gang members in their community. In fact, many of their cousins are in gangs. You might recall that thirteen-year-old Nadya had acknowledged, "Like my cousin, he got into jail like three times already because he's, like, stealing and doing drugs and he's a gangster. I don't want to be like him." Or you might remember the words of eighteen-year-old Veronica, who said, "My neighbor just sleeps, smokes drugs, and then, like, he goes and eats and he doesn't even help his parents." The children in this study are not sheltered from interactions with gang members, drug users, or street violence. That is the reality of their neighborhoods in Boyle Heights. But that is not their only reality. They are also exposed to hardworking community members and close family ties that are a positive influence on them.

Segmented assimilation theory was developed in the early 1990s to help explain the incorporation experience of post-1965 immigrants who hailed predominately from Latin America, the Caribbean, and Asia.[15] However, this theory still drew on classical assimilation theory, with its Eurocentric perspectives that presented assimilation to the mainstream middle class as a unidirectional process. This model is still intact in segmented assimilation theory, whose model still characterizes the mainstream as White Anglo Saxon Protestant (WASP). Assimilating to this mainstream is the primary pathway of incorporation in this theory. It was not until the turn of the twenty-first century that Richard Alba and Victor Nee provided a nuanced understanding of the mainstream to include more than just Whites, and proposed that the mainstream is expanding.[16] In her study of the Mexican middle class, sociologist Jody Agius Vallejo found that Mexican Americans are incorporating into a minority class culture and community.[17] In other words, they are assimilating to other middle-class Mexicans. These findings challenge the dissonant acculturation pathway in segmented assimilation theory, which homogenized Mexicans into an underclass. In the minority culture of mobility theory, the main contribution is that class has been overlooked in analyses of the Mexican population and its incorporation patterns.[18] In other words, Mexicans are a heterogeneous group in terms of class, and their "class background affects different spheres of social life and mobility pathways."[19] Class does matter, and so does citizenship. Vallejo found that the advantages enjoyed by the second generation were due to the adjustment of legal status of their parents, thanks to the policies in place that granted the ability to legalize through native-born infants.[20]

The street vending families that shared their stories for this book are still disadvantaged by class, context of reception, undocumented status, and labor opportunities. According to Vallejo,

> The majority of research on the Mexican origin population in the United States unintentionally contributes to the idea that Mexican Americans will never assimilate into the middle class, by focusing primarily on poor and unauthorized workers and their similarly low-income children who remain in disadvantaged or working-class ethnic communities.[21]

Vallejo is absolutely correct. In fact, when I was on the academic job market, I was told by one prominent university in Southern California that its department wanted to move away from studying poor Latinx communities in the informal sector of the economy, and instead wanted to focus on Latinx professionals. For these very reasons, moreover, *Kids at Work* is a study that primarily focuses on "poor and unauthorized workers and their similarly low-income children who remain in disadvantaged or working-class ethnic communities." But the findings of this study reveal so much more than a typology of upward and downward mobility. While it would be much easier to dismiss this population as unworthy of being studied because of their possible downward mobility, I decided to dig a little deeper, and my time with these families allowed me to see how these household dynamics among street vending families impact socioeconomic transitions without focusing on unidirectional assimilation processes into the American mainstream or a minority class culture of mobility.

Focusing on classical definitions of success and upward mobility overshadows the agency, resiliency, and resources within working families. Contrary to what segmented assimilation theory would predict, I found that parents' authority over their children is not diminished as a result of children's faster acculturation. Rather, parents who work with their children are more vigilant of their children because they spend more time with them. Children also respect their parents' work efforts and report feeling closer to them. The children in this study earn income alongside their parents and are language and media brokers as well. These skills and resources are important because they allow children to contribute to the family's social and economic adaptation in a unique way. In fact, having legal status, which their parents lack, serves another function for the family business. Street vending children use their own citizenship not as an individual right and privilege, but as a resource that can help the family as a protection mechanism against the police. These resources are unique and important to the street vending children in Los Angeles precisely because this activity takes place in the United States. In other words, their faster acculturation in the United States is the asset. For example, in Mexican and Peruvian household studies, children, like their mothers, are portrayed as victims of the patriarchal father, where the father has power over the resources and the decision-making process in the household.[22] While citizenship, language skills, and popular culture knowledge of children may be irrelevant resources in countries where children and their parents speak the dominant language, my study shows that in the United States, these are valuable resources for the street vending children and their families precisely because parents do not have these resources.

These American generational resources are crucial to the family enterprise and provide the youth with leverage and negotiation power in both the household and the family business. Children are not single objects of socialization; they are actively helping their parents establish community and work life in the United States with their AGRs. The following section details how English language skills, knowledge of popular culture and technology, and citizenship are (1) resources unique to the children, (2) valued by their immigrant parents, and (3) useful for the family business.

English Language Skills

The ability to speak English gives immigrant children an upper hand in day-to-day interactions in U.S. society.[23] For young street vendors, however, the ability to speak English becomes a crucial resource for the entire family, as knowing English mitigates the illegality of their work. It also helps them expose their business to non-Latinx/Spanish-speaking clientele.

Lack of English language skills makes street vendors more vulnerable to police harassment and discrimination. Being able to communicate with the police eases the aggression against street vendors. Marisela explains that she feels comfortable letting her daughters (ages seventeen and eighteen) street vend alone because they speak English.

> The police approach the people that don't speak English and they get mad. But when my daughters respond back to them in English, "Okay, then, I'll move," . . . then the cops say, "Well, you know you can't street vend here because someone called us and they don't want you to be here." But the cops do discriminate when you don't speak the language.

Like others in this study, Marisela recognizes that speaking English is an important asset for the business and is a skill that mostly children possess. According to Marisela, the police approach the street vendors assuming that they do not understand or speak English. When they come with these preconceived assumptions, they are loud and rude to street vendors who do not comply with the police officers' orders or who cannot defend themselves verbally. Children, on the other hand, comply with the orders both by putting away their street vending goods and by telling the police they understand.

Speaking English also serves to increase clientele. Contrary to the common belief that street vendors are patronized only by Latinx Spanish speakers,[24] the street vendors' clientele was becoming increasingly diverse, as is the case in New York City.[25] For example, Susana (age fourteen), told me that "Koreans, Latinos, and White people" purchased pupusas from her family. When asked about her experience with these customers, she replied, "It's the same because I speak English; and then I ask them what they want so I treat them the same. I speak both languages." For Susana, being bilingual made her comfortable when interacting with non-Spanish speakers. Susana's mother, on the other hand, was a little uncomfortable communicating with non-Spanish speakers. Below is an excerpt from my field notes when Susana translated for an Asian couple eager to taste pupusas for the first time.

> An Asian couple approached the pupusa stand and asked the cook, Hilda, what she was selling. Without saying a word, Hilda turns to her daughter Susana and immediately Susana explains to the couple, in English, that pupusas are like Mexican gorditas but traditionally from El Salvador and

Honduras: "We put cheese or chicharrón inside and then put cabbage and sauce over it once they are cooked."

Meanwhile, Hilda remained silent, continuing to make the pupusas with a clap-like motion. She molded the pupusa to an almost perfect flat circle and carefully softened the rough edges with her index finger. Susana and other children provided a type of customer service that parents could not provide due to language barriers. This in turn made customers more comfortable and willing to spend their money on new and authentic Salvadoran food.

For many Latinx families, it is common for children to serve as translators and mediators between their parents and schoolteachers, doctors, or even lawyers.[26] Among street vending families, speaking English and translating for the parents also has positive consequences for the family's income. Customers were often surprised to learn that street vendors spoke English. When I went street vending with Martha (age eighteen), two young men approached us on the street. They spoke to one another in English and switched to Spanish when they addressed us. Martha rolled her eyes, annoyed by the customers' assumption that she did not speak English. During my interview with Martha she explained,

> Customers are like, "I can't believe you are helping your dad. And you know English!" I mean, even most of the people are like, "Oh my God! I can't believe you know English!" And I am like, "Dude, I was born here, what is wrong with you?"

Martha's ability to speak English challenged the customers' stereotypes of street vendors as undocumented monolingual Spanish speakers. But most importantly, speaking English allowed her to establish rapport with diverse customers, build a steady clientele, and ultimately generate more revenue for the family.

Similarly, sixteen-year-old Sofia also sold corn on the cob to non-Hispanic and non-Spanish speakers. Sofia street vended alongside her father and uncle at the same park. Each separately pushed their own cart around a large park with a lake. Sofia had South Asian customers who purchased corn on the cob only from her. She boasted,

Figure 3.1. Children create signs in English for English-speaking customers.

There are these Indian people and they always come to me. My uncle would pass or my dad would pass and they would not go with them, they would go with me. And a lot of people do that. They are like, "Yeah, we were looking for you." And I could be, like, on the opposite side and they will go all the way over there just to look for me.

Even though her relatives sold the same food she did, Sofia believes that customers liked her better because she spoke English. Unlike her father and uncle, she was able to establish a customer-vendor relation by simply having informal conversations with clients in English.

I also saw children write or type signs in English so that parents would not have to translate for their customers when selling alone. For example, Joaquín laminated three cards that contained a picture of a carrot, a beet, and an orange. Each card also had the name of the fruit and vegetable. Joaquín laminated the small cards, hole punched them, and then tied them to his mother's cart. When I street vended with Rosa, one Saturday morning she showed me the cards and told me that this made it easier for her to explain to customers the kind of juice she could make for them. Joaquín also sold juice, but he did so around the block. Since he could not be there to translate for his mom, these cards offered a perfect solution.

Access to Technology and Knowledge of Popular Culture

It is common for children to serve as media brokers for their immigrant parents.[27] Child street vendors were into technology (computers, video games, cell phones) and U.S. popular culture like music, movies, and clothing. Parents and children alike used cell phones to communicate while street vending. However, children also used their smartphones to promote the family business by creating and updating social media pages, including Facebook and Twitter, with information about their business. One Facebook message from eighteen-year-old Patricia read, "We don't Sell Today Due To The Weather :/ *Hoy No Vendemos Pero Los Esperamos Mañana*!!" This task was solely the child's responsibility. When I asked parents whether they knew how to update the pages, they usually replied, "I don't even know how to turn on a computer." Patricia tried to teach her mother to use Facebook, but after a while she took on the responsibility of updating it for her. Patricia elaborated,

> My mom isn't really into technology. I've noticed that a lot of people who come here, they're on Facebook. So I told my mom, "I'll make you a Facebook page." I showed her how to use it and update her status and she is getting a lot of people following her. . . . I help her update her status, like, where we are located, where we work, when do we start, what we have, what we sell. So it helps a lot. And people have said, "Oh, I saw you on Facebook." We also post stuff like, "We're on our way." . . . It helps a lot.

Facebook was a valuable resource for street vendors that helped them communicate directly with their clients. This was important because vendors had to take many things into consideration before going to the streets. For example, on rainy days, some canceled their sales, but if they saw the rain mitigating, sometimes they would take a chance. Consequently, Facebook allowed them to inform customers of their decision to street vend. Another point of consideration was police raids. More than once I went to La Cumbrita only to find an empty parking lot on days when vendors typically gathered to sell their food. The threat of police raids in places like La Cumbrita dissuaded vendors from street vending on certain days. However, missing a day of sales was not feasible for some vendors, who would opt to vend at other locations, including their own front yards. I often saw vendors at La Cumbrita hold signs written in Spanish informing customers of their new location. They would hide these signs when the police passed by. Children's ability to use the Internet to communicate directly with their customers helped avoid this extra burden and stress on their entire families.

Children were also aware of Internet blogs mentioning La Cumbrita and their *puesto* (street vending stand). Some Internet blogs were from Los Angeles foodies, while others were from recognized newspaper reporters. La Cumbrita was "a must," according to some of these bloggers, who recommended the place for its authentic ethnic food. Children sometimes used these blogs to lure in customers. On one occasion, one of my respondents and his family catered for an event attended by the Los Angeles mayor. The young street vendor showed me a cell phone picture of them with then mayor Villaraigosa. While this picture was taken, he matter-of-factly told the mayor, "The police tell us that you sent them," referring to their current struggle with the police. He also directed him to the website where people praised their food.

Sonia (age thirteen) sold DVDs and CDs with her parents, and her knowledge of popular culture benefited the family business. I had a chance to see her in action when the movie distributor dealt directly with teenage Sonia and not with her parents. During one of my field site observations, I was invited to a Halloween party. Since the vendors at La Cumbrita had organized this party for the vendors in the neighborhood, most vendors that night decided to stop street vending early, around 10:00 p.m., and attend the party. Because I had been shadowing them all day, Sonia's family invited me to the party, and I agreed to go. They had an extra space in their 2007 Yukon truck, so I squeezed into the back seat next to Sonia and her little brother. On our way to the party, they decided to stop by their house to pick up sweaters for the kids. When we opened the car door, we were met with a man holding a box full of movies. He was their movie distributor. Sonia's mother got out of the car and went up the stairs to their apartment to get the sweaters. Meanwhile, Sonia made sure they got the correct number of movies and requested more of the popular movies. "I need three more *High School Musical*," she told their distributor. She passed the movies to me and asked, "Have you seen this one?" and then confidently stated, "This one is good. We sell this one a lot." Sonia knew what movies were popular not only because she enjoyed watching them as a kid herself, but because she knew her clientele.

While street vendors do not depend on social pages for their business, children are applying their knowledge of popular media and culture to outreach to a larger audience. In fact, this is already a popular strategy among sophisticated food truck businesses in Los Angeles and New York.[28] In this realm, the children of street vendors are the experts and the parents take on a more auxiliary role.

Parents were reluctant to use technology for their business. The distrust or lack of knowledge of new technology is common among first-generation, Spanish monolingual vendors. New technology and applications are being developed and the youth are spearheading this new trend. For example, in June 2017, Latino USA aired a podcast titled "No Money More Problems."[29] In this podcast, they featured an *elotero* from Santa Barbara, California, who has been street vending his roasted corn for over twenty years near a university and recently started using Venmo, a digital method that helps customers pay him directly from their smartphones. Students reacted with amazement when they saw this technologically advanced *elotero*: "Mira un elotero con Venmo. Un elotero con Venmo? Se le hacía curioso. Les daba risa. Se sorprendían" (Look, an elotero with Venmo. An elotero with Venmo? They thought it was funny. It made them laugh. It surprised them), recalled the *elotero*. He then explained how the idea of using Venmo came from a group of Latina students who introduced him, encouraged him, and even helped him open an account. Now students use Venmo to pay him all the time. He is very successful and proud of being a very technologically advanced *elotero*. Similar to these students, the children of street vendors are technologically savvy and constantly finding ways to incorporate what they learn to help the family business.

Citizenship: "Dude, I Was Born Here"

Undocumented status made parents vulnerable to local authorities, but the children's U.S. citizenship extended protection to their undocumented parents. U.S. citizenship for these children and their families is a valuable resource. Only five parents in my sample were legal residents. Yet three-fourths of the children in this sample (thirty-three out of forty-three) were born and raised in the United States. Children often cited their parents' lack of citizenship as a reason to explain their choice of occupation. "My mom can't work [elsewhere] because she doesn't have papers," said Esmeralda (age twelve). Similarly, Norma's father, a sewing operator, was fired after his employer did a mass document verification search at the factory. The family then turned to street vending. Patricia (age eighteen) said with resignation, "Before I wasn't planning to help them street vend . . . but now, like, I have to because they can't get hired or else they're going to get sent to México." The underlying fear for these young street vendors was that they would be separated from their parents due to deportation. Indeed, this is a national concern among immigrant families.

According to the Migration Policy Institute, there were "5.1 million U.S. children under age 18 living with at least one unauthorized immigrant parent during the 2009–13 period."[30] The majority of these children (4.1 million) are U.S. citizens. The number of mixed-status families is even higher: 14.6 million people are living in a mixed-status home where at least one family member is unauthorized. This fear was well justified during the Obama administration, with a record mass deportation of 2 million. By 2014, the Department of Homeland Security under the Obama administration had removed 2 million noncitizens.[31] The deportation rates in 2011 surpassed previous deportation figures—359,795 individuals, not to mention the countless family members and loved ones actually affected—under the second Bush (2001–2009) administration. Those fears have amplified since the 2016 election as Trump's administration constantly threatens to deport all undocumented immigrants.

Street vendors are the most vulnerable representatives of undocumented immigrants since their work exposes them so publicly. Even having legal permanent residency afforded little security for street vending parents. For example, Katia's mother is a legal permanent resident with legal authorization to work in the United States. Katia's mother worked as a janitor for many years, but for the last sixteen years she has been selling fruit with her daughter because she makes more money and street vending allowed her to take care of her children when they were younger. Even though street vending is a better work arrangement for her, the criminalization of street vending makes her vulnerable to citations and even arrests. According to Katia, she has gotten many tickets from street vending:

> *Mi mamá agarraba* [my mom would get] tickets and tickets. *Mi mamá* [My mom] has papers, so you know, [it] is bad for her record. It's bad for her record because she could lose her papers.

These interactions with the police made Katia very nervous because as a legal permanent resident, her mother could still get deported. Katia's concerns are not far from reality. The Illegal Immigrant Reform and Immigrant Responsibility Act (IIRIRA) of 1996 imposed provisions that would deport current U.S. residents deemed likely to become a public charge.[32] In her book *Deported*, Tanya Maria Golash-Boza states that many of the 2 million deportees under the Obama administration were in fact legal permanent residents. Katia was very aware that being a U.S. citizen gave her an advantage over her mother. She mentioned that often she would tell her mom to leave her in the fruit stand when the police were near. Other kids developed similar strategies. Fifteen-year-old Elvira told me,

> I can't get in trouble as much as my mom can. . . . Like, the worst thing they [the police] can probably do is give me a ticket 'cause I'm still a minor. And, well, with my mom, they may take her to jail and who knows.

Despite their young age, children saw greater risks to having their parents street vend alone due to their legal status. Being able to articulate in English their right to be in this country was empowering to the children and served to extend protection to their parents.

The children's citizenship was not only an immediate resource for the family, but also a future investment. Little Esmeralda, at just twelve years old, saw her own citizenship as an opportunity to invest in her education with the purpose of helping her parents in the future. Esmeralda, who sells fruit with her mother, plans to go to school to become a lawyer in order to help "fix . . . [her] mom's problems." Esmeralda explained that with a law degree she would help people, like her mother, who did not have papers, "so she [her mom] could have a good work . . . 'cause she doesn't really like that job [street vending]." I continue this discussion in chapter 7.

U.S. citizenship also enabled these children the opportunity to get a driver's license. Street vending requires these families to drive and transport heavy wares such as skillets, tables, chairs, canopies, and pots full of food. During my time in the field, California passed a law—vehicle code 12500 (a)vc—that prohibited undocumented immigrants from obtaining a license to drive. Most parents in my study drove without a license, thus violating the law and putting themselves at risk. They risked getting their cars impounded for up to thirty days, with fines exceeding $1,200.[33] Leticia, introduced in chapter 1, was excited to turn sixteen in order to legally drive. She had been saving money to get her driver's license and looked forward to helping her mom drive their van without constantly fearing the police. As it did for her peers in this study, citizenship offered Leticia a level of protection and belonging that she was able to experience and identify at a young age. The youth recognized that privilege and saw it as a resource they could share with their undocumented parents to offer them protection from local authorities.

Resilient Agency

The youth in this study can communicate in English with peers, customers, and even the police, and they also have considerable knowledge of American popular culture and technology. In fact, most youth are U.S. citizens. Rather than serving as a disadvantage or as a springboard for a dissonant form of acculturation, as Alejandro Portes and Rubén Rumbaut would argue, the children in this study benefit from these American generational resources and in turn benefit their street vending family business.[34] In this context, children's participation in their parents' street vending work serves as a resource that helps buffer against downward mobility. Working together as a family unit provided many benefits for the family and the children. Essentially, children's work provides immediate financial resources for the family and the children. With these extra earnings, families could stay afloat, and some could even help pay for the children's schooling.

These children are in many ways apprentices to their parents, who carry the cultural knowledge of cooking traditional ethnic foods.

However, the children's American generational resources enable the youth to support their parents' work and make it possible for them to sell to more people. The children in this study are not disenfranchised, exploited family members, but rather economic co-providers with parents. This type of family work relation allows us to see that parent-child relations do not always fall into a socialization pattern in which children learn from and are socialized by their parents. Instead, parents also learn and benefit from their children's skills and knowledge, most of which are a result of their faster acculturation.

Street vending with children served a functional component in the household, whereas children's American generational resources helped the family business. It also helped children develop an economic empathy toward their parents because they can directly relate with their parents' struggles. Ultimately, children develop economic empathy for their immigrant parents and forge deeper ties of family connection through the time spent together.

4

Making a Living Together

Communal Family Obligation Code and Economic Empathy

I Work Too MUCH To Be 17,
I Sleep Little && Dnt Get Tireed Caause I'm YOUNG,
I Have Never Had A Normal Teenage Life,
Buut I Guess That's Whaat Maakes My Life So Unique, &&
So Full Of Adventuress
Sad/Mad/Happy/Unforgettable Memories That Shall Last
Forever{:
There's Always Time For The TeenageDream♥
—Leticia, January 2012

Leticia had taken on many new responsibilities months before she posted this poem on her social media page, three years after I interviewed her for the first time, when she was only fourteen years old. On December 28, 2011, her mother, Nilda, suffered a stroke and was hospitalized for three months. I visited Nilda frequently in the hospital, and on numerous occasions I saw Leticia stop by after school and then go to La Cumbrita to street vend. Leticia had decided to continue street vending without her mother because she was the only one able to bring money into the household. In order to manage their street vending business, Leticia enlisted the help of two high school friends and other street vendors at La Cumbrita. Leticia's American generational resources were pivotal during this time, as she used her smartphone and Facebook page to communicate with their customers to inform them that they were still making and selling their famous quesadillas, fried tacos, and more.[1] She also used her Facebook to keep her friends and family informed of her mother's health. Leticia coordinated hospital visits with her mother's friends and relatives to ensure that someone was always at Nilda's bedside while Leticia was at school or vending.

Although it was difficult for Leticia to leave her mother alone in the hospital, she needed to keep vending in order for their family to avoid eviction from their home.

One evening, we sat together in Nilda's dark hospital room. Nilda lay prone on the bed with her eyes closed, and Leticia stared at her mother with tired eyes. Leticia had woken at six o'clock that morning, prepared the sauces for their business, attended school, then went to La Cumbrita to street vend. She was exhausted. "Es el pinche estress," said Leticia while she tenderly caressed her mother's hand, trying to avoid touching the heart monitor clipped onto her index finger letting us know she was still alive. "It's the fucking stress," she murmured again and again, switching from Spanish to English. Leticia blamed the stress they endured street vending for her mother's stroke. She told me countless stories of them getting citations while street vending. This made it difficult for them to stay afloat financially. On that night, I could see that the stress was getting to Leticia as well. She looked tired and overwhelmed, but she never lost faith that her mother would open her eyes again, and she did. Nilda was released from the hospital in March, three weeks before her birthday. Leticia felt that she had no choice but to continue the arduous schedule of waking up early, cooking, going to school, and then going to La Cumbrita to sell food. In fact, Leticia's street vending kept the family economically afloat for six months after her mother was released from the hospital. "I wouldn't let my mom do anything," said Leticia. "But I went to sell one day and she showed up and said she wasn't leaving because that was her *puesto*."[2]

The multiple intersections of oppression that push first-generation immigrants to work as street vendors also spill over to their U.S.-born children like Leticia. As an economic family strategy, the children of street vendors learn to labor side by side with their immigrant parents. As we saw with Leticia, sometimes the children of street vendors take on additional obligations in the household and in their street vending business when parents cannot work. Why?

The children of immigrants develop a special connection to their immigrant parents because they understand the sacrifices their parents make by immigrating to the United States and the social and economic marginalization they experience as immigrants. As sociologist Jody Agius Vallejo argues, the second generation retains strong social and financial obligations to their families and adopts an *immigrant narrative* that is born out of their parents' migration experience, economic marginalization, and a shared struggle for mobility and belonging to explain why they give back socially and financially to their immigrant parents. Vallejo captured this immigrant narrative among the Latinx middle class. Vallejo also finds that the children of immigrants who grow up poor are more likely to give back financially to family or extended kin and are also more likely to provide social support than those raised in more economically stable households.[3] Giving back can affect the mobility and economic security of the second generation because they are financially stretched due to the high financial demands that come from poor family and extended kin. The compulsion to help kin is a pattern that has been observed among African Americans as well.[4]

This chapter builds on Vallejo's work with the Mexican middle class by shedding light on how and why children adopt an ideology beyond an immigrant narrative. The child street vendors in this study are experiencing firsthand this form of immigrant sacrifice faced by immigrants in lower-sector occupations. The children in this study are not just adopting an immigrant narrative from their parents' harsh working conditions, but they develop a *communal family obligation code*, which holds that U.S.-born children must work with immigrant parents in myriad ways to make ends meet.[5] This code differs drastically from the typical expectations of children in American society. Child street vendors in this study experience compounded disadvantages stemming from their parents' social locations rooted in unauthorized status, informal work, and stigma from their work. Yet street vending also sets the stage for children to develop *economic empathy*, resulting from experiencing their parents' position of oppression and their family's economic marginalization. Economic empathy is a behavior toward immigrant parents that is born out of the experience of working together to sustain the household and derives from a *shared* struggle that exposes the children of immigrants to their undocumented parents' labor struggles. In other words, economic empathy is fostered by the practice of communal family obligation to work together.

Communal Family Obligation and Remuneration

Day in and day out, child street vendors work with their parents, and many become integral to the functioning of the family business and the family's economic stability. Child street vendors know firsthand the hard work that is required to make a living. They wake up early. They prepare food. They set up the tables. They handle money.[6] They negotiate with clients. They devise marketing strategies to increase business. The children and the parents who work together have developed a communal family obligation code by which both parents and children benefit from making a living together. In this parent-child economic productive unit, kids must work, but they also reap economic benefits. The communal family obligation code is born out of necessity and derives from structural constraints and in turn creates stronger bonds and obligations among children and their parents. Children understand that their family's very economic survival depends on their contributions as well. Their relationship to money—how money is earned, distributed in the family, and spent—is central to street vending families because children are vital to this decision-making process.

The communal family obligation code is expressed in several different ways. The first way is that children do not expect to be paid for work. Among all my participants, the typical expectation that one should be paid for a day's work was rejected in favor of helping the family. The idea of receiving payment for work was almost insulting to children. For example, when I asked fourteen-year-old Susana whether her parents ever paid her for her help, she immediately said no. She explained it this way: "No, I'm not that kind of person, 'cause I don't ask them, like, 'Oh, I helped you, so are you gonna pay me or something?'" However, this does not mean that children never feel that their parents owe them some form of compensation. Susana clarified, "If we work here on Fridays, we'll go to the mall the next day, and I'll be like, 'Okay, can you buy me this?'" With confidence, Susana added, "I think I earn what they buy me." Children knew that if they worked with their parent, they had earned the right to ask for things.

Rather than getting paid an hourly wage for their work, they engage in *family bartering*, or rules of exchange and remuneration between parents and children. When children sell merchandise by themselves, they typically hand all of the day's earnings off to their mother, father, or even an older sibling. Fewer than half of the interviewees said they receive cash regularly from their parents as compensation for vending. And when they did, the amount for a day's work varied between five and thirty dollars, a small sum compared to a typical day's take. With this cash, they buy everyday necessities, items such as shoes and school supplies, but also some nice extras that children and teens desire in a consumer-driven society, such as video games and brand-name jeans. The majority of the kids, however, do not ask their parents for money. Rather, they barter for specific items. In her book *Consuming Citizenship*, sociologist Lisa Sun-Hee Park studied the children of Korean and Chinese immigrant entrepreneurs in thirty-six different types of businesses and found that most kids do not get paid and very few get twenty dollars a day for their help.[7] In contrast to the children of street vendors, some of the kids in Park's study who did not get paid did not want to receive payment because they did not want their parents to feel more entitled to boss them around.

On the other hand, child street vendors have expressed feelings of appreciation toward their parents and do not demand payment because they feel that the food, clothes, and education that they get from their parents are payment enough. In some cases, the children in my study feel empowered and know that they can get anything they want because they help their parents. Alejandro explained, "I don't really ask her for money because . . . I'd rather ask her for things like shoes." Similarly, when I asked Leticia whether she got paid for keeping the family afloat during her mother's illness, she paused for a second, tilted her head, looked up, and after a short "ummmm" sound, she explained,

> Like, for example, I can work all these days and I can tell my mom, "Can I go to the movies?" And she will give me, like, ten dollars to buy the movie ticket or buy some food or to go out with my friends. Or she will give me money to buy shoes or something like that. Oh yeah! She also pays my cell phone bill.

These children received from their parents what most middle-class children receive without having to work.[8] Rather than feeling entitled to these privileges—money for social outings with friends, clothes, food, and payment of their cell phone bill—they felt that they had to earn them. As thirteen-year-old Nadya explained, "If I want some new clothes, I have to earn it, like I have to work. I have to help my mom. . . . Whatever we want my mom buys it for us, like the *comida* [food], all the clothes, the shoes, so, like, that's how it works." Gloria added, "My mom buys more for my older sister because she works more with them. My other sisters, the one who is fourteen, does not get a lot of things because she only stays home and takes care of my brothers and sisters." Early on, children understand that the work done outside the home is valued and rewarded more. Tasks like cleaning and taking care of siblings are not valued or compensated as much, an issue that I will discuss in the following chapter. Children recognized their communal family obligation code as a matter of fact. Their street vending work helps parents, but it also helps them. To put it in Alejandro's words,

> It's help, because sometimes she gives me money and sometimes she doesn't. It's not that I want the money. I just do it for the help, because I know she is the one that needs the money the most. Well, we both do because we live under the same roof, so most if not all the money goes to our house, our rent and to stuff that we need.

Economic incentives blended together with children's moral obligations to help support their families. This communal family obligation code is developed early in their childhood. Parents recognize that like most children, their own children crave the latest technology and material goods, but they also have limited resources to buy their kids what they desire. In addition, they cannot afford to hire help, and so children's labor becomes integral to their ability to support the family unit. Parents like Lorena recognized that the only way to give their children what they wanted was if the children contributed their labor. Lorena elaborated,

> Yes, they do help. For example, I have to cut fruit, make the jam and prepare the dough. Then imagine if I had to pay someone else. Then, it is not that I am saving money. I tell my son, "Here is five dollars" or whatever. On Monday, he bought an iPod. He had to sacrifice a lot to save up and buy his iPod. Look, they want their little luxuries. Then, it is help for us and for them, too.[9]

Almadelia also believes it is better to obtain help from her children instead of hiring anyone else. "Si alguien tiene que contratar alguna persona, es mejor que se venga el hijo. Se ayudan." (If someone has to hire a person, it is better for it to be your child. It's mutual help.) Similarly, when I asked Nilda, Leticia's mom, whether she paid her kids for helping, she replied with a firm "No" and then burst into laughter and added, "Pero me saca lo que quiere." (She gets whatever she wants out of me.) Nilda elaborated,

> I don't pay my little girl, but she gets whatever she wants out of me. I tell her, if you help me I will pay for your cell phone, if you help me I will buy you pants, if you help me I will buy you this.[10]

The communal family obligation code leads to intimate knowledge of family needs typically associated with adult responsibilities. Parents and children learn that they must work together in order to fulfill these family needs as well as their personal desires for material goods. In our current consumer age, sociologist Allison Pugh reminds us, childhoods have become more commercialized, and children in the United States want too many material things.[11] According to Park, consumerism is key for Asian American children and their parents to demonstrate their U.S. citizenship.[12] Furthermore, for the children and the parents in Park's study, the participation of children in the family business was a stepping stone to getting an education. Most of the parents pressured their children to go to prestigious universities and study majors that would lead to profitable careers. Ensuring that their children had prosperous futures guaranteed parents a retirement. In addition, a high-paying career would allow their children to buy cars, houses, and clothes that would show their success in this country to fellow Asian immigrants and to White Americans.

A major difference between the children of Asian entrepreneurs and child street vendors is the context of their work. The Asian entrepreneurs were small business owners; the Latinx street vending children work with their parents in the informal sector of the economy. According to Park, the Asian entrepreneurs were seen as hardworking and model minorities, while the Latinx kids and their parents are criminalized on a regular basis for the work that they do in very public and visible spaces.[13] Despite the different nature of the job, both Asian and Latinx kids expressed pride in their parents' work and said that they were happy that their parents worked for themselves. Notably, none of the children who shared their story with me desired to have a "White boss."

Economic Empathy

Compared to children who do not work with their parents, working children are more mindful of how they spent the money they received from selling on the street. The children who worked with their parents developed an empathetic stance toward their parents that I call economic empathy, a resiliency that results from experiencing their parents' position of oppression. Economic empathy develops not just from working together but from working tirelessly to help support the family. Scholars refer to the work that children do for their parents based on obligation or deep feelings of guilt, love, and concern as the labor of love.[14] Children often make sacrifices to work in order to help their parents or their younger siblings. This is often the case with farmworkers and their families.[15] In her book *Voices from the Fields: Children and Migrant Farmworkers Tell Their Stories*, S. Beth Atkin assembles a collection of autobiographical stories of young children who work with their parents doing farm work in California. In these essays, the children describe their everyday lives, which include going to school and sometimes missing school in order to help with the farm work. Atkin writes, "One of the most disturbing yet also heartening situations I encountered were older siblings who chose to drop out of school to work in the fields so a younger sister or brother could finish school and improve her or his life."[16] Atkin captures the sacrifices that individual family members make for the good of the entire family.

Additionally, most children who worked with their parents as street vendors feel that it is their responsibility to help relieve some of their parents' economic burden. For example, fourteen-year-old Amanda earns five dollars every time she works with her mother, and she saves her hard-earned money in a box inside her clothing drawer in case her mother ever needs money. She confessed to wanting to use her money for toys, but, because she has worked in the business and understands that their income from street vending fluctuates, she knows that there are days when one can come up short of cash or that unforeseen economic emergencies are frequent. At a young age, she realized that helping her mother was more important than indulging in material things like toys. Rather than buying things for herself, she frequently loans her mother money to buy fruit for the business. This type of labor of love is relatively unusual in most contemporary Western societies.

In addition, street vending children *experience* their parents' pain, which is also their own. Children feel a strong empathy with their parents and often frame their work as a responsibility. Leticia told me, "I don't really see this like a job. I see it more like our responsibility. Like, I have to be there to help my mom, so she won't get that tired." Similar to Leticia, seventeen-year-old Clara choked back tears as she said, "We feel my mom's pain for working." Clara and her mother sell fresh cut-up fruit. Many times, she has helped her mother hide their wares and fruit behind parked cars in the parking lot during police raids. These moments help Clara value her mom's work and the risks involved. These experiences transcend an immigrant narrative and are the substance of daily dialogues, even something that parents talk about with their children after work or over dinner conversations.

Parents also describe having closer relationships with the children who worked with them. The parents emphasize that economic empathy results from working together and sharing the common struggle of running from the cops and selling in all kinds of weather. For example, despite having two older brothers, Leticia is the only one who helps her mother street vend. One son is Leticia's twin and the other is eighteen years old. During my interview with Nilda, she distinguished between the relationships she had with her kids. Nilda confessed that she was more attached to Leticia and attributed this attachment to gender, but she also emphasized the fact that they worked together. Nilda said that her relationship with her children, especially her daughter, would be different if she worked in the formal sector, like at a factory or a restaurant, because they would not witness her struggle.

> My daughter is living what I am doing. She knows, for example, Leticia knows that I get tickets [citations], about the police, [having to work in] the rain, the water, everything. All of my kids also know about this, but they don't live it. . . . My relationship with Leticia is more of attachment [*apegamiento*]. What happens is that she is a girl and I have more trust

[*confianza*] in her for everything. And with my sons, we talk less. They are less attached to me. Why? For the same reasons . . . They don't interact [*conviven*] with me.

Nilda reiterates her realization that both interaction and spending time together at work help create not only empathy, but economic empathy. Héctor's words help to better clarify this concept:

> When our children realize how we earn our money, it is difficult for them to take the wrong path. Because they say, "My dad or my mom work hard to earn money and how could I waste it."

Parents were confident that if children experienced firsthand the conditions under which money is earned through street vending, children would have a stronger appreciation and respect for parents and the money they earned. Parents also believe that working together buffers children from joining gangs or doing drugs, or what they described as "taking the wrong path." This sentiment is echoed by the children. Seventeen-year-old Clara told me that her relationship with her mother was special. She told me that she does not ask her mother for many things because she knows how much work it takes to earn a dollar. She compares her life with the lives of friends who splurge on consumer items carelessly. She believes that if her friends worked as much as she did, they would not be as demanding with their parents. Clara told me,

> I would like people to come here and see that it is not easy. We see my mom suffer. I see friends that don't do anything. They go shopping and I tell them, "Dude, while you're shopping I'm working my ass off over here." A lot of people make fun of my mom or me, but if they only knew. Then they would be saying, "Don't buy me this, don't buy me that." I think my relationship with my mother is special.

Clara's quote encapsulates the meaning of economic empathy. Clara explains how she sees her mom suffer and she connects that to her own pain as well. She states that many people make fun of her mom and they also make fun of her for street vending. She recognizes that she works hard just like her mom does. She then shows us what economic empathy is not. In comparing herself to her friend, she implies that if they had economic empathy toward their parents, they would not ask for excessive material goods. Clara ends by saying that the relationship with her mother is special. Their shared struggle creates economic empathy and brings them closer.

Rejection of Parental Work

Economic empathy and a communal family obligation code develop only among the children who work with their parents and who had first-hand experience of the difficulty of earning a living doing street vending work. I also interviewed families in which children do not work along-side their parents, and they espoused ideologies about work and family that were very different from those of their working peers. Street vending youth also spoke extensively about their siblings, cousins, or friends who did not street vend. Paradoxically, the children who develop a sense of communal family obligation and economic empathy see themselves in sharp contrast to their nonworking peers, whom they view as lazy and irresponsible, and as bad sons and daughters. Fourteen-year-old Linda compared herself with her cousin of the same age who did not help. Linda's aunt sells tamales. Linda describes the difference:

> I learn to understand my mom. When one of my aunts started losing days at work, like, my cousin wouldn't understand. She would want to do the same things when her mom couldn't afford it anymore. So it's like, I learn to understand that when my mom has money, I feel comfortable asking my mom, "Can you buy me this?" But when I know, like, the sales didn't go good, I won't ask [my mom] for money.

Linda's economic empathy helped her know when bartering with her mom was appropriate and when it was not. Linda's cousin, on the other hand, lacked economic empathy and as Linda points out, her cousin did not understand that her mother could not afford the things she used to buy when she was working more hours at her employment. Linda makes it very clear that she "learned to understand" when not to ask.

Sixteen-year-old Josefina also had a cousin, Angela, who did not work with her street vending parents. Josefina expressed frustration over her cousin's lack of support and economic empathy toward her parents. She explained, "My cousin takes everything for granted." Unlike Josefina, Angela frequently asked for money even if she knew sales were slow. Josefina expressed economic empathy when she added, "My aunt would bust her butt and everything and my cousin just doesn't care." Josefina contrasted her experience with that of her cousin this way:

> I try to look for things I like and I ask myself, "Do I really need them?" . . . I look for specials and everything and my cousin . . . just, like, makes her mom make food every night. Like [my aunt] barely gets sleep and [my cousin] doesn't care. It came to a point where my aunt hired me to come help her every night. And, you know, having a daughter. We are the same age. I'm four months older than her.

Josefina's body language could not hide the frustration she felt toward her cousin. She would tighten her fist, shake her head, roll her eyes, and even extend her arms to demonstrate her lack of understanding when she said, "And, you know, having a daughter." Josefina found it perplexing that a daughter would not help her own mother. Her own gendered expectations were not met, and that was frustrating for her. Here it is important to remember Nilda's words, "All of my kids also know about this, but they don't live it." Economic empathy is the result of practice and a shared work struggle, one that Josefina's cousin simply did not have.

Intrigued by Josefina's description of her cousin, I interviewed Angela as part of my comparison group of children who do not work with their street vending parents. Most interviews with street vending children took from one to three hours, but my interview with Angela was only fifteen minutes long. She had very little interest in her mother's street vending business and mostly shrugged her shoulders, followed by an "I don't know" to questions pertaining to the business. Similar to other children who did not street vend with their parents, Angela told me that her mother had made the fateful decision to street vend. Angela also spent a lot of her free time with her father, who had remarried and lived in Pasadena, a town a few miles away from Boyle Heights, where her mother lives. Being removed from her mother's daily struggle prevented Angela from developing economic empathy, a sharp contrast to Josefina, her cousin.

The lack of economic empathy among children who do not street vend with their parents did not mean that the nonworking children do not love and appreciate their parents. However, the youth in this group were removed from their parents' street vending struggles, and some even expressed feelings of embarrassment about their parents' work.[17] For example, fourteen-year-old Glenda relayed, "I hate it when she sells tamales outside my school." Children who did not work with their parents ignored the social structures that pushed their parents to street vend. They also missed out on the opportunity to develop an economic stance that would have proved useful in countering stigma associated with street vending. Nonworking children did not understand how difficult it was to find employment and the sacrifices required to earn money street vending. These children often developed a level of resentment toward their parents for "choosing" to work as street vendors. Some could not understand why their parents could not get a "normal" job instead.

Fourteen-year-old Betty is an example of this pattern. Betty did not work with her mother and she was embarrassed that her mother was a street vendor. She wanted her mother to get a "normal" job cleaning houses, working as a janitor, or distributing newspapers. Betty perceived these service sector jobs as higher in status than street vending. When I interviewed Betty in the kitchen of her family's small two-bedroom apartment, she was eating a cup of instant noodles. Her mother had left tamales that morning for both of us to eat. As I ate two tamales, Betty made a face of disgust and said she was tired of tamales and preferred to eat noodles. I could not relate to Betty; in my own house, we eat tamales only during Christmas, so eating tamales in July was a treat! Later in the interview, I asked Betty whether she had saved money from her allowance. She responded with a cutting "No."

During our interview, furthermore, I asked, "Why don't you save money?" "Usually I just spend it all. I just don't save it," replied Betty. Unlike the youth who worked with their parents, Betty was very detached from her mother's work and even came to view the tamales that her mother sells as emblematic of an abnormal occupation. When I asked her what she liked about her mother's work, she replied in a high voice, "Nothing. Nothing. I'm tired of it. It's her decision to sell them [tamales] because we need money." Betty failed to recognize that her mother's undocumented status pushed her to the underground economy. Betty was certain that, like her father who worked as a newspaper distributer, her mother could also find another type of work.[18] Rather than feeling empathy toward her mother, though, she expressed frustration and saw it as her mother's decision to do this type of work.

Just because children who work with their parents have developed a sense of economic empathy does not mean that they do not experience tensions with their parents. The chief complaint relayed by working children is that they work too much. This is a common complaint among children of Asian entrepreneurs as well. For example, in her study on Chinese families in Britain, Miri Song stated, "All of the young people interviewed in this study stressed that the shop ran their lives."[19] Similarly, the street vending children I spoke with saw their work as stealing their childhood and golden teenage years that should be spent hanging out with friends, going to theme parks, and extracurricular activities. You might recall Leticia's poem in the opening of this chapter, when she states, "I Work Too MUCH To Be 17," followed by "I Have Never Had A Normal Teenage Life." Although children rationalized their work as a family obligation, they did feel overworked at times. Patricia, who is just one year younger than Leticia, reflected,

> I think there is a limit, because, you know, we are young and we wanna, like, have fun. Have our *juventud* [youth], you get me? But, I mean, it's good that we help. It's just—there should be a limit.

Other children also complained about not having time to go out with friends because they had to work. For example, Josefina, who is also sixteen, complained about not being able to go out with her friends to the movies or to Disneyland. These social outings with her friends often clashed with the time she worked on the weekend. During our interview, she confided,

> Sometimes it sucks because, I mean, I do give up a lot of things. Like, there are times that my friends are like, "Oh, let's go to the movies," and I'll be like, "No." . . . We finish [street vending] at five, so, like, after six I could go. My mom would give me permission, but they always want to go early. Last week they invited me to Disneyland but I'm like, "No, I can't go because I have to help my mom." My sister wasn't here to help her and

then my stepdad goes to work somewhere else, so I'm like, "How is she gonna work with two kids?" and then I'm all like, "No." But I have given up stuff, but, I mean, I guess I have to.

Josefina was very mature and felt responsible for helping her mother. She did not see herself going to the movies or to Disneyland while her mother worked alone. These types of conflicts with her work and her social life created tensions between daughter and mother. Josefina was allowed to go out with friends after work, but after work hours was typically too late for her friends.

In contrast, nonworking children lacked economic empathy because they did not take part in the communal family obligation code with their parents and because they did not see their works as normal. Context makes a difference in how children and families make sense of their work and family obligations. Miri Song found that "expectations that children should help out emerged in a context where there was an awareness that other Chinese children in Britain also helped out in their takeaway businesses."[20] The Chinese children saw the take-away business as a normal job for immigrants. Some accepted this completely and believed that it was the best option for their parents since they did not speak English. They also saw that other families like them had similar businesses. Their work and their business seemed normal. In fact, not working was the exception. According to Song, some parents even used shame or guilt to get their children to help. These parents compared their children to model Chinese children who helped their parents.

The difference here is that the children I interviewed did not see street vending as a normal job for their parents. The informality of street vending made it difficult for families to openly talk about their business and it was seldom seen as a source of pride. In fact, parents and children constantly challenged negative stereotypes so that they could construct their work as dignified (see chapter 1). In addition, the children who worked with their parents did so in isolation from other children. This was evident in many ways. When I asked children to refer me to other street vending children, many of them could not think of people to recommend for my study. Also, when I asked them whether their school friends worked, many said that their friends did not work. One kid even said that her friends' parents worked for their children. In this context, the economic empathy that results from a communal family obligation code serves as a buffer against these intergenerational tensions. The children who work with their parents as street vendors *conviven* (interact or spend quality time) with their parents. While the children of Korean and Chinese entrepreneurs can prove their "Americanness" through the consumer items that their work offers them,[21] street vending provides the children in my study the exact opposite. Street vending helps confirm the "otherness." Even though the majority of the child street vendors are U.S. citizens, some attended private schools, and most lived in homes owned by their parents, once on the streets, their immigrant shadow surfaced, and so did their economic empathy.

"I Get Mad and I Tell Them, 'Guys Could Clean, Too!'"

Many Latinx parents in the United States go to great lengths to keep their daughters confined at home when not in school or chaperoned by a family member. They generally try to protect them from dangerous streets, neighbors, and especially boys. For example, sociologist Robert Smith found that Mexican immigrant parents in New York restricted their daughters' spatial mobility, keeping them home "on lockdown" as if they were in a prison, while boys were allowed to roam the streets.[1] Why do Latinx parents do this? Many believe that protecting their daughters' virginity is important. Sociologist Gloria González-López conceptualizes virginity as *capital femenino*, a strategic, life-enhancing resource that will allow girls to have a better future and marry better husbands. Although some Mexican immigrant parents are changing their views on the necessity of maintaining their daughters' premarital virginity, many still want their daughters monitored at home.[2] This is true of immigrant parents from other nationalities with strong Spanish Catholic traditions, including the Philippines. As Yen Le Espiritu has noted of Filipina girls in the United States, they are expected to be family-oriented, chaste, and willing to serve the family.[3] While these parents push their girls to strive for education, achievement, and elite college admissions, some have been known to forbid their daughters to go away to college.[4] These parents construct their daughters as morally superior to their White, Anglo counterparts, but this emphasis on the family burdens the girls with unpaid reproductive work and domestic confinement.[5] Morality is expressed through dedication to family and protection from public streets and sexual danger.

The daily practices of street vending daughters of Mexican immigrant parents call into question what we think we know about childhood in the United States in the early twenty-first century, as well as the lives of working-class Latina girls. Not only do these daughters of Latinx immigrant workers attend to their schoolwork, but they are saddled with significant household work responsibilities—cleaning, cooking, laundering, and looking after younger siblings. On top of that, these young Latina daughters dedicate time to income-generating street vending work. This chapter extends the feminist literature on intersectionality by exploring the world of Latinx teenage street vendors from a perspective that takes into account gendered expectations relating to age as well as the familiar intersecting relations of race and class.

While I was conducting observations in the field, I often witnessed young girls performing many household domestic duties. On a Friday afternoon, for example, Lorena, a parent highlighted in chapter 2, introduced me to thirty-nine-year-old Monica Martinez and her family. The Martinez family sells hot dogs, chips, sodas, and bottled drinks outside two schools during the week, and huaraches and natural orange, carrot, and beet juices on Saturdays near downtown Los Angeles.[6] After meeting me in her front yard, Monica agreed to participate in my study. I followed her through a narrow corridor on the side of her house leading to the large concrete patio resembling a mini food factory. This large patio was completely covered with several blue tarps that protected the patio from the sun and rain. I saw an old Chevy van parked in the patio with its side doors opened. Inside were crates filled with oranges and *pencas de nopal* (cactus leaves). In front of the van were two folding tables where Monica and her husband meticulously removed the thorns from the cacti with incredible agility. Twelve-year-old Metzli, their youngest daughter, politely cleared a corner of the folding table topped with crates full of cacti so that I could place my small digital recorder and my interview guide.

When I started the interview with the parents, each of the kids resumed their chores independently. Their only son, Pedro (age eighteen), helped unload some of the crates from the van and then drove the van to buy oranges. Yesenia, the oldest in the family (age twenty-three), walked in and out of the house doing household work. She also cooked some of the food for Saturday's street vending sales. Two hours later, toward the end of my interview with the parents, Yesenia came out to the patio and arranged another folding table and placed a red tablecloth over it. Metzli helped her set the table for six people. When I finished the interview, Yesenia said to me, "Véngase a comer." (Come and eat.) Each plate had freshly cooked cacti fried with egg and accompanied with beans, chipotle sauce, cheese, and tortillas. I joined them for a delicious lunch that Yesenia and Metzli prepared without a single instruction from either parent.

When I interviewed Yesenia the following week, she explained that cooking was among her main responsibilities at home, especially when her mother was busy, tired, or unable to cook for the family. Over dinner, I found out that Fridays are the busiest day for this family because this is when they prepare for their biggest street vending day—Saturday—when they sell huaraches and fresh-squeezed orange juice. This is also the day when they make the majority of their week's earnings. On average, they make $1,300 in one day.

During my time in the field, I saw the daughters of Latinx immigrant street vendors, such as Yesenia and Metzli, saddled with significant household work responsibilities believed to be a mother's obligation—cleaning, cooking, doing laundry, and looking after younger siblings. Many of the girls in this study cooked for their entire families or prepared food for family businesses. Street vendors who sell prepared food spend a good deal of time purchasing ingredients and making the food at home. Kenya, an eighteen-year-old who sold tamales with her parents, reported, "My responsibilities [were] to get home from school and help my mom do the tamales and clean the leaves and do everything you're supposed to do [for] the tamales and help around the house and then clean everything in the house." Eighteen-year-old Patricia sold birria with her mother on the weekend and she, too, helped prepare some of the food at home. Patricia confessed not feeling comfortable cooking the birria on her own, but did help by making the salsas and dicing the onions.

These girls carry substantial loads of housework at home. When I asked the children in this study whether they did any type of work at home, almost all of the girls quickly recited a list of household responsibilities that included a combination of cleaning, cooking, and taking care of their younger siblings. Esmeralda, who is twelve years old and the second oldest of six siblings (three girls and three boys), said,

I do the beds, I do the dishes, and sometime I [clean] the balcony with my other sisters. . . . [My brothers] just stay there and watch TV and do *tiradero* [a mess] and everything and we [my sisters and I] have to sometimes pick it up.

Girls of all ages took on more household work while their brothers contributed by only making a mess, or a *tiradero*, as Esmeralda would say. Similarly, Gloria, a fourteen-year-old who sold tacos with her parents, revealed how gender and not age essentially shielded boys from household work:

> Well, I go wash with my mom on the Laundromat . . . I have to help her because it's my clothes also. My [ten-year-old] sister sometimes goes, too, and then my [twelve-year-old] brother, he doesn't go. He stays with my dad. But it is usually me, her [pointing at mother], and my grandma.

Gloria, the oldest in her family, did a lot of the household work. While her younger siblings did relatively less work at home, it was the boys who were never held accountable to help with household work, including laundry. Even the younger sister would go at times, but the brother stayed with his dad at home.

Taking care of younger siblings was also a responsibility these young girls had to endure as part of their daily lives. Over half of the girls in our sample (twenty-five out of thirty-two) reported having some type of childcare responsibility for their siblings or extended family members. Mariana, a sixteen-year-old who sold fruit with her parents, told me,

> Well, when I get out of school . . . I start school at seven and I get out at around two. . . . My sister takes care of them [my siblings] when I am in school and then when I get home from school I take care of them. I'm the one that takes care of them when I get home.[7]

Street vending girls shared household work with older sisters who stayed home. Josefina, for example, whom I introduced in chapter 1, was the oldest and stayed at home watching over her two brothers and her sister while her parents street vended during the week. Rather than working during the week, she helped only on the weekend, when her siblings could join them while they street vended at the park. This way, the children played while she and her mother sold food and drinks.

Childcare responsibilities shift as children grow. Carmen, for example, now eighteen years old, does not have to take care of her ten-year-old brother. During our interview, she remembered having to take care of him when he was younger. Carmen's story is similar to those of the other girls in this study who had to take care of their younger siblings. Carmen elaborated,

> When my brother was three or four years old I took care of him. Well, I took care of him, I fed him while my mother worked. But now that my mom has more time, she takes care of him.[8]

Although she was no longer in charge of looking after her little brother, she told me in no uncertain terms that she still bore the brunt of household cleaning responsibilities: "My brothers just get up and go, well, they work and all. But me, I have household work. I have to make the beds, sweep the floor, and, well, many things."[9] Carmen's routine was more complicated than that of her brothers, who, as she puts it, "just get up and go."

Second-wave feminist scholarship has taught us to see the largely unrecognized private sphere of household work as legitimate work and alerted us to the "second shift" work obligations faced by many employed women.[10] In a study conducted in México, Liliana Estrada Quiroz found that girls were expected to assume more household responsibilities than boys. While boys also did chores, these chores were gendered. At a young age, girls were relegated to domestic activities (*quehaceres*) inside the home and boys seldom performed such chores.[11] These household burdens on female children seem to increase with migration. Ethnographic observations by Marjorie Faulstich Orellana in Central American immigrant households showed that girls as young as seven do numerous household chores (unpacking groceries, bathing and dressing a younger sibling, and cleaning) without being asked to do so by their parents.[12] This demand for young girls to help out in the home increases not only when their mothers go to work but also "when families are detached from the support networks of extended kin."[13]

Furthermore, in addition to cleaning and taking care of younger siblings, the girl vendors in this study also helped prepare food for the family business. Salvador, introduced in chapter 1, was the only boy who helped cook birria in the backyard of his home. Street vendors who sell prepared food on the street spend a good deal of time, first purchasing the food and then preparing it at home before they go out to sell on the streets. Monica told me she was responsible for helping to make the tamales after school. She added that she also had to "help around the house and then clean everything in the house and help with my brothers." Monica's quick response sums up the girls' household responsibilities. After school, they must help cook the food for the business, clean the house, and take care of younger siblings.

By contrast, the boys in this study, like the brothers of the girls in this study, relied on their sisters and mothers for help with household domestic work. Most boys whom I interviewed simply looked puzzled when asked whether they had any household responsibilities. For example, Juan, a ten-year-old boy who sells homemade jewelry with his father, responded to this question with a "Mmmmmm, no." Juan's sister is only a few years older than him and also sells jewelry with her father and two brothers, but she said she was also in charge of cleaning the house. When asked whether her brothers also cleaned the house, she responded with a quick "No!" and burst into laughter. Her tone of voice changed when asked how she felt about having to do more household work than her brothers. She clearly was bothered as she said, "Well, not good, because they don't do anything. They slack off."

This theme of boys being able to "slack off" from doing household work was echoed by many of the girls interviewed. They said that very little, if any, household work was expected of their brothers. Doing household work was a task that fell under their duties as daughters.

Contesting the Gendered Roles

Although street vending takes place in an open space where girls are exposed to many dangers, girls are seen as more apt for these kinds of jobs. While the girls prepared the food at home and later sold it on the street, most of the brothers helped with tasks girls were unable to do, such as peeling coconut with a *machete* (a large sharp knife) and driving. Mariana said that she woke up early every day to peel the fruit. When I asked her whether anyone helped her, she responded, "Yes. My sister. But the only one that did not help was my brother, . . . he would just help peel the coconut." Sixteen-year-old Linda and her younger sister Susana (age fourteen) sold pupusas with their mother and father at La Cumbrita. Before they sold at La Cumbrita, they used to sell their pupusas door-to-door from a basket and shopping cart. When I asked whether their brother accompanied them, Linda responded with a quick "No." She then explained,

> He was older. . . . He would just drive us there [to the park]. And we [sister and mother] used to just get the little cart out and we would just go sell. And when we finish we used to call him. So, he was, like, the driver.

Similar to Linda, other girls used age to justify the fact that their brothers did not street vend with their parents. They were either too old or too young, they rationalized. The boys did help in other ways, by peeling the hard fruit and driving the girls to their vending site. These tasks, however, did not require the boys to work long hours. In comparison with the girls, the boys put in relatively little time and effort.

Some girls also referenced their brothers' lack of skills to prepare food at home or cut fruit. For example, when I asked Adriana whether her brother helped cut the fruit, she was quick to say "No" right before she burst into laughter. Adriana told me, "Él deja echar más [fruta] con la cáscara." (He leaves more fruit on the skin he cuts off.) Adriana found it funny that her brother could not peel the fruit like her. Since he was too careless and wasted more fruit, he was released from this duty.

Other girls found it less amusing that their brothers were able to "slack off" simply for being males and contested the unequal division of labor between themselves and their brothers. Veronica, for example, believed it was unfair that she worked more than her brothers simply because she was female. She stated,

> So then I'm the one [who cleans because] las mujeres limpian, no los hombres [women are the ones who clean, not men]. And I get mad too, yeah, and I tell them, "No, guys could do the same thing, all humans are the same . . . guys could clean too and everything." And, like, [my brothers mock me by saying] ay ay muy trabajadora. Cállate! [Ay, ay, what a hard worker. Shut up!]

Veronica was not only required to do more domestic work, she was also the only one who helped her parents with their street vending business. Veronica saw her brothers as capable of doing the domestic work she was assigned. With her statement "all humans are the same" she spoke against labor burdens caused by gendered inequalities. Her brothers were unwilling to share their male privilege that shielded them from doing "women's work." They held on to their male privilege by mocking her and ignoring her plea for gender equality in her own home.

Veronica was not the only girl I interviewed who complained about the extra work she had to do at home. Other girls were also conscientious and unhappy about the tasks they were assigned or expected to do simply for being female. In the case of Martha, it was not her brother, but her father who reinforced a gendered division of labor at home. Martha explained,

> My brother did not do anything. . . . My dad is like those old Mexicans and, like, [he thinks that] guys are not supposed to do anything. . . . Like, once my brother was ironing his pants and [my dad] yells at us [my sisters and me] and says, "Why aren't you ironing your brother's pants?"

Martha replied to her father, "He irons his own pants. He doesn't like the way we iron." Martha was very upset when she told me this story. She was even more upset when her dad responded, "Well, he's not supposed to iron!" Martha defied her father's orders and left the room. She challenged the gendered position her dad had relegated her to by labeling her father an "old Mexican" for thinking that ironing was a task not suitable for a male like his son, but rather a task for his daughters.

Even though girls believed it was unfair that their brothers were able to "slack off" from doing domestic and street vending work, they also believed that girls could sell more food than boys. Veronica told me, "If I don't come, I don't think that they'll make that much money." Moreover, customers, like close family members, constantly reinforced the gendered belief that made girls more suitable to handle and sell food by requesting that girls rather than boys prepare the food. In these instances, girls internalize these gendered justifications and even pity male street vendors for not selling as much as they.

The boys' ability to slack off on private household work extended to the sphere of public street vending. Even boys who do not have sisters at home to pick up the household workload have light responsibilities. Edgar, a thirteen-year-old boy who sells tejuino with his mother, is an only child. When asked about household work, he reported that when he was not selling tejuino he worked out at a local gym with his friend. When I asked him what other type of work he did at home when he does not have to sell, he responded without hesitation, "Well, my mom just lets me take the day off. Or when I finish working here I go to the gym." Edgar was not only free from household work but was also able to withdraw time from street vending work in order to pursue leisure activities with friends. At his young age, he was very interested in body building and spent time with older friends who were teaching him how to lift weights at a local community gym.

This was not always possible for girls. Katia, who was twenty-one years old when interviewed, remembered selling fruit with her older brother and mother. Katia stated, "[My brother] was more wild. He used to go help my mom and then go home. He was not like us. My cousin and I were stuck to my mom." Katia did not resent the fact that her brother was able to go home while she had to stay with her mother and sell fruit. Even though she recognized that she worked more hours than her brother, she justified their work arrangements along gender lines and "natural" gender differences between her and her brother. Below is a quote from our interview it its original Spanglish form, followed by a full English translation.

> I think as a girl, you know? I am a girl, he is a guy. I guess he had a girl-friend already, you know? *Él se iba más temprano*, you know? He would leave with his friends. *Le ayudaba un ratito a mi mamá y se iba con sus* friends. *Y yo me tenía que quedar ahí* 'cause I was a girl. I was with my mom. And he is a guy. You know? Guys, they just leave with their friends.

> I think as a girl, you know? I am a girl, he is a guy. I guess he had a girl-friend already, you know? He would leave earlier, you know? He would leave with his friends. He would help my mom for a little bit and then he would go with his friends. I had to stay there 'cause I was a girl. I was with my mom. And he is a guy. You know? Guys, they just leave with their friends.

Although I was unable to interview Katia's brother Carlos, I heard a similar refrain from other girls. The girls explained that they were typically brought to the street vending site by their parents or by an older sibling. Once at their street vending site, they were allowed to return home only when escorted by a family member, and after they finished street vending at the end of the day. This was a strategy predicated on the belief that girls require family protection to maintain their virginity and family honor, a belief that is widely shared in Mexican Catholic culture, as well as among Filipino families.[14] This strategy yielded an added family economic benefit, as the girls were required to put in many hours of work. Yet the parents were then faced with a paradoxical dilemma: How to protect the girls while having them work on the streets?

Gendered Justifications

"Girls Are More Clean Than the Guys"

Gendered beliefs that girls sold more than boys surfaced repeatedly in conversations. Girls were associated with being clean and not threatening to customers. For example, Katia told me that customers saw her as cleaner than her brothers. It wasn't that she performed cleanliness in front of customers by managing the food with extra care or by washing her hands multiple times. Her cleanliness was taken for granted simply because of her gender. During our interview she said, "Some people think, 'Oh, she's more clean because she is a girl.'" Then Katia quickly contrasted how customers saw her brothers: "And a guy, 'Oh no!' They say that a lot. . . . 'Oh, she is a girl, she is clean.'" To Katia it was therefore rational that she, instead of her brother, would do street vending for the family; it was simply better for business.

In this thinking, girls were associated with cleanliness, soap, and purity, and boys with dirtiness and dubious hygiene. As Veronica, introduced earlier, said,

> I feel bad for the guys because, like, they're in the sun too and, like, they don't sell as much as girls because we see guys as more dirty, like, they think that girls are more clean than the guys. That's what some of the customers told me before too. Because they say that the guys don't even clean their hands. They don't wash their hands when they get the money or they do the stuff [prepare the tejuino]. So I think that's why they buy more from the girls too.

Veronica was fully convinced that she was indispensable for the economic success of the family business. Young "virginal girls" and "maternal, nurturing women" are socially constructed as natural purveyors of food. They are seen as clean, and their "natural" service in the kitchen is extended to the public sphere of street vending. Veronica expressed empathy for the male street vendors who did not sell as much as she. She suggested that it was common knowledge among all customers that boys are dirty. Veronica stated that she sold more tejuino than her father on the basis of being a girl and being seen as cleaner than her father and brothers. She surmised, "If I don't come, I don't think that they'll make that much money."

Ethnographic observations with Veronica and her family affirmed that customers did indeed prefer to have a girl like Veronica prepare the tejuino instead of the other male workers. The field note excerpt below shows how this dynamic unfolded one day when a customer asked Veronica, rather than the older man her family had hired, to serve him.

> The customer asked Veronica if she could prepare the tejuino instead because he liked the way she prepared it. Veronica rinsed her hands with water from one of their jugs and went to help her customer. She grabbed a large cup, put ice and salt inside the cup and then began to cut and manually squeeze about five limes into the cup. She later filled the cup with tejuino and covered the cup with a lid. Placing one hand over the lid and the other under the cup, she began to mix the tejuino, lime, salt and ice preparing the tejuino just the way her customer liked it.

During these field notes I did notice Veronica performing cleanliness. After spending time with this family, I noticed that her father and the man they occasionally hired also adopted similar handwashing routines, especially after handling money or stepping away from their cart.

Furthermore, when I asked Veronica whether it was common for customers to request that she prepare the tejuino, she responded,

> Yeah, because, like, sometimes, like, customers say that . . . they like how I mix it. . . . So they say that they like how I make it because last time, you know, that guy [pointing at a male vendor they hired as help], the guy helping me right now, like, he was by himself before, like, the customers

Figure 5.1. Girls preparing food.

> were complaining because . . . it tastes good but not as good. . . . So then after my mom is like, no, then I'm just gonna put you with that guy because otherwise the customers are not gonna wanna come no more.

Veronica and Katia's experiences were not isolated incidents. Street vendors were acutely aware of presenting themselves as clean cooks, and their work involved hygienic routines. Street vendors constantly cleaned their stands while customers lingered nearby. They also made sure their surroundings were clean at all times. Women often used hairnets and plastic gloves. Families with more children had the luxury of assigning one of the children to handle the cash transactions, so that clean hands could remain in contact with the food. It was usually boys or the fathers who were in charge of cash transactions while the mothers and daughters prepared the food with their hands. It was also common to see jugs of water that the street vendors constantly used for washing their hands. Bottles of water were also available for the customers' own handwashing.

The street vendor's hygienic performances matter, but so did their gender. On one occasion, a young boy was selling tamales at La Cumbrita. He declined to do an interview, but during my field observations with other vendors at my site, I noticed something worth noting. He sold the tamales alone from a grocery pushcart. He was modestly dressed with a black cap, a black sweatshirt, and blue jeans. Even though his clothes were not new, he looked clean. Like the rest of the vendors, he used plastic gloves to handle the tamales when he would put them inside plastic bags or plates for the customers. Even though he followed the same routines as the other street vendors, he was asked by one customer, "Did you make the tamales?" The boy immediately responded, "No, my sister did, but she asked me to come sell them for her. I only sell them." He attempted to reassure the potential customer. The customer ended up not buying the tamales and instead purchased two pupusas from Linda and Susana.

While it is possible that this customer's decision to buy pupusas and not tamales was simply a desire for a particular type of food, it is also likely that the customer was concerned with whether the boy made the tamales and whether or not he was clean enough to sell them. Here it is important to recall Katia's remarks about the customers' preferences:

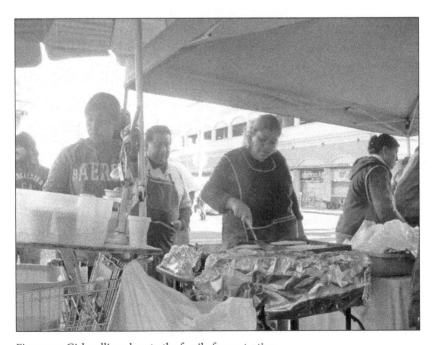

Figure 5.2. Girls selling close to the family for protection.

"'Oh, she's more clean because she is a girl.' . . . and a guy, 'Oh no.' . . . Like, people don't think about it but they do see it."

"Guys Buy More from Girls"

The appeal of attractive young girls was a good asset for the family's business. Katia remembered selling with her cousin at age fourteen or fifteen. She also remembered that when she and her cousin were left alone to tend the fruit stand, they sold more than when her mother or brother was in charge. Katia explained, "You're a girl and you are growing up and you know how guys are, *que quieren mirar a las muchachas* [they want to see the girls], you know?" She explained that guys frequented her stand because they wanted to see young girls. She later exclaimed, "You know guys *les compran más a las muchachas que a* [they buy more from girls than they do from] ladies or guys. You know?"

Mariana, a sixteen-year-old girl who sold fruit with her parents and sister, said that she and her teenage sister played games and engaged in what she called *travesuras*, which loosely translates to pranks or playful banter, with male customers. This was enjoyable and fun for them. As she noted, it made long hours pass quickly, and they especially enjoyed these games because they could sell more fruit. Below is an excerpt from the interview:

> EE: What kind of *travesuras* do you do?
> M: Well, when cars pass by my sister says, umm . . . [for example] some guys will pass by and the guys will say "hi" to my sister, right? And my sister will say "hi" back to them.
> EE: What does your sister say to them?
> M: She says, "Hi, how are you," stuff like that, and the guys ask questions to us and all.
> EE: When you are both alone, do a lot of guys try to talk to you?
> M: Uh huh, yes, yes.
> EE: Yes? And how does that feel?
> M: Oh, well, it feels good because we don't get bored there and we sell more.

These flirtatious encounters were very frequent and often initiated by the customers. The encounters were also normal for teenage girls. In small towns throughout Latin America it is common for youth to meet in the plaza. Adolescent boys and girls meet, and in this very public, group context, it is acceptable for them to chat, laugh, and flirt.

Typically, in these street vending encounters, young men would drive by and initiate the flirtatious game with a witty comment or a simple "Hi," as Mariana related above. And, as we saw in the interview transcript segment reproduced above, Mariana and her sister experienced the encounter as pleasant, and they made a sale. While the girls enjoyed doing what they called *travesuras*, they also were aware of the dangers they faced. In an attempt to protect themselves from male customers, they gave false names and claimed to be older. Mariana and her sister Amanda called themselves "Maria" and Amanda called herself "Tania." When I asked why they changed their names, Amanda innocently said that she changed her name in case the customers wanted to look her up on Facebook.

What were the parents' responses to these encounters? Parents either were unaware of these flirtatious games or looked the other way. Mariana and Amanda said that their father had no clue about these street vending interactions. During my interview with Mariana I asked, "Si tu papá llega y mira que están hablando con muchachos, no se enoja?" (If your father arrives and sees that you are talking with young men, he doesn't get upset?) With a half-smile Mariana replied, "Pues, a lo mejor sí [se enoja], pero pensará que está comprando fruta." (Well, maybe he will [get upset], but he will think that he [the male customer] is buying fruit.) Other parents were more vigilant of their daughters. Linda and Susana's mother, for example, reprimanded her daughters and made it clear to the customers that she disapproved of them flirting or disrespecting her daughters. During my field observations, a local gang member and customer called Susana over. Susana started walking toward him and before she took a few steps, her mother called her back and told her to sit down. Angry and in an overprotective manner, she told her daughter that she did not want to see her near that guy.

Girls Benefit from Their Work

Even though no one can deny that these girls and their families worked very hard, these girls managed to see their work positively. Leonor said,

"Well, it's tiring," in reference to her long work hours on the weekend, but then in the next phrase, without skipping a beat, she added, "I like helping my parents." Leonor's sentiment was echoed by many of the respondents. Monica, an eighteen-year-old who sold fried plantains with her parents, said, "You are doing it [street vending] because you have to help your parents out. But it's fun at the same time because you have fun seeing different people every day."

While it may appear that girls in this study are constrained, most girls enjoyed as many benefits from their work as their families did. Some, like Monica, expressed feelings of freedom because street vending allowed them to see "different people every day." Similarly, Gloria, a fourteen-year-old who sold tacos with her parents, said with excitement that after they started street vending, "Every Friday there is something different going on over there [street vending site]." Gloria remembered being bored at home before she started street vending: "Before we sold tacos, I was at home Fridays and . . . it would be boring. Like, just watching TV, and going on the computer and the same things." Unlike her brother, who played soccer, she did not participate in extracurricular activities that would give her a reason to be out of the house; before her family decided to street vend, she was more confined to the home, similar to the girls in sociologist Robert Smith's study.[15]

In addition to experiencing more physical freedom and distraction from their work, the girls also acquired purchasing power. Those who were paid by their parents liked having the freedom to buy their own things. Carmen, age eighteen, said, "Sí, si me alcanza [el dinero que me pagan], pues yo no soy una persona que quiero todo, pero compro lo necesario. . . . Pues compro mis cositas." (Yes, [the money I get] is enough, because I am not a person who wants everything, but I buy what is necessary. . . . I buy my own things.) In addition to being able to buy their own things, these girls also helped their parents invest in their own business. When I asked Adriana, age thirteen, what she did with the money she got paid, she replied, "I save it and sometimes when they don't have [money] to buy fruit I lend them [money]."

In addition to seeing their work as beneficial for their entire family, these girls saw their work as preparation for their own future. Some, like Katia, believed that street vending helped instill the skills, strength, and courage to do any other type of work in the future. Katia posited,

Selling fruit is, like, you know how to work—how to be in the sun, how to run from the cops, or whatever. And if you get another job [it will be], like, easy, you know. If I was selling fruit, I could do this. . . . And how to get along with people, 'cause you have to talk to people, you know.

While some of the girls complained about heavy workloads and very full schedules, the majority of them saw the work as opening new opportunities for them. Street vending made them feel useful and responsible, it ended the boredom that many felt at home, and it offered what the girls perceived as useful socialization experiences for their future. Most importantly, the girls saw real tangible benefits: their street vending labor brought more money into the household, and thereby allowed the parents to purchase special items—trendy jeans or simply school supplies—for themselves. On the balance, the girls saw street vending as an empowering experience for them, one that opened doors to new possibilities and better life opportunities.

6

Street Violence

"I Don't Put Up a Fight Anymore"

Thirteen-year-old Edgar was born and raised in Boyle Heights and attended a private Catholic school in the area. His mother, Renata, had decided to put her son in private school to protect him from the violence and gangs in the public schools.[1] Renata feared that her only son would be recruited to gangs or hurt by the *cholos* in the local schools.[2] Her fears were not irrational. According to sociologist Edward Flores and the Los Angeles Police Department, Los Angeles is known as the "gang capital" of the nation, with over 450 active gangs.[3] Yet Renata's efforts to protect her young son were futile because the protection he received at school did not extend to the streets, where he spent a great deal of time helping his mother sell tejuino.

When I met Edgar, he was sitting on a small stool next to his mother's tejuino cart. He was wearing a shirt he had purchased in México City a few days prior. Renata sent him to México for nearly three months. He did not go for recreational purposes, to visit family, or on a study abroad program. On the contrary, Renata sent Edgar to México to recuperate from a beating he received from what she believed to be *cholos*. These *cholos* had been bothering Edgar after school for a while. Renata had noticed them before, but they never did more than verbally tease him when she was there. For instance, they called him "tejuino boy" and made fun of the work he did. Although these insults hurt Edgar and made him very angry, Renata reminded him why their work was important to them. One day, though, when Edgar was street vending alone, the teasing turned into a fight that left him with a couple of broken ribs and bruises all over his face and body. It was then that Renata decided to send Edgar to México with his grandparents, where she believed her son would recuperate from his injuries, and most importantly where he would be safe from future attacks.

Across the street from the tejuino stand, thirteen-year-old Sonia sells bags of mixed fruit such as mango, watermelon, cucumber, and jicama. She has been street vending with her parents since the family emigrated from Puebla, México, when she was five. For the last two years, she has been street vending alone every Saturday and Sunday and on select school nights using her own fruit cart. Her parents and her uncles also sell fruit nearby, where they can keep a vigilant eye on her to protect her from any dangers, including from boys and male customers.

While both boys and girls like Edgar and Sonia diligently work alongside their parents on the street, my time in the field revealed that the daughters of Mexican and Central American street vendors in Los Angeles are more active than the sons in street vending with the family. As we saw in the previous chapter, a gendered analysis helps us understand why girls are seen as more fit for this activity. It is also useful in helping us understand why boys are less likely to help and why they face certain risks associated with male violence.[4] Sociologists Ann Arnett Ferguson and Nancy Lopez demonstrate that Black and Latino boys are more vulnerable to violence and punishment than their female counterparts in the school setting.[5] In this chapter we will see how this vulnerability also extends to the streets. As we saw with Edgar, when street vending boys do help with the family street vending business, they face aggression from other males. Paradoxically, while the street is more appropriate for males, in this context, male vendors of all ages report more instances of violence from gang members, other school boys, or male customers. The freedom their male privilege affords them also leaves them unprotected from the family and more vulnerable to street violence while peddling on the streets of Los Angeles.

This chapter sheds light on this paradox. First, while "the street" is generally viewed as a dangerous, disreputable place for women and girls, it is the boys and the men who are more likely to be victims of physical violence and aggression from gangs, the police, and the community.[6] Consequently, the families develop different gendered strategies for protecting their sons and daughters. Second, in this context, the presence of women serves as a protective mechanism for adult and adolescent male vendors alike, thus challenging what we know about a space that has been male-centered.

Paradoxical Gendered Disadvantages

Almost all of the young Latino boys I interviewed had experienced physical violence from peers who teased them for doing "Mexican" work and local gang members who sought to extort their earnings from them. Their fathers and uncles had had similar experiences. The majority of the boys— nine out of eleven—reported being in fights at least one time while street vending. None of the boys I interviewed said they were affiliated with any gangs, but several had been victims of gang aggressions. Street violence committed by Latino gang members in Los Angeles is a serious concern to residents and to street vendors who peddle the streets for a living.[7] According to journalist Dakota Smith, street vendors generally do not report gang crimes or any crimes against them because they also fear the police.[8] In response to their vulnerable situations, Latino street vending boys and their parents need to learn how to navigate and survive while street vending. Vendors face not only the threat of violence by gangs, but potential arrest and citations. In 2016 the city of Los Angeles collected $9,880 in fines.[9] In 2014 the police made more than 1,200 vendor arrests.[10]

Sociologist Victor Rios, who has devoted his career to understanding the criminalization of Latino youth, found that even the non-delinquent youth in his study learned to navigate multiple worlds within and outside school. They knew how to avoid getting in trouble in school or with the police—and they also learned how to survive on the street among their delinquent peers by "keeping it real" and learning what sociologist Elijah Anderson calls the "code on the street."[11] Anderson argues that "simply living in such an environment places young people at special risk of falling victim to aggressive behavior." It is important to know the code of the street, "set of informal rules governing interpersonal public behavior, particularly violence," as a survival mechanism.[12] The code is so powerful that even the families that Anderson calls "decent" encourage their children to know the code in order to be capable of negotiating the inner-city environment. For example, someone who knows the code of the street knows that maintaining eye contact for too long is a sign of disrespect. Anderson adds that the code of the street is a cultural adaptation and a response to the lack of faith in the police.[13] This is further illustrated in Rios's book, in which he describes how kids who were victimized by teenage gangs turn to violence in self-defense.

Furthermore, this was often the case when victims of violence did not find support from the police or parents. A similar narrative is expressed in Geoffrey Canada's autobiographical book, where he narrates his personal story of violence. Canada's first encounter with violence was at age four, when neighborhood bullies took his money.[14] Similar to the young men Rios interviewed, Canada reached out to the police, only to get a response of laughter and a reaffirmation that police "had better things to do." Rios calls this the overpolicing–underpolicing paradox. Rios states, "Policing seemed to be a ubiquitous part of the lives of many of these marginalized young people; however, the law was rarely there to protect them when they encountered victimization."[15]

According to Rios, non-delinquent boys in his study were often "guilty by association": "Non-delinquent boys held the conviction that they had been criminalized in the same systematic way as their delinquent peers."[16] He adds that non-delinquent boys often avoid associations with neighborhood friends and even relatives who are delinquent in order to stay out of trouble, and they also avoid being on the street at specific times of the day, such as from 3:00 p.m. to 6:00 p.m., when violence is at its peak. Most of the street vending children in this study, however, could not avoid the street during these hours. This was usually the time when the kids I interview sold food outside schools, at parks, and at various street vending sites in East Los Angeles, and often as late as midnight or a little after.

The boys in my sample talked about their violent encounters on the street. Sixteen-year-old Alejandro was still very angry when he told me about the day he got stabbed by "some fools." Alejandro had been working with his mother at their pancake stand one night when he got "jumped." His mother, Lorena, appeared at the scene just minutes after he was stabbed. He was rushed to the hospital immediately, and days later, Lorena sent him to México to recuperate with his older brother. Sending the youth to México is a common practice among Latinx immigrants in the United States. Sociologist Robert Smith also noticed that his respondents sent their children to their hometown where they could enjoy their freedom, party, and relax far from the busy city, where children often lived in a state of lockdown.[17] In my study, I found that children were sent to México in order to recuperate from serious beatings they had received while street vending, such as the cases of Alejandro and thirteen-year-old Edgar, whom I introduced earlier in this chapter.

This was not the first time Alejandro was assaulted on the street. I had the opportunity to shadow Alejandro and his mother, Lorena, for a little over two months. One sunny Saturday morning, I met Lorena and Alejandro at Grand Central Market in downtown Los Angeles. I invited them to eat Lorena's favorite Chinese food in gratitude for all of the help they had offered to me during my study. At the time, I was without a car and I relied on the metro to commute from Long Beach to East Los Angeles, where I interviewed most of my respondents. Grand Central Market was in the middle of my destination. I still needed to take two more metros and a bus to get to one of my interviews in Boyle Heights later that afternoon. After breakfast, Lorena offered to take me to my next interview in her car. The door on the passenger's side was broken and could not open. Therefore, I sat in the back seat with Alejandro. On our drive to East Los Angeles from downtown, we made several stops related to Lorena's street vending business. At one place, she dropped off greeting cards, then she exchanged party balloons with another client, and finally she collected money from another vendor.

During this time, Alejandro and I talked about his school, his upcoming birthday, and the many times he has been bothered on the street while street vending. Alejandro complimented my new iPhone and told me he had a new iPod, but could not use it outside the house because "them fools" would "jack it" like they did before. Instead, he used an old iPod Nano—a less expensive music device—he had bought at the swap meet for twenty-five dollars. "If they want to take it, I just give it to them," he told me. "I don't put up a fight anymore," he continued, but this time, in a lower tone of voice, looking down at his old iPod Nano while shuffling through his songs.

Again and again, I heard parents advise their children to not put up a fight if gang members or the police ordered them to give up their merchandise or money. Although this was their "code of the street," the advice was still difficult for the youth to understand. They could not comprehend how they could be victims of both gang members and the police, and why the police could not go after the real problem, the gangs, rather than people like them and their parents who were trying to make an honest living. For example, eighteen-year-old Joaquín had negative experiences with both gang members and the police.

At the time, Joaquín was completing his second semester at the California State University, Northridge, where he is studying criminal justice and sociology. For the last three years, he has been street vending with his parents on the weekends. Joaquín has his own juice stand, and on a good day he makes an average of $200. He uses this money to help his parents with the bills and with his new 2009 Honda Civic payment and insurance. He also has a part-time job at a large department store, where he earns additional money to fund his education. Joaquín said that customers are often surprised to learn that he is in college and wants to become a police officer, a theme that I discuss further in the next chapter. While talking about his school with some of his customers is a source of pride, he cannot reveal this information to other people he encounters on the street, such as the gang members in his neighborhood or even the police. He sees it as pointless to explain to gang members about his school. The best strategy for him, as he explained during our interview, is to "act dumb."

Joaquín has had several encounters with gang members due to the nature of his street vending business. For example, in addition to selling juices in the morning, Joaquín and his mother drive around his neighborhood to see whether anyone is having a birthday party by paying attention to the ubiquitous jumpers or party decorations. As he drives up and down the streets of East Los Angeles, his mother writes down several addresses on a piece of paper. After dinner, they load a small cart with toys and head to the parties. This is a profitable business, but it is also dangerous because it takes place late at night—after 7:00 p.m. and often until the parties end at 1:00 a.m.—in neighborhoods that are not that safe and that do not offer the inherent protection of other vendors. Here, instead of trying to stand out as a college student, he needs to distinguish himself from any affiliation with gangs. One day while street vending with his mother at night, a gang member called him over and asked him what gang he was from. Joaquín mimicked the gang member's tone of voice and body posture to show me how the gang member tried to intimidate him:

> He [the gang member] asked me where I was from because I was wearing a hat. I told him, "Just because I have a hat on, it doesn't mean that I am in a gang." It was then when he started telling me, "Well, you know this is Maravilla."

Joaquín knew that Maravilla was the gang that controlled that neighbor-hood, but he pretended not to know. Knowing the "code of the street" does not always mean that you play along or keep it real. In Joaquín's case, it was best to appear oblivious of the code in order to not be linked to any gang.

Like Joaquín, eighteen-year-old Pedro also said that gang members have asked him for his street vending earnings: "Muchas veces me han seguido y me dicen que tengo que darles dinero." (Many times they have followed me and they tell me I have to give them money.) Eighteen-year-old Eric has also been stopped several times on his way back home after selling his homemade ice cream. Even though the youth are ad-vised to give up their money in order to avoid fights with peers or gang members, some are reluctant to do so. The first time the gang members stopped Eric, they took all of his money. He learned his lesson, and now he keeps only a few dollars inside his pocket and hides the rest of the money—about $150 to $200 each day—under the barrel of ice cream in a plastic bag. He has also opted for pretending that he works for someone else and that his boss picks up the money before he goes home. Here again, pretending to act innocent, being submissive, and playing dumb help them survive in the streets where they work.

When I interviewed eighteen-year-old Pedro in his parents' dining room, he told me about a couple of fights he was involved in while street vending. Pedro believed that it was more common for male street ven-dors to get into fights. He emphasized that it was also more dangerous when men got into fights. With a tone of common sense, he told me, "Es más común en los hombres." (It is more common in men.) He then mocked the women who got into fights with other women, saying that they only scream at one another during fights: "Las mujeres nomás se gritan." (Women just yell.) Then, shifting to a more serious tone, he said with a concerned hand gesture, "Pero luego que se meten los hombres, oh! Con cuidado!" (But if men get involved, oh! Watch out!)

Strategies for Protection

Edgar, Alejandro, Joaquín, and Pedro agreed that it was most dangerous when they were alone. In fact, Edgar and Alejandro got attacked when their mothers left them alone to run errands. It was most common to see the boys selling alone. The young girls sold alongside their parents or in close proximity to relatives who had a clear view of them. In some cases where the girls sold alone, the families and the girls employed other protection strategies. One strategy was to have the girls stationed in public parks where a familial environment prevailed, such as a children's playground. Another family did a variation of this by allowing their daughter to sell cut-up fruit alone at a park, one where relatives were nearby also selling fruit on Sundays. While these girls sold in parks or busy street corners on their own, their parents often sold at more dangerous spots, and sometimes they sold merchandise that was considered more dangerous than food. This was the case for Adriana, who at age thirteen was already selling fruit by herself at a popular park in East Los Angeles. While she did that, her mother sold fruit and flowers at a spot perceived as more dangerous for a young girl (by a freeway entrance), and her father sold more dangerous merchandise—pirated CDs and DVDs. Even though Adriana lacked a permit to sell fruit, being inside a park offered more protection than being near the freeway or selling pirated CDs and DVDs, which would merit time in jail if confiscated by the police. An added level of protection was that while Adriana's mother sold bags of fruit from a shopping cart, Adriana used their only "official"-looking metal cart.

Similarly, Sofia, a sixteen-year-old who sold corn on the cob, mangos, and churros, was dropped off at a park south of Los Angeles every weekend. Early every Saturday and Sunday, her father dropped her off inside a park and picked her up at the end of the day. Her father then would sell the same items, but he did so while walking down the street. This made him more visible and vulnerable to police harassment. Sofia, on the other hand, sold in a more controlled environment where many Mexican immigrant families went to spend their weekend days.

Another parental strategy was to monitor the girls through a cell phone. The girls were instructed to use the phone in case of an emergency, and they also received instructions from their parents. During one of the fieldwork observations, I accompanied Sofia's sister Martha, an eighteen-year-old girl who also sold corn on the cob, churros, and raspados, to a park and to a gathering spot in front of a church. Martha used her phone to ask her father for instructions related to the business. For example, one day when I went selling with her, Martha received a call from her father telling her to walk to a nearby park where his friend was having a big party and wanted to buy a sizable order of corn on the cob and raspados for his guests. Before we went to the party, she called her father to notify him that we were on our way. Once we arrived, she called him yet again to confirm that we were there. Cell phones allow the girls to remain tightly tethered to parental instruction and monitoring.

Women Contesting a Gendered Public Sphere

The findings above challenge the belief that the street is more danger- ous for females and more appropriate for males. The girls in this study did not report having any issues with gang members in their area. To be sure, though, this does not mean that women are immune to this type of street violence. In 2015 journalist Dakota Smith published a story in which her main informant, Mariposa Gonzalez, told her she received the following advice from her mother: "Talk back to the gang members who demand money. Say you don't have any cash. Throw a pineapple if need be." This was the exact opposite advice the parents in my study gave to their young boys. Talking back to gang members, refusing to give them money, or even attacking them with their merchandise would escalate to a bigger fight if men followed this advice. Here it is important to recall Pedro's words, "Las mujeres nomás se gritan. . . . Pero luego que se meten los hombres, oh! Con cuidado!" (Women just yell. . . . But if men get involved, oh! Watch out!)

The girls I interviewed reported neutral experiences with gang mem- bers who purchased food from them and even engaged in small talk with them. They were never asked whether they were affiliated with any gang. For example, Martha told me that her interactions with local gang members were amicable. She said, "I know all the gangsters around there, it's pretty funny, all the Eastsiders. . . . They are really cool 'cause every time they see me they are like, 'You are still around?' And they ask me, 'Did you graduate from high school?'" Martha enjoyed these conversations with these young men and it did not bother her that they were affiliated with gangs. Teenage gang members often flirted with the girls I interviewed. Linda told me, "Some boys flirt with us, but I usually don't pay attention because some look like if they're irresponsible. Like, I usually don't like the kind of guys that dress all *cholos* and things, so it's like, I don't really mind." Linda and her sister sold pupusas with their mother and she kept a close eye on them; many times she also protected me from male advances. Since I spent many hours with the families, I often just walked around or sat near street vending stands to observe various dynamics. Men often sat next to me and started small talk to find out who I was and where I was from. Hilda quickly would answer for me with a firm, "Ella está con nosotras." (She is with us.)

After a while, Hilda suggested that I move my seat closer to her stand. While I appreciated her protection, this gave me a sense of the limited spatial mobility that the girls I met talked about. Unlike the girls, the boys did experience greater spatial mobility. Girls worked closely with their parents so that parents could protect the girls from sexual advances and other dangers from men. This preventive measure worked. The young men in this study also worked with their parents, but most had their own stand or were given time off from street vending to roam around on the street and hang out with friends. This often made them more vulnerable to harassment from both gang members and peers.

The presence of women in the public sphere, the street vending site, mitigated violence and aggression from gangs. Older women talked to gang members the way they did with their own children. Some of the parents I interviewed also knew the parents of these young *cholos*. One night at La Cumbrita, a young gang member visited all of the street vendors asking them if things were okay. I was shadowing a family who sold pupusas when the gang member ordered a pupusa and asked the family how they were doing. Hilda, the mother making the pupusas, gave him one for free and said they were doing okay. Hilda knew the gang member and his mother. When he left, Hilda jested, "I know him since he was in diapers" and continued making her pupusas.

The dangers of the street were neutralized with the presence of women and young girls. As seen above, boys in these spaces were more vulnerable. One night, months after Alejandro had been stabbed, he left the street vending stand to go to a fast-food restaurant around the corner. I turned to Lorena, his mother, and I could see she was worried about her son. Quickly Lorena turned to five-year-old Kimberly, a girl she was babysitting, and asked her to accompany Alejandro. Little Kimberly ran in the dark street and caught up to Alejandro and held his hand. Lorena believes that the presence of a little girl will shield her son from the attention of gang members.

Lorena's instinct was not too far off. One night while eighteen-year-old Joaquín street vended with his mother, a gang member asked him to come over. Once he had him face to face, the gang member told him he had to pay taxes for street vending. Joaquín's mother, Rosa, standing only a few feet away, heard the exchange. In tears, she told her son to give the gang member anything he wanted. "Dale lo que quiere!" she screamed. In response, the gang member told her, "Cálmese, ruquita. Yo no les voy a decir nada, pero si pasa otro de la Maravilla, le van a tener que pagar a él." (Calm down, old woman. I'm not going to say anything, but if someone else from La Maravilla comes by, you'll have to pay him.) After that incident, Joaquín and his mother decided to work at another spot. During the interview Joaquín wondered whether the gang member would have done something to him had his mother not been with him:

> I think that if I was by myself they would have done something to me already. But they saw my mom and said, "No, well, we have to cool it a little bit." But I think they go more towards the guy than the ladies. So, if they see a guy, they know that he will stand up to them. Do you understand? With an old lady they are not going to stand up to her.

Rosa's presence saved Joaquín from a fight with a gang member. She instilled a sense of respect for both that helped assuage a potential extortion or a fight. *El respeto por la mujer*, or respect for a woman, is common in Latinx culture, where women, especially motherly figures, are rendered extra respect and deference.

This theme of women instilling respect on the street emerged among many of my male respondents. Forty-three-year-old Isidro began to street vend when his daughters were still babies. During our interview, he told me that when his daughters were younger, he would bring his wife to street vend with him because gang members did not bother him when his wife and daughters would accompany him.

> The gang members would not bother you if they see two people. Many times in that zone, if they see you alone they would try to take your money away. Then, I would sell with my wife. She would push my daughter's stroller and I would push the cart with raspados.[18]

Females passively protected men just by being present on the street, but they also actively tried to shield young male street vendors from street violence. Specifically, mothers helped prevent fights by reminding their own children not to fight back. Unlike the female vendors described by journalist Dakota Smith, none of the parents in my study ever said they encourage their children to fight back.[19] Rosa said, "Yo siempre le digo a mi hijo que no conteste." (I always tell my son to not speak back.) Similar to Rosa, other parents worry when their boys sell alone because they feel that boys are less compliant with gang members and even the police. Pedro (age eighteen) told me that he "controlled himself [from fighting] only because his mother was around." Pedro's mother threatened him with her health condition and told him that if got into a fight her blood pressure was going to rise. Similarly, Leonel recognizes getting out of trouble only because his mother and father told him to calm down and obey the orders of the police who were trying to confiscate the toys he was selling on New Year's Day in Pasadena. Leonel said,

> The cop told me to put my stuff on the truck. And I pushed the cart and went like this with my hands [lifting his hands in the air angrily and showing defiance]. And they told me, "If you don't put the stuff in the truck we will arrest you." . . . My dad and my mom told me [by patting my back] to be quiet and to load the merchandise. I was very mad. I was not scared. I was mad. Why do they do that if we were not even selling drugs or doing anything of that sort? . . . I understood it as that saying that goes "adding insult to injury." In addition to taking the stuff away they make you carry them and put them on the truck.[20]

The families in this study took more precautionary measures to protect their daughters, while sons were given more freedom. These strategies for protecting the girls were very effective. However, I found that it is more dangerous for boys to roam the streets unaccompanied. Many of the boys in my study had been victims of gang aggression. In this context, the presence of women, young and old, mitigates violence because women instill a general respect from men in the neighborhood. Street vending women, especially when selling in large groups, help create a family ambiance that contests the street as a male-centered space.

As Mexican and Central American immigrants make their way in subordinated and saturated Los Angeles labor markets, many of them find that their best economic options are to utilize the labor of all possible family members, including their children. In this chapter, I find that gender shapes the work experience of adolescent street vendors in Los Angeles. While both sons and daughters engage in the family business, it is more common for girls than boys to help their parents. Street vending families have produced an adaptive culture that involves using femininity—in combination with boys using naiveté—as protections against street violence. This is in part due to a combined influence of culture-of-origin gender beliefs and their current environmental demands.[21] The benefits of freedom granted to the sons by their male privilege came at a great expense for the boys, many of whom had been victims of gang violence. This is a difficult situation for boys to assimilate because they have to play down their masculinity and act submissive in the face of gang aggressions.

"My Parents Want Me to Be Something in Life, Like a Lawyer or a Hero"

When I met sixteen-year-old Josefina, she was very excited about her upcoming high school graduation. She almost had the $486 she needed for her graduation regalia and senior field trip. For an extra $100 she could have gotten the next most expensive package, which includes a class ring, but she assures me she does not care about the class ring. According to her, she could always buy the ring later at an indoor swap meet. Josefina, like other children in this book who had economic empathy toward their parents, made these types of financial sacrifices often. Josefina told me that for the last six months, she has been allocating part of their street vending earning for her graduation expenses. Pointing at the top drawer of an old dresser where she keeps the family's money, she told me that after she and her mother finish selling hot dogs, Gatorades, and chips, she puts the money in that drawer in three different stacks. One stack is to save up for the rent, the other for their street vending merchandise, and the third one is for her high school expenses, which she knows will be particularly higher in her senior year.

Josefina, like many children of Latinx working-class immigrant parents, faces strong parental expectations to do well in school. Latinx parents often underscore their own migration sacrifices and hard work at low-paying jobs to motivate their children to study. Some scholars have referred to this as part of the "immigrant bargain" that second-generation, U.S.-born children must make with their parents.[1] The idea is that parental sacrifice will be redeemed by the children's American success story, one that includes a professional educational degree.

This immigrant bargain narrative is common among other immigrant groups as well. Sociologist Lisa Sun-Hee Park, for example, found that Korean and Chinese immigrant entrepreneurs who also rely on the help of their children in their family businesses steer their children to majors that will offer them prestige and the means to help their parents retire comfortably.[2] The idea here is that parental sacrifice will be paid in full with material goods such as luxurious cars and comfortable houses. However, Park observed that while Korean and Chinese entrepreneurs often rely on the help of their children, they do not want their children to take over the family business. Instead, the earnings from their family business provide Korean parents with the means to pay for a good education. This offers their children alternatives to working in the family business within the ethnic enclave economy.[3] Sociologist Dae Young Kim has observed that these entrepreneurial parents encourage their children to go into "safe professions" such as law or medicine, because they believe that such professions, in addition to being profitable, will shield their children from the racism they will encounter once they leave their ethnic communities.[4] Kim argues that the exodus of the second generation into professional positions is achieved in the context of their parents' social and human capital as well as their legal status.

While parents often steer children into "safe" and high-paying professions, some students are systematically tracked into low-paying professions.[5] Sociologist Glenda Flores found that the Latina teachers she studied in Santa Ana, California, were tracked into teaching, one of the fastest-growing professions for Latinas in the United States—and also one of the most underpaid.[6] In her study of Black and White undergraduate students, sociologist Maya Beasley discovered that talented Black students steered away from high-paying and high-status careers for fear of anticipated discrimination in particular fields.[7] In both studies, discrimination had an impact on the educational trajectory of Black and Latinx students.

In comparison, the parents in this study encouraged their children to pursue higher education, but I found that they preferred careers that would give their children the knowledge and tools to help their community and themselves with social justice issues. The children and the parents revealed a level of social consciousness that goes beyond giving back to their parents in the form of doing well financially, behaviorally, or in school. This reveals what I call a *collectivist immigrant bargain*, in which parents expect that their children will do well in school and become a critical resource for their community. The collectivist immigrant bargain that inspires their educational aspirations is born out of their street vending experience and exposure to life and inequality in their community.

Collectivist Immigrant Bargain

Unlike the parents in Park's study, the street vending parents I met did not express interest in their children's education so that they—the parents—could benefit themselves. They did not use their own story of sacrifice as an immigrant bargain with their children. The parents in my study expected a return from their children's education that went beyond the family. They instilled in their children a commitment to a collectivist immigrant bargain. For example, the parents in my study used street vending as a platform to show their children the injustices in society and to instill in them a sense of responsibility toward their community. Almadelia, for example, said this about her son:

> I have always said to him how I have seen many injustices with the police here in my community, and in reality we do need legal representation. . . . At first my son told me that he wanted to be a lawyer and then he said, "No, I don't just want to be a lawyer, I want to be a judge."[8]

Parents encouraged their children to become doctors and lawyers. None of the parents who spoke to me wanted their children to become street vendors. When I asked the children whether they wanted to continue street vending when they were older, all responded with a quick "No!" Thirteen-year-old Arnulfo said his parents wanted him to be "something in life. Like a lawyer or a hero." When I asked him to clarify, he elaborated, "Like a person, like a lawyer, a police officer. They save people, like a firefighter. Someone that is considered a hero." Many of my respondents wanted to become heroes for their community and for their parents. Professions such as law and criminal justice came up many times during my conversation with children. When they talked about these two professions, they sounded empowered and committed to serving and helping people like their parents. For example, Alejandro wanted to be a police officer who focused on real crimes and not on people trying to make a living through street vending. He made sure to clarify that he was going to be a "good" police officer and not a corrupt one:

> I'm not gonna be those types of cops. I mean, I'm gonna see how it is. Like, if it's something dumb, like, why am I gonna be bothering them if

they are not even doing anything? I'm gonna be chasing the guys that are killing people. . . . How are you gonna stop somebody who is not doing anything? Yeah, I understand they [street vendors] are not supposed to be here because of the fire and all of that, but I mean if you know they are not really doing anything, if they are trying to make profit the same way everyone else is, why bother them?

The children framed their career dreams through a collectivist immigrant bargain framework. During this part of the interview, Alejandro's body language expressed a lot of frustration despite his usual calm demeanor. I could tell that the criminalization of street vending had given him added stress. Being a police officer seemed to him like a possible solution to this larger social problem that affected so many of the people he knew in Boyle Heights.

Seventeen-year-old Clara also wanted to study criminal justice and work as a probation officer. Her goal was to help and work with youth. During my time in the field, I helped the students I interviewed with their homework and school assignments. Clara is a senior in high school and was working on her graduation portfolio, which included a personal statement, a résumé, sample essays, and letters of recommendation. During one of my visits to her home, she asked me whether I could write her a letter of recommendation and whether I could review her résumé and personal statement. Below is an excerpt from her original personal statement, which she explains why she wants to major in criminal justice:

> I want to study criminal justice so that I can assist those in my community to prevent them from taking the wrong path. . . . I feel that these experiences have prepared me to take on the challenge of college and new situations, because I have become very determined and focused on wanting to become a probation officer and help all the troubled youth to correct their path and do something beneficial with their lives. It will benefit everyone and will make our community a safer place.

When we revised her personal statement, I asked Clara to clarify what she meant by "these experiences." She told me that while street vending with her mother she often saw young kids in gangs hanging out at the park. She felt bad for them, and also did not feel safe because she often witnessed fights among these young *cholos*. The students I spoke to gravitated toward careers in criminal justice because they felt that it was a profession what would allow them to solve the immediate issues they saw on the streets of their own community.

Other children wanted to study law because they felt that with such a profession, they could help people like their parents. Twelve-year-old Esmeralda sells fruit with her mother and her dream is to study law in order to "fix . . . [her] mom's problems." Here she is referring to her mother's legal status and inability to find a job in the formal sector. Similar to Esmeralda, Leticia said, "Ever since I was four I wanted to be a lawyer. . . . For a while I wanted to be a cop, but then I went back to lawyer." Héctor's daughter also wanted to be a lawyer. He told me that his youngest daughter has dreams of becoming an immigration attorney. With a huge smile on his face, he said, "One of them already dreams. The youngest one is the one who dreams the most. She already dreams that she will defend all immigrants."[9] When I asked him why his daughter wanted to defend immigrants, he said that it was because they had relatives who were undocumented and suffered when crossing the border. He explained, "Because she has a lot of communication with her mother's relatives. She realizes that many of them suffer, that many arrive and then go back. And most of all, many of them share stories of how they got hurt."[10] Working with their parents allowed children to be more aware of the issues surrounding their community and also increased communication with their parents, as mentioned in my discussion of economic empathy in chapter 4.

By contrast, the five children in my comparison sample did not have a collectivist immigrant bargain framework when they talked about their educational aspirations. They spoke about their school in more individualistic terms. For example, Betty and her two sisters do not help her mother sell tamales. During my interview with her, she projected very little economic empathy toward her mother and knew very little about her day-to-day street vending struggles. Below is an excerpt from my interview with sixteen-year-old Betty:

EE: What do you want to study after you graduate high school?
B: I don't know yet.
EE: Do you have any careers in mind?

B: I want to be a teacher or a vet.

EE: Why a teacher?

B: Because I had this teacher in elementary school and I liked how she teaches, so I want to be an elementary school teacher.

Like Betty, fifteen-year-old Bianca, who does not work with her father, said that she was not sure what she wanted to study but was leaning toward engineering. She told me she became interested in engineering after she was able to fix her bike on her own.

The children who worked with their parents and those who did not had contrasting educational aspirations. Those who worked with their parents and experienced firsthand discrimination and police harassment knew how difficult it was for them, their parents, and other community members to live in their neighborhood. They were more exposed to discrimination and racism. You might recall the children in chapter 1 being told to "go back to México." These children were committed to a collectivist immigrant bargain, and they and their parents saw their education as an opportunity to help each other and their community.

"No Seas lo Mismo Que Yo!" (Don't Become Like Me!)

All of the parents in my study said they wanted their children to go to school and become professionals. When I asked Olga whether she wanted her daughter Karen to continue street vending when she became older, she immediately replied with a sharp "No!" Money was not driving her decision, but rather the hardships endured through street vending. In fact, she believed that a street vendor could earn as much as a lawyer. Olga suggested, "A street vendor can make as much money as a lawyer. But we suffer a lot because there are times when we are chased by the police."[11] Olga did not want any of her U.S.-born daughters to suffer the hardships endured by street vendors, including stress and humiliation resulting from constant police harassment. Instead, having a real business or a professional diploma would protect her daughters. Here again, we see immigrant parents pushing their children to professions that will protect them from discrimination and racism.

Olga, like most parents interviewed for this study, wanted her children to go to college, but did not look down on her own work. Some, including Olga, saw street vending as a source of valuable teachings for their children, a sentiment that was echoed by their children as well. One parent said that she did not want her son to be a street vendor, but she believed that street vending gave her son something to fall back on if things did not work out in his future. For example, Gina sold hot dogs outside a church on Sundays with her three children. I interviewed Gina outside the church during Mass. Meanwhile, her kids helped her set up the cart on the sidewalk in front of the church. During our interview Gina said that she liked having her children work with her because they were learning as they worked. She believed that their street vending experience helped them be self-sufficient when other opportunities were not available for them.

> Well, I like it that my children are with me, that they help me, that they learn. I tell them that there are a lot of people who do not know how to do this kind of work . . . and I tell them, "Learn how to sell anything, do not be ashamed." . . . Because there are people who do not know how to do this and there are times when they only know how to do one type of work, and then when they don't have that work they feel like the world is closing in on them because they don't know how to do anything else.[12]

Parents reinforced the importance of acquiring multiple skills. Gina and most parents I spoke with reminded children not to be ashamed of street vending and instead highlighted the valuable skills they were gaining from their experience. For Gina, being a street vendor made you resourceful and a person of strong character who would not crumble when work was scarce.

Similarly, Olga wanted her daughter to go to college and get a degree, but she believed that street vending was a good backup plan in case problems came up that would require her to work for extra money. Olga also believed that it gave her the skills to face any adversity in the future:

> If she has her degree, she can do both things. There are singers who have stores. You can't only live off of your singing because sometimes you can lose your voice. You must always have two things and be well prepared. Yes, this way, you know how to clean, you know how to clean your house, you know how to make tamales, you know how to work and you are a lawyer.[13]

With this example, Olga tried to explain that obtaining a degree was not enough. Asian immigrant entrepreneurs want their children to leave the ethnic economy or the family business once they obtain a professional degree. The family business is simply a "springboard" for them to obtain their educational goals.[14] However, their definition of success is often too narrow, since only high-paying professions such as law and medicine are seen as acceptable.[15] The street vending parents believe that to succeed in life you need to work hard and have pragmatic life skills such as cooking and cleaning. Being entrepreneurial did not detract from being a professional. On the contrary, as we see with Olga, street vending offered her daughters opportunities to become well-rounded individuals and fearless professionals not dependent on just one source of income.

Children and teens, especially in the middle class and affluent social classes, are highly scheduled, monitored, and subjected to what Annette Lareau calls the practice of "concerted cultivation."[16] Middle-class and upper-class parents work to reproduce their familial class status by enhancing their children's high achievement in education with a barrage of extracurricular activities (music lessons, sports, tutoring, enrichment programs, and so forth). This intensive focus on educational achievement is not only class-based but also a historical construction. The elite aristocracy of feudal times, for example, did not require their children to prepare for competitive college placements.[17] Their children simply inherited their high status and wealth. According to authors Clayton Christensen, James Allworth, and Karen Dillon, a major problem is that parents outsource these lessons to other professionals such as tutors, coaches, and teachers, and in doing so, parents miss important bonding opportunities with their children.[18] Street vending gave parents the opportunity to instill in their children these important life and money lessons directly by virtue of the time they spend together.

Street vending was a good Plan B, but for street vending parents, Plan A was for their children to get an education. I asked all of the parents in my study what they wanted their children to study. "A mí me gustaría como doctora" (I would like something like a doctor), said Carolina. Almadelia said she wanted her son to be a lawyer or a judge. Like most immigrant parents, they wanted their children to be better than them and to take advantage of opportunities they did not have growing up in

México or in the United States when they immigrated. Children have frequently heard their parents remind them that they have to be better than them. During my interview with Josefina, she told me that her education was very important for her mother. She recalled her mother's words during our talk:

> "You're set to do something better than just be here. I do this because I'm stupid and I didn't stay in school, but I did it for the need of money. . . . And you have more opportunity so you might as well take advantage of it." And I mean, it is true, so that is why I've been trying to boost up my grades right now.

On a similar note, Rosa, who sold fresh orange juice on Saturdays with her son and daughter, also described how she wanted something better for her kids:

> More than anything so they won't fall like we did. No job is bad, says my husband, but don't kill yourselves like we do. Don't let them [employer] step all over you just because you are undocumented or without an education. On the other hand, you are able to work and make good money. . . . You guys with your bright little head. We don't force them to work. Their only obligation is to study.[19]

Taking advantage of the educational opportunities available in this country was payback for the immigration and work sacrifices made by the parents.

Scaring Them Off to School

The parents I interviewed used street vending as a scaring mechanism to push the children to succeed in school. For example, Sonia recalled her mom telling her, "Yo no quiero que ustedes vendan fruta en el calor y en el frío." (I don't want you to sell fruit in the hot and cold weather.) Children certainly received the message loud and clear from their parents. During my interviews, some of the children echoed the sentiment expressed by Arnulfo, who said that street vending with his parents made him realize that he "should work more and study more because"—he paused for a moment and then continued—"I don't want to be outside in the cold, freezing, making tacos." This was evidently the message that parents wanted to send to their kids. Genaro, for example, who works with Nilda and her daughter Leticia, knows that Nilda does not want her daughter to street vend. During my interview with Genaro, he explained,

> Nilda does not want her daughter to end up selling quesadillas. . . . It is like an important subliminal message that says, "I don't want you to become what I am." It is like inculcating it in a very subtle manner because many times we don't find the right words to tell them, "See how I am suffering and running from the police. Don't fall into this." It is up to them if they get it or not.[20]

Similarly, Almadelia's message was clear to her son: "Tienes que ser más inteligente y tienes que estudiar más y prepararte más." (You have to be smarter and you have to study more and you have to be more prepared.) The alternative was street vending like them. She elaborated:

> We do it so he can see that it is not easy to have his things. The things, we have to work hard and earn them. I tell him, if you don't do anything in this life, what do you expect from this life?[21]

Parents did not want their children to street vend as adults. Street vendors in Los Angeles are constantly humiliated, under constant stress, and fear getting arrested or deported. These experiences motivated parents to instill in their children a social consciousness and study a profession that would empower them to give back to their community as they engaged in a collectivist immigrant bargain. Parents also used street vending to scare them off to school. For these families, the immigrant bargain took a collective perspective because the educational achievement of the children could potentially benefit disenfranchised communities and not only the immediate family.

In many respects, the work kids do is seen as problematic and anachronistic because it interrupts the Western idea of a period of childhood in which children are supposed to be free from adult responsibilities. Observes may think that street vending deters children from school and leads to the erosion of parental control. A good deal of the literature on children and informal sector street vending remains predicated on the idea that work detracts from children's appropriate activity—their education.[22] Some scholars argue that it is simply a matter of time allocation: the more time children spend at work translates to less time spent studying and preparing for school.[23] For some kids, grades may suffer, and in extreme cases, scholars show, too much work can even push youth out of school. In some cases, children may not be able to balance school and work responsibilities and decide to drop out of school after they are too far behind in their schoolwork.[24] Others may choose to drop out of school because they like the independence they gain from their earnings.[25] This is of great concern to many scholars and policy makers, since education in today's hourglass economy is the key to securing well-paying jobs at the top of the labor market. The premature work, adult-like responsibilities, and extra earnings can also have a negative effect on parent-child relations in the form of erosion of parental control.[26]

Alternatively, work deemed socially appropriate for children, such as household chores, babysitting, or after-school part-time jobs for teens, are seen as virtuous activities that will help develop good character. Also, volunteer service and unpaid internships are expected of youth on elite tracks. Some scholars conclude that this type of work teaches children "adult roles."[27] According to this group of scholars, children who work develop positive interpersonal skills that help them deal with customers and coworkers.[28] In addition to learning these interpersonal skills, children gain in self-esteem and become more responsible family members.[29]

Contrary to the idea that work deters children from getting an education, these scholars have suggested that some working children place more value on their education.[30] In this view, work adds to rather than detracts from education. According to this line of thinking, children learn to better manage their time and focus on their studies. Some scholars in developing countries also argue that the work children do enables poor children to go to school because children are able to pay for the necessary school materials with their earnings.[31] In her longitudinal study with one thousand students, Jeylan Mortimer found that high school students who work part-time during high school are, in many ways, better off than children who do not work.[32]

Opting Out: "Don't Worry about What I Do, Just Worry about School"

Most of the children I interviewed said that street vending did not inter-fere with their studies. I was often skeptical when I heard this, because when I visited the families I would always see the kids working. Also, seeing Josefina work so hard taking care of her siblings after school wor-ried me. Josefina learned to make the best of her time while in school and did most of her homework in an after-school program that ends at 6:00 p.m.

Leticia used any opportunity she had to study or do her homework. She told me, "I study at home or when I'm here [street vending], at school in my advisory class. I study everywhere." Furthermore, sixteen-year-old Flor explained, "Yeah, sometimes when there is not a lot of people I do my homework." The only time kids said that street vending got in the way of their school was during finals. During finals, students struggle to maintain a balance between their school and work responsibilities. Karen, who works with her mother selling pupusas on Saturday, told me,

> When it comes down to finals, that's when I'm like, "Oh my gosh I need to concentrate a lot," and then I just get really mixed up with everything I'm doing. . . . That kind of affects the whole Saturday, how the day goes. But it only happens when finals come.

Similarly, Josefina, who seemed to have a good school and work bal-ance, confessed to feeling overwhelmed during finals and when she had important homework assignments due. During my interview with Josefina, she said,

> There's time when I'm, like, I want to go with my mom, but I have this due next week. My personal statement was due today, so on Saturday I took my folder and I was just writing all this stuff when people weren't there. . . . But I mean, there are some times where I wish, like, specially when I have finals, it's super crazy for me. But I try my best to balance ev-erything out, like, going to school, helping in my house, working with my mom, and spend time for myself. But it's really hard. Because sometimes I wish I could just close the door and not talk to anybody.

While finals is a stressful period for all students, the children in my study navigate the difficulties of managing their time in order to study *and* help their parents.

For the most part, though, children said they could opt out of street vending if they needed to work on a project or study for finals. Over and over, children said that their parents would always remind them that their priority was their school and not helping them. Alejandro told me, "Like, my mom always tells me don't worry about what I do, just stay focused in school, but if you are able to help me then help me, but don't worry about what I do, just worry about school." I was able to see this during one of my field visits when I met Daniela and her mother. After meeting them, I invited both to participate in my study. Daniela quickly accepted, but her mother reminded her that she could not help me with the interview next Saturday because she needed to study and take her PSAT exam. For the same reason, she was not coming to work with her that Saturday. Her mother then asked me to call her after she finished her exam. I interviewed Daniela three weeks after she took her PSAT and she told me she felt confident she would get a good score.

Street Resources for School

Most parents I interviewed for this book had an average of a sixth-grade education. While they wanted their children to go to college, the parents themselves were not equipped to help them get there. My own mother, a high school teacher in México, was unable to help me navigate the intricate education system in the United States, but she helped me in other ways. She did not edit my papers, pay for prep courses, or take me to see a counselor, but she stayed up late when I wrote midterms and served me fresh cups of coffee at night to help me stay alert. She constantly motivated me to do my homework, and bragged about me publicly to her friends. Similarly, I saw the parents in this study do a combination of these acts of educational care.

The youth in this study also had very little academic guidance from their parents. Street vending gave these students the opportunity to increase the social and human capital that would help them in school. Street vending offered these children resources and opportunities they would not receive if they were just at home. The first thing, as already mentioned, was an appreciation for education. For many of them and their parents, school was the way to get out of street vending. Others, however, said they developed tangible skills that helped them do better in school, including math and social skills. For example, Héctor said it was better for children to work because they developed math skills and learned to value the dollar:

> Well, it's support for the family. It is even better for them because the children start to develop math skills. Because they do math problems, they know how much we make and they know how to earn money.[33]

Not all children were good in math. Some, like Alejandro, really struggled with his math homework. However, street vending offered an opportunity to interact and study with other children who were also helping their parents. I interviewed Alejandro on the street while he was helping his mother sell pancakes. We sat on the steps adjacent to his mom's stand. He told me that his friend Noelia, who also sells with her mom, is "really smart" and would sometimes tutor him while they worked. He said, "I would tell that girl right there," as he pointed at Noelia selling tamales.

Alejandro continued, "I would tell her, 'Hey, help me with my homework.' I would ask *la tamalera*"—he laughed—"that is what we call her. *Tamalera*. She is good with math." The youth in my study lacked many resources at home. Some did not have Internet access, private tutors, or a place to study. Children helped one another when they could. More than once I saw Leticia and her friends study at a fast-food restaurant near her mother's street vending stand. Leticia would take breaks from helping her mother to go study with her friends. They liked working at the fast-food restaurant because they could drink coffee and had free Internet access. Twice I joined their study group. I also brought my computer and took field notes while they worked on their English assignment, which involved writing a song that later had to be performed in class. Using the Internet, they listened to music and changed the lyrics. Another time, they worked on their math homework. There, too, they used the Internet to figure out how to solve some of their math problems by searching for online math tutorials.

Some of the youth also developed social skills at work that proved useful at school. Josefina was able to transfer the confidence she had gained from selling with her mother to her school activities. When they are asked to sell chocolates for school, she usually sells her own and also helps friends who are too embarrassed to ask people to buy chocolates from them. Josefina explained,

> Well, the thing about me is, I guess, that, like, I don't get shy or nervous. Like, I mean, for me, like, in my school they have to sell chocolates for fundraisers. Other students are like, "Oh, I don't know how to sell." And I'm like, "Oh, give me the box, I'll sell them for you."

Josefina's friends could not understand why she was not embarrassed to sell chocolates to strangers. Josefina had a lot of experience selling food on the street with her mother in more stigmatized settings. Selling chocolate was not a source of stigma to her, but rather a skill she had acquired from her mother that helped her be more confident at home and at school. Her mother would constantly remind her not to be ashamed. "You're doing nothing wrong. The day they find you, like, stealing or something, then that's wrong," Josefina quoted her mother. Then in a more optimistic tone of voice, she exclaimed, "That's where I get my shoes, that's where I get my clothing."

In addition to shoes and clothing—all necessary for their school and everyday life—going to school required extra expenses. For Karen, these expenses included a laptop she really wanted and needed. Karen had declared, "Well, I really want a laptop." And instead of asking her parents for a laptop, she said, "I'm gonna try to save, even though my mom told me she might get me one for Christmas." Similarly, thirteen-year-old Jenny acknowledged, "The money I get from street vending helps me. . . . Like, it helps me buy my materials, everything I need for school."

However, some of these skills and resources remain invisible. College-bound kids are taught to do community work, fundraise, build houses for the poor, read to the blind, and more in order to build their college résumé and stand out from the rest of the students. Everything these kids do counts for them, and they boldly proclaim these accomplishments in their personal statements and often high school transcripts. Jeylan T. Mortimer argues that in today's competitive world, young professionals who have work experience are more likely to be employed because of the social capital and job experience acquired through their early employment.[34] She asserts that this is the same for students who are college-bound and those who are not. The youth in my study, however, rarely report their work experience in a résumé because of the criminalization and stigma attached to street vending. The youth in this study do work with their parents that is seldom recognized by school authorities, and is even minimized by the youth themselves. As we have seen throughout this book, since their stigmatized work is framed as simply help and a family obligation, they often feel shame and refuse to share it with teachers or friends.

During the two months I followed Josefina and her family, I helped her and her friend Clara with their graduation portfolio. Part of their assignment was to create a résumé. I used a template of my own résumé and I started asking them questions to replace my information with theirs. When we got to the work experience portion, they looked at one another and said they had none. Clara had recently started working at a shoe warehouse in downtown Los Angeles every Saturday and Sunday with a Korean lady who paid her fifty dollars each day. She asked me whether that would count. I said yes and asked, "How about the work you do with your mother?" They both laughed and said they could not include that. "How can we write that in the résumé?" asked Josefina. With a sarcastic tone she asked, "Do I say I'm a street vendor?"

We spent a while talking about their street vending responsibilities and the skills required to do this type of work. They listed the following: They had to sell food, offer good customer service, wake up early, manage money, buy merchandise, be on time, and be consistent. In the world of street vendors, this is very important because another street vendor will take your spot if left unattended for a period of time. They also said they had to be flexible and resourceful. For example, if they went to a park, but the park was closed or the game was canceled, then they had to think of a new place to go and sell their merchandise. In addition, they had to take care of siblings, clean the house, and cook.

After they listed all they had to do, they still could not imagine that this kind of information would be on a résumé. I finally convinced them to include it, though. Under the subheading "Family Business Entrepreneurship," we listed the skills and responsibilities described in this chapter. Both thought that was a funny title for their work and were surprised to know that this part of their lives could be included in their college portfolio. For the vast majority of the population, street vending is stigmatized as an immigrant occupation and is not recognized as a real job. Even though I convinced them to include this in their résumé, I too did not write the term "street vendor" anywhere in the résumé. Rather, I unconsciously disguised it under a more "appropriate" title for a résumé. Although this is a small example of how informal work renders invisible the important and tangible life and work skills that are not translated in formal sector work, it is not the only example in Latinx communities. For example, we all know that having a work history and a high credit score is vital in the United States in order to receive a loan for a car or house, and even to rent an apartment. Among Latinx communities, however, it is common to save money through a collective group or lending circles. In México, such groups are called *tandas* or *cundinas*.[35]

The practice is very simple. For example, in a group of ten people, each puts in $100 per week so that the group collectively saves a total of $1,000 each week. Each person is given a number at random that indicates a specific week, and then one fortunate individual will receive the total sum of money being raised by the group. For example, the person who gets the first number receives $1,000 in the first week, but continues to contribute with $100 for the remaining ten weeks. This method of saving or receiving a quick loan is informal and based on trust. While financial needs are met within the community, these community members do not get recognition for honoring their payment commitment the way someone would when paying a credit card statement on time. José Quiñonez formalized this practice by creating a Mission Asset Fund (MAF), "a nonprofit that helps poor and unbanked immigrants get access to loans and improve their credit scores."[36] Through MAF, Quiñonez formalized this practice to help record that loan as well as report the loan to the credit bureaus. This earned Quiñonez a 2016 MacArthur Foundation "genius grant" for turning immigrant traditions into credit scores.

In a parallel comparison, the children in this study also gained invaluable skills from their work, including math, social skills, and a strong work ethic. They also continually benefit from street resources, including free Internet and peer tutoring. Equally important, they help generate extra income that is invested in their school and education, including school clothing and computers. While it is beyond the scope of this research to predict whether or not any of the students I talked about in this chapter will graduate from college, I was able to see that children harnessed vital resources and learned lifelong skills that revealed a level of maturity, commitment, and professionalism. Yet, while real and tangible, these skills remain invisible and hidden in the dusk of an already invisible profession.

Conclusion

"So, Are You Saying Children Should Work?"

I have spent many years thinking about the question of whether children should work, and I have to admit that I too have been seduced by the concept of a normative childhood in which, in an ideal society, children would not have to work to help make ends meet. Yet that was not my experience growing up, it is not the experience of many students in my own classroom today, and it was not the experience of the street vending children who shared their stories with me. For almost a century now, childhood has been defined as a period of freedom and play.[1] This, however, is all too often just a social construct, an impossible ideal. In the United States, families disadvantaged by class, race, and/or immigration status are oftentimes unable to fulfill this expectation as well.

Every day throughout Los Angeles, many Latinx children and their undocumented parents struggle to balance school, family, and work responsibilities. This study set out to understand the work experience of a segment of these Latinx children who work alongside their parents. *Kids at Work* goes beyond moral value judgment questions of whether or not children should work. The reality is that children *are* working. Rather than ask whether children should work, in this book I show why families resort to working together. I highlight the social structures that constrain and enable families to resort to street vending as a family. I present children's voices as they explain why and how they started street vending and what working with their undocumented parents as street vendors means to them and their family. In this conclusion, I return to the initial queries about childhood, family work relations, intergenerational family dynamics, and ethnic entrepreneurship. In doing so, I also summarize the book's findings and address some broader implications of a study of child vendors in Los Angeles for other working children.

Mutual Support and Protection

Childhood is such a powerful social construct that even the families in this book struggled to create meaning of their work arrangement around what they also believed should be expected of them in a postmodern society that sees the dissociation of childhood from the performance of work as a yardstick of modernity.[2] For example, one night while I was shadowing the Martinez family, two priests from their parish came over for dinner. Since this entire family was very involved in their church, such dinner visits were very common. Twenty-three-year-old Yesenia, their oldest daughter, was the youth group leader at the church. Everyone in the family was very spiritual and attended church, retreats, and Bible studies on a regular basis. During the two months that I spent with this family, I accompanied them to several of these events, including a concert by Gela, a Christian singer. We took pictures with her, and I even got an autographed CD. They also frequently volunteered to sell food to raise money for their church. Before I could say goodbye for the day, Yesenia fixed a plate for me and placed it on their large, eight-seat dining table next to the priest and invited me to stay for dinner. As always, I happily and respectfully accepted their invitation.

During dinner, one priest asked me questions about my study. He had seen me at previous church events, and was curious about how I knew the family. I provided him with the same information I did to the families that agreed to participate in the study. I told him that I was interested in learning about families that worked together with a specific focus on how children experienced their work and what that meant for them. I also shared with him a little bit about my own experience working with my parents both in México and in the United States when I was a little girl. As often was the case, the conversation quickly shifted to child exploitation. On this occasion, it was Salvador, Yesenia's father, who steered us onto that topic.

Enjoying his large bowl of meatball soup topped with big chunks of carrots, zucchini, and corn, Salvador said in a loud voice, "Dicen que exploto a mis hijos." (They say I exploit my children.) He was referring to his neighbors who criticized their family work arrangement. There was a short silence, but before anyone could make a comment, he continued, "Pero miren como andan sus hijos, todos acholados y de flojos." (But look at how their children are doing, they are in gangs and they are lazy.) Salvador was convinced that working as a family had helped prevent his children from joining gangs or being unproductive and lazy. In other words, he believed that working with *la familia* helped buffer against what immigration scholars would call downward assimilation or dissonant acculturation.[3] This was a sentiment also echoed by other parents and reinforced by the children who constantly defined themselves in opposition to their "lazy" cousins or "troubled" and "drug-user" neighbors. The priests, whose church was in the heart of Boyle Heights, nodded their heads in agreement and even recited a well-known biblical quote: "Una mente ociosa es el taller del diablo." (An idle mind is the devil's workshop.) As always, I did not weigh in on the issue and kept enjoying my large bowl of meatball soup.

The children at the table, on the other hand, tried to control their laughter, because Salvador spoke with so much passion and because they too often joked around about being exploited by their parents. For example, a day before Valentine's Day, a very busy day for street vendors in Los Angeles, the Martinez family arranged an elaborate flower stand in the corner of a gasoline station. Twelve-year-old Metzli was not her usual cheerful self that day. She was dressed nicely, with a brown leather jacket and matching boots she had been wanting to buy for some time. I knew this because on weekends they sell food near the fashion district in downtown Los Angeles, and many times I had seen Metzli window shop and had noticed that she had her eyes on that jacket. Quietly she multitasked between playing games on her phone and arranging the flowers on the handmade wooden shelves. Her oldest sister, Yesenia, spontaneously started video recording her with her own phone and began to tease her, saying in a mocking yet playful tone, the kind that only a sister can get away with, "Look at that poor girl being exploited by her family." Amid laughter, Yesenia continued teasing Metzli, but Metzli kept her eyes fixed on her phone. She looked upset. Yesenia continued and added, "Look at that poor girl with her new jacket." There was more laughter from Yesenia, and this time she got a smile in response from Metzli, who did not interrupt her activities. "Look at that poor girl with her new boots. . . . Oh, nice boots," Yesenia added, trying to keep a straight face. This time, Metzli laughed and said, "Stop it!" But Yesenia did not stop. "Look at that poor girl with her new phone." This time, both burst into laughter. They later posted the video on Facebook and before long, Metzli got over the fact that she had to work that day with her family selling flowers and stuffed animal bears, holding red hearts in the corner of a busy intersection.

These types of conversations, questions, and interactions were very common during my time in the field. The families I interviewed constantly battled and even played around with the expected ideals that define childhood as a protected period free from work and adult worries. Children also struggled with the dream of having a "normal" childhood, the realization that their parents needed help in the family business, and their own desires to also have material goods such as new clothes and technological gadgets. How do you have all of this if you are among the nation's poor? According to the National Center for Children in Poverty (NCCP), 41 percent of all children under age eighteen in the United States are low-income and 19 percent live under the federal poverty threshold.[4] The NCCP report also states that 51 percent of children (9.3 million) with immigrant parents live in low-income families.

Kids at Work captures a preindustrial form of family work life in a postindustrial urban setting in the heart of one of the largest metropolises in the United States—Los Angeles.[5] A long time ago, the ideal childhood expectation came about in the context of industrialization, urbanization, and the rise of compulsory education laws that made school mandatory for children under fourteen.[6] The Fair Labor Standards Act of 1938 restricted child labor and required employers to check legal documentation that certifies that minors are at least fourteen years old, the legal age to work in the United States.[7] The U.S. Department of Labor, however, does not have an age restriction for children who work with their parents. Still, the expectation is that children should not work. Sociologist Viviana Zelizer documented this shift at the turn of the twentieth century. Children had formerly been valued for their economic contribution and involvement in the economic life in the household, but now they were regarded as "emotionally priceless" and, rather than contributing to society, they were in need of protection from it.[8]

The Latinx street vending families I observed and interviewed gave me an opportunity to understand something different. Their experience did not lie in just one of these polar opposites; they were not just being protected or being contributors. The relationship between parent and child was mutually protective and supportive. In other words, children were not only the passive recipients of protection and support from the parents; rather, they too protect and support their parents. A child's role within the family is in constant evolution as the world around us also changes. The role that children play in the family expands as children take on new economic responsibilities. In a society where the poor have few resources, the household members become what anthropologist Mercedes González de la Rocha calls the "resources of poverty."[9] In other words, street vending families in Los Angeles decide to work together to provide their children with a safe place to live, toys, games, clothes, school supplies, food, college tuition, and in some cases, a private Catholic education.

We currently live in a U.S. society that is increasingly xenophobic toward immigrants, and street vendors have become easy targets in the current anti-immigrant movement. The current service economy offers scarce opportunities for undocumented immigrants to earn living wages, and many are pushed out or blocked altogether from formal sector jobs. These types of inequalities trickle down to their U.S.-born children, who are very aware of them. In turn, some street vending children choose to help their parents at a young age. These decisions are not easy, but to quote fourteen-year-old Flor again, "Si no les ayudo yo, quién?" (If I don't help them, who will?) Many children interviewed for this book feel that they are their parents' last hope.

While the children told me that they chose to street vend with their parents, it is clear that their choices are constrained by their parents' labor opportunities. First-generation immigrants resort to street vending because of their undocumented status and the few opportunities to work in the formal sector of the economy.[10] The work that child street vendors do with their parents is not a pathology, but a symptom of a larger structural problem intertwined with our immigration system, which has kept immigrants in the shadows of our society for decades.

Children and Immigration: Family Work Relations

Kids at Work highlights the experience of children, as economic contributors, among Latinx families. In the immigration literature, children are often framed as the "luggage" that immigrant parents bring along with them.[11] This implies a level of invisibility and a position of dependence. Not so long ago, women were also invisible objects in the migration experience, and only the male immigrant served as the protagonist and a subject worthy of analysis. My research builds on the important work of scholars such as Hondagneu-Sotelo, Fernández-Kelly, Espiritu, and Menjívar, which provided the much-needed gender analysis in the immigration debate and the foundation for this book.[12] In addition, a growing body of literature has examined the intergenerational dynamics among parents and children.[13] The bulk of this research, however, considers only the role of children in the home and in school.[14] Much of this research has also taken place in a transnational context among children in México or Central America and parents in the United States.[15]

Street vending families gave me the opportunity to witness how children experienced the kind of work that places them in a very public and visible space and at the same time renders them invisible. After each interview I conducted, I asked children what they wished they could tell the readers of this book. Most children told me that they wanted to be recognized and respected for their work. Seventeen-year-old Clara summarized the overwhelming responses I heard most often: "I would like people to come here and see that it is not easy. We see my mom suffer. A lot of people make fun of my mom or me, but if they only knew." I hope that this book has accomplished the children's desire to bring awareness to their work and family contributions.

In the United States, the literature on street vending has referenced children as an afterthought.[16] Much of this also happens in the current political debate surrounding the legalization of street vending. For example, in early February 2018, Senator Ricardo Lara proudly stood in front of Los Angeles City Hall to champion Senate Bill 946, a bill that was later signed into law decriminalizing street vending across the entire state. He said, "Sidewalk vendors are overwhelmingly women, seniors and vending provides a means to put food on the table, pay the rent, buy school supplies and even put their kids through college." After Senator Lara's address, two street vending women gave their testimonies. Isabel Rodriguez was one of them.[17] "My crime has been to be a street vendor," she said. "My son was seven years old when a police officer cornered us with his car as if I was a delinquent, a criminal." She conveyed how that experience has been difficult to overcome.[18] As I listened to Senator Lara and to Isabel's testimony, I wondered about the children they referenced. In their narratives, children were described as passive recipients of protection and goods and services from adults. I wondered how Isabel's seven-year-old son might have experienced that encounter with the police and how it might have impacted his life as well. What would his testimony have been, had anyone asked?

While I did not interview Isabel and her son, her testimony took me back to the sixty-six interviews I conducted with individuals like them. I interviewed these young entrepreneurs and their parents after school and on the street when business was slow or in between their sales transactions. Some interviews also took place inside my car near their stand to offer some privacy. Many more interviews took place in their homes. The children I spoke with were not passive children waiting to receive goods and services from their parents. Rather, I saw them actively creating opportunities and generating income for their schooling, their family household, and their future.

When Isabel mentioned the police, I remembered the fear I also felt the first time several police cars drove up and down La Cumbrita with their flashing bright lights and announcing through their loudspeakers that we needed to leave the street vending site. As a participant observer helping the families street vend, I remembered feeling paralyzed and not knowing what to do. I remembered how families quickly dismantled their stands and stored away their wares to avoid getting them confiscated or simply thrown away. "Hide the juice maker!" I recalled hearing Joaquín yell to his young sister. The juice maker is the most expensive piece of equipment they own and he needed to make sure it did not get confiscated. The families also feared getting fines or, worse, getting arrested.

As my mind wandered back to those field moments, I was thankful that I never saw any of the families I studied get arrested. Before I could finish my thought, the next speaker shattered that memory:

Good afternoon, my name is Rosalba Flores. Marcelina Ríos is my cousin. Her only crime was to sell corn. She is the mother of five children. One of her daughters has special needs. . . . They detained her for selling corn and took her to the police station to check her criminal record. They found that she had no criminal background. When she was released from jail, immigration was outside waiting for her. She is currently in Adelanto [a detention facility and ICE processing center] and is being held by immigration.

Rosalba's statement put in perspective what fifteen-year-old Elvira told me during our interview a few years ago. In a worried tone she said,

I can't get in trouble as much as my mom can. . . . Like, the worst thing they [the police] can probably do is give me a ticket 'cause I'm still a minor. And, well, with my mom, they may take her to jail and who knows.

Elvira knew that her mother could get deported, and that was her biggest fear. That was the biggest fear for all the children who shared their stories with me.

Family separation through deportations is not a unique fear to street vending families. Over the last decade, immigrant deportations have become a real threat to families with mixed-status members. In her book *Deported*, sociologist Tanya Golash-Boza stated, "Nearly one quarter of the more than 400,000 people deported in 2012 were parents of U.S. citizens. Tens of thousands of these children will grow up in the United States knowing that the U.S. government has taken away their right to grow up with one or both of their parents."[19] Furthermore, the threat of deportation has only intensified under the current Trump administration.

Ultimately, street vending families show us how families work together in order to survive in the United States by becoming mutually supportive and protective. However, this is a phenomenon that transcends the United States with the increase of deportations and family separation. A new form of transnational family is emerging as parents are forcibly removed and sent back to their country of origin while U.S. children are left behind. What new economic responsibilities do children who remain in the United States take on after one or both parents have been deported? This is an area of study that merits more attention. I would hypothesize that economic support through remittances will continue to flow from the United States to México, and this time, the economic support will come from children. What explains this type of mutual protection and support?

Through street vending families, I was able to understand the inter-generational family dynamics that result when parents and children work together on the streets of Los Angeles to make a living. Street vending families that work together developed a communal family obligation code that resulted in a deep bond between parents and children that I call economic empathy. In other words, the need to work together fostered stronger ties and mutual understanding between children and their parents. Economic empathy motivated children to work with their parents and helped them appreciate and take care of the business earnings with maturity. In a way, developing economic empathy discouraged kids from joining gangs, wasting money, and being lazy. These findings also open a window to analyze similar work arrangements in other occupations in which children also play key economic roles. Future research should study the experience of children who work with their parents in other sectors. Many more children toil in other informal sectors such as gardening,[20] domestic work,[21] and farm work; increasingly, more children are entering the garment industry as well.[22] What role do children play in these other sectors and how does their *economic* contribution alter parent-child relations?

Ethnic Economy: Centering Children's Experience

Street vending was learned and adapted by parents and their children after they immigrated. None of the adult vendors immigrated to the United States with hopes of becoming street vendors. Instead, they resorted to street vending as a *cultural economic innovation* to combat unemployment or discrimination in the workplace. As my analysis shows, rather than being a cultural transplant, street vending has been a constant economic strategy by disenfranchised communities in both the United States and México. The children of street vendors help bridge the gap of this cultural economic innovation and a growing U.S. "foodie" culture that seeks "authentic" ethnic food. The child street vendors bridge this gap, with their own skills and assets I call American generational resources (AGRs), which include their ability to speak English, their knowledge of American culture and technology, and most importantly, their citizenship. Rather than seeing these forms of rapid acculturation of children as problematic and a dissonant form of acculturation,[23] my research shows that AGRs are valuable assets unique to the children and highly appreciated and respected by the parents. Future research could benefit from exploring these individual-level assets in the context of family dynamics beyond upward or downward mobility outcomes.

Ethnic entrepreneurship has served as a springboard to educational achievement for the children of Chinese and Korean entrepreneurs.[24] The literature on Latinx entrepreneurs is less optimistic. For example, in her book *The New Entrepreneurs*, sociologist Zulema Valdez argues that it is not clear whether ethnic entrepreneurship among disadvantaged Mexican-origin immigrant parents provides a similar prospect of economic mobility and success among their second-generation children. While I cannot make claims on outcomes because this study was not longitudinal, *Kids at Work* shows that children's educational aspirations are shaped by their lived experiences as street vendors. Street vending exposed the children of immigrants to inequality beyond their school and the household, and these children want to do something about it by entering professions that in their view will enable them to make a change in their communities. Some want to be police officers and others want to become attorneys, so they can help people like their parents. The child street vendors in this book are committed to a collectivist immigrant bargain, and their educational aspirations go beyond an effort to repay their parents for their immigrant sacrifice. What does the future hold for these children and their families? I cannot answer that question now, but below I present a few promising cases worthy of future analysis.

Throughout the journey of writing this book and presenting the findings at different conferences in the United States and abroad, I always encountered successful young professionals who met with me after my presentations and shared their stories about working with their parents as children. When I began recruiting families for my study, I met Janet Favela, former community organizer at East Los Angeles Community Corporation (ELACC). She was in charge of the street vending campaign. Soon after meeting her, I learned that Janet used to help her dad sell watermelons when she was a little girl. In a *Los Angeles Times* article, Janet is photographed holding a poster that reads, "My dad put food on the table by selling watermelons."[25] At an interview with *Narratively*, Janet said, "I grew up helping him sell watermelons. He drove his truck to Bakersfield and we hit the street. . . . Those are the things people do in order to make their families survive and, ideally thrive."[26] At ELACC, Janet devoted ten years of her professional career to helping low-income communities and street vendors in particular.

Not so long ago, while giving a talk on this book at UCLA, I met a professor and a teacher who also worked with their parents during their childhood. The workshop was for teachers in the Los Angeles Unified School District (LAUSD) as part their ongoing professional development. Given the major street vending campaign aiming to legalize street vending in Los Angeles, the UCLA Latin American Institute, in charge of organizing the workshops, decided to focus on the topic of street vending.

When I received the invitation to present my work, I gladly accepted for two reasons. First, I was excited for the opportunity to share my research findings with the teachers who possibly interact with children who work with their parents to make a living together. The stigma attached to informal work is so powerful that children who do this type of work seldom talk about it. I see that every time with my own students when I teach on the topic of children and work. For some, my class offers a space where their childhood work experience is recognized and represented. What if K–12 educators help develop class curricula that include the realities of children who work with their families? This is important so that children can understand their situation in a broader context and feel less stigmatized. The children I interviewed gained valuable skills from their work. They learn customer service, time management, budgeting, and the value of the dollar. These skills, however, often remain invisible beyond the private sphere of their homes because of the stigma attached to street vending. While children, together with their parents, flip the script and find pride in the work they do by appealing to "timeless American values" of hard work and devotion to family, this counternarrative seldom makes it to another important sphere of the children's daily lives—school.

Education scholar Angela Valenzuela acknowledged the importance of incorporating culture into academic curricula in early education.[27] Tara J. Yosso builds on this notion and demonstrates that communities of color have a community cultural wealth, consisting of knowledge, resources, skills, and abilities that students bring to the classrooms.[28] Knowledge of the work kids do could help educators, specifically those in working-class schools, better understand their own students. This is a goal I hope this book accomplishes.

Second, I was happy to return to the university where I began to learn about my own immigration history. The workshop took place in a small conference room in Bunche Hall, a room that was very familiar to me from my time there as an undergraduate student. This time, and for the first time, I walked into that room as the professor. I took my mom with me that day. I wanted her to see what I did for a living. That was the third time my mom had been to UCLA. The first was when she helped me move into my dorm; the second was when I graduated. During the workshop, I had her sit among the teachers, and she felt welcomed and included.

I had the honor of sharing the panel with Dr. Lissette Aliaga Linares, who is a professor of sociology and Latino/Latin American studies at the University of Nebraska. Dr. Aliaga Linares presented on her research related to street trade in Latin America.[29] I presented after her. I talked about intergenerational family dynamics between parents and children and spent some time talking about the concept of economic empathy. I described how children are mindful of how they spend money because they know how much work it takes to earn it. I noticed that Dr. Aliaga Linares was eager to make a comment. I figured she wanted to compare my findings with some of her own data. To my surprise, she explained, nearly teary-eyed, "That is what I felt growing up in Peru." She told us that she used to street vend with her mother in Lima and that she too used to worry about money matters when she was a young girl. She recalled choosing to walk to and from school in order to save the bus fair—two soles (Peruvian currency). "I was very happy and proud to be able to give my mother two soles at the end of the day," she added. I could tell that her story was heartfelt and that the concept of economic empathy took her back to her childhood memories in Lima. As I looked around the room, I could tell that several of the teachers were also relating to the children in this book, but none decided to share with the group.

When the workshop ended, Tamara Taylor, an African American teacher, approached me and gave me a hug near the exit. She pulled me to the side and told me that she too worked with her mother when she was a little girl. She used to help her mother clean offices late at night.

She told me she often felt upset at the "messy" and "privileged" people who worked in those offices because her job, back then, was to help her mother pick up the trash that was near the trashcans. "The trashcan is right there!" She gestured with her hands in frustration as she relived those childhood days. With a wide-eyed expression on her face, like a person receiving an epiphany, she stated, "The kids in your book are my students." She made the connection as she recalled some of her students selling food inside her school just like Joaquín, the child introduced in chapter 1 and highlighted in my presentation that day. Then she murmured, "My students are like me." In that moment, in that small conference room in Bunche Hall at UCLA, an African American teacher in LAUSD found a little bit of her own childhood story in the stories of the Latinx child street vendors I share in this book. She left knowing that she had more in common with her Latinx students. And I left with the realization that there are more stories that need to be told. For now, and in this book, I tell the story of Latinx street vending children who work with their undocumented parents in Los Angeles, but this book also sheds light upon countless untold stories of individuals who also had to work with *la familia* as an act of mutual protection, support, and love.

ACKNOWLEDGMENTS

And, when you want something, all the universe conspires
in helping you to achieve it.
—Paulo Coelho, *The Alchemist*

The journey to writing this book started many years ago and, as in any journey, I met many generous people who made my dream of writing this book possible. First, I want to thank the children and the parents who participated in this study. I am honored to have met them. I am deeply grateful to them for trusting me with their stories and for allowing me into their homes. I hope I have accurately captured their stories in this book and that my analysis does justice to their family and work experience.

This book would not have been conceived without the unconditional support of my intellectual mentor, Pierrette Hondagneu-Sotelo. I'm grateful that Pierrette believed in me and in this project from the start. Pierrette is *muy exigente*, as she should be, and she is also the most committed, diligent, efficient, and kind person I have ever worked with in any capacity. Without her critical revisions of multiple drafts of this manuscript, coupled with her words of encouragement, this book would not have been completed. Thank you for your friendship and for continuing to set such a great example.

Throughout this journey, I was blessed with other extraordinary mentors who selflessly shared their passion for the study of Latinx families. Marjorie Faulstich Orellana stimulated my intellectual curiosity pertaining to the topic of children and work. From the early stages of this research, she offered suggestions on how to enter the field and how to interview children. I feel profoundly indebted for the time she dedicated to support and nurture my work. I'm also grateful for Jody Agius Vallejo, Veronica Terriquez, and Roberto Suro, who provided extensive feedback on early drafts of this book.

I would also like to thank and recognize Cecilia Menjívar, who is a great part of the reason I am now at Arizona State University. I am forever indebted for all that she has done to support me in my academic and personal life goals. My family and I thank you deeply.

Since moving to Arizona, I have built a great community of liked-minded scholars outside my school who have nurtured my soul and supported my scholarship. I am especially thankful for Eileen Diaz McConnell, Nilda Flores-González, Sujey Vega, Rudy Guevara Jr., Iesha Jackson, Sybil Durand, Michelle Tellez, Adriana Janette Umaña-Taylor, Mary Romero, Rebecca M. B. White, Aggie Noah, Angelica Afanador Pujol, Ersula Ore, and Nilanjana Bhattacharjya. All of them read and commented on selected chapters and sections of this book. I also had the honor of meeting scholars such as Alejandro Lugo, Karen Leong, Carlos Vélez-Ibañez, Maria Cruz-Torres, and Lisa Magaña, who asked thought-provoking questions and offered extraordinary guidance and encouragement for this book.

I want to express sincere gratitude to Takeyuki "Gaku" Tsuda, Alexandra Brewis Slade, Kaye Reed, and Amber Wutich for serving as my faculty guidance committee in the School of Human Evolution and Social Change. Special thanks to Alissa Ruth and Cindi Sturtz-Sreetharan, my office neighbors, for creating such a welcoming and fun office work environment. I feel blessed to be a part of such a large (sixty-seven faculty members) but collegial body of faculty members. Thank you all.

I would also like to thank and recognize Michael Messner, Leland Saito, Lynne Casper, Elaine Bell Kaplan, Rhacel Salazar Parreñas, Tim Biblarz, Sharon Hays, Ruthie Wilson Gilmore, Rubén Hernández-León, Vicki Ruiz, Zulema Valdez, Tanya Golash-Boza, Vikki S. Katz, Norma Chinchilla, and Kristine Zentgraf for their support and unofficial mentorship throughout the years.

My peers Hernan Ramirez, Lata Murti, Edward Flores, Radheeka "Rads" Jayasundera, James McKeever, Suzel Bozada-Deas, Kristen Barber, Evren Savci, Jazmin Muro, Hye Young Kwon, Glenda M. Flores, Stephanie Canizales, Edson Rodriguez, and Xiaoxin Zeng continue to be a great inspiration for me. At one point during our early careers we commented on each others' work. I am grateful to have them in my life and I continue to celebrate their personal and professional success.

I want to thank my writing coach, Silvestre Vallejo, for instilling in me his passion for the telling of human stories, my editor Jordan Beltran Gonzales, who carefully revised the entire manuscript, and Ilene Kalish, New York University Press editor, and her team, who believed in the book project and provided invaluable support throughout the entire process.

I also want to recognize the Federation of Zacatecas, the Ford Foundation, the National Science Foundation, and the University of Southern California Graduate School's First Summer Institute for the grants and fellowships that made this research possible.

I want to give special thanks to my three best cheerleaders: Norma Fernández, Adriana Palomares, and Elvira Cortez. I met these extraordinary Latinas when I was an undergraduate at UCLA, and for more than a decade we have treasured and nourished our special friendships. I also want to thank Dr. Barbara Martinez, Steven Meckna, Marcela Meckna, Jessica Flores, Larry Whiten, and Alberto Gutierrez, who have been great friends and mentors outside academia. In addition to offering emotional support throughout the difficult journey of writing this book, they also read parts of this manuscript and offered valuable feedback.

I spent a great deal of time writing this book in two coffee houses that are dear to my heart for the community that they help create. I am thankful to Viento y Agua in Long Beach, California, and to Goldbar Coffee House in Tempe, Arizona. I met extraordinary people there who expressed interest in my research and lent an ear as I worked through various drafts of my book.

Mil gracias to my family members who have been so understanding every time I had to miss a family reunion or a special gathering because of my work obligations. I want to give special thanks to my brothers Eloy, Eric, Esly, and their families. The memory of my father, Salvador Estrada, has helped me overcome many obstacles. Even though he is not physically with me, he has been with me in spirit throughout the entire process of writing this book. I am eternally grateful to my mother, Leonor Estrada Rivas, for giving me my most valuable inheritance, my education. Thank you for taking care of me for so many years. It is my turn to take care of you. *Te quiero y te respeto mucho, mami.*

My daughter Xitlali has been with me since the start of this project. She was only two years old when I started recruiting street vendors for this research on the streets of Los Angeles. Many times, vendors agreed to participate in this study solely because she was with me. I remember that Xitlali was in the field with me when I started potty-training her. One day, confident that Xitlali was fully trained to go to the bathroom on her own, we ventured to MacArthur Park for the first time to recruit vendors for my study. In the middle of attempting to recruit a potential respondent, I discovered that she was, in fact, *not* fully potty-trained as a steady stream of pee trickled down my side while I carried her. These are, literally, *warm* memories I will treasure forever. Xitlali is also a lively presence in almost all of my field notes. Even when she was not with me, vendors always asked about her. As she got older, we both learned to sacrifice time away from each other when I had to do field work at night or when I had to write. Without a doubt, my life and my work are enriched because of you every single day.

NOTES

INTRODUCTION

1 My study design included participant observation. I conducted ethnographic field observations for three years and shadowed five families for two months each.

2 Most of the street vendors engineered their own street vending carts.

3 Vikki S. Katz, *Kids in the Middle*; Kwon, "The Hidden Injury of Class"; Orellana, *Translating Childhoods*; Abel Valenzuela, "Gender Roles and Settlement Activities."

4 Enriquez and Saguy, "Coming out of the Shadows"; Gonzales, *Lives in Limbo*; Nicholls, *The DREAMers*.

5 Atkin, *Voices from the Fields*; Canizales, "American Individualism"; Ramirez and Hondagneu-Sotelo, "Mexican Immigrant Gardeners"; Romero, *The Maid's Daughter*.

6 Castells and Portes, "World Underneath," 12.

7 I am grateful to Professor Gail R. Mummert Fulmer, who gave me great tips for entering the field.

8 La Cumbrita and El Callejón are pseudonyms given to the sites I studied in order to protect the anonymity of my respondents.

9 I have always loved art. Ever since I can remember, I loved to draw and paint. Since I was fifteen years old, I started selling my art as a means to generate income for my family and myself. To this day, I continue to paint and do art in *repujado*. I started a scholarship fund for street vending children in 2016 and 100 percent of the income that my art generates goes to this fund.

10 Hondagneu-Sotelo, *Doméstica*.

11 Orellana, "The Work Kids Do."

12 In order to protect the anonymity of my students, I have changed their names.

13 Basu, "Child Labor."

14 Zelizer, *Pricing the Priceless Child*.

15 In U.S. agrarian societies before the turn of the nineteenth century, children were loved, but they were mostly valued for the service they performed and their contribution to the family economy. Fass and Mason, "Childhood in America"; Zelizer, *Pricing the Priceless Child*. These farm families were typically large in numbers with two parent and an average of seven children. Hernandez, "The Historical Transformation of Childhood." As soon as children were physically able, they were expected to work and contribute to the family economy. Fass and Mason, "Childhood in America"; Jenkins, "Childhood Innocence"; Zelizer, *Pricing*

the Priceless Child. Some scholars recall agrarian societies as the ideal form of child labor, since children "performed a diversity of tasks under parental control and alongside other family members." Horrell and Humphries, "The Exploitation of Little Children," 486. Others have a less romantic view of agrarian societies and argue that children worked long hours, often from dawn to dusk. Pinchbeck and Hewitt, *Children in English Society*, vol. 2. Up until this time, however, child labor was generally honored at the macro political and economic level as well as at the level of micro morality. For example, laws in the seventeenth and eighteenth centuries "reflected prevalent Puritan views on the virtue of work by providing employment for dependent children." Zelizer, "From Useful to Useless," 83. During this time, the real threat was idleness.

16 In the classic book *Centuries of Childhood*, Philippe Aries reminds us of how recent our current understanding of childhood is and how conceptions of what is appropriate work for children varies across time. Aries and Baldick, *Centuries of Childhood*. Aries points out that in the Middle Ages the category of child did not exist because those who could fend for themselves—typically at the age of five—participated in adult activities, including work, and were treated as small adults. This was also an era of extraordinary mortality among infants and, according to Aries, "people could not allow themselves to become too attached to something that was regarded as a probable loss" (38). Other historians have "pushed beyond Aries's account to suggest that premodern parents had little attachment to their children, treating them with neglect and abuse." Jenkins, "Childhood Innocence," 16. This argument, however, remains much debated to this date. See also Hecht, *At Home in the Street*.

17 Thorne, "The Crisis of Care."

18 Harvey, *The Condition of Postmodernity*.

19 Nieuwenhuys, "The Paradox of Child Labor," 237.

20 During the second half of the nineteenth century, developmental psychologists and pediatricians spearheaded the study of childhood. They represented children as "adults-in-the-making" and childhood as "a distinct stage in the human life cycle," defined by purity, biological immaturity, and dependence on adult care. Buckingham, *After the Death of Childhood*; Prout and James, "A New Paradigm." Childhood was, in other words, a pre-social stage or a period of apprenticeship for adulthood. During the late nineteenth century it was also common to depict children as victims in need of protection from some adults, including their own parents, who could abuse or exploit them for their labor. Fass and Mason, "Childhood in America." According to scholars of the time, childhood should be a "golden age" of freedom and play. These Western definitions of childhood were seen as "natural" and "universal" and were often imposed on societies that were different in economic development, religious practices, racial/ethnic composition, and culture. Prout and James, "A New Paradigm."

21 Invernizzi, "Street-Working Children," 323.

22 Invernizzi, "Street-Working Children."

23 Hecht, *At Home in the Street.*

24 Industrialization was the period that brought most attention to the work per-
    formed by children due to its increased reliance on child labor and the visible
    concentration of children in factories. During this time, the number of children
    working in factories increased while the age at which children started working
    decreased. Horrell and Humphries, "The Exploitation of Little Children." The first
    factory that opened in the United States in 1790 hired nine boys from poor fami-
    lies; by 1801, "the number of children increased from ten to one hundred children
    of ages [ranging] from four to ten." Bremner, *Children and Youth in America*, vol. 1.
    By 1820, 55 percent of the workers in the textile mills in Rhode Island were young
    boys and girls. Zelizer, "From Useful to Useless." During industrialization, it was
    also common for every member of the family above age seven to work in the fac-
    tory. Over time, child labor in the factories started to receive negative attention.
    In 1904 Robert Hunter, a child labor advocate, stated, "This evil of child labor is
    a new evil. It was brought into existence by the factory system. . . . Children have
    always worked, but their labor was not an evil, rather it was a good thing in the
    early days. . . . The labors of children in the days of the craftsman and artisan were
    educative, and the process of learning how to weave, spin, and brew and do work
    in their fields or home, were not such as to overburden and break down the little
    workers." Quoted in Grotberg, *200 Years of Children*, 264. Similarly, mothers who
    worked side by side with their children were accused of not loving their children
    the "right way." Zelizer, "From Useful to Useless." The twentieth-century child
    was beginning to lose its nineteenth-century economic worth and instead was
    becoming sentimentally priceless. Empirical evidence of this shift exists in public
    attitudes toward adoptions. Before, older boys were favored for adoption because
    of their economic utility; later, families looked to adopt babies and young girls who
    were cute and cuddly. Zelizer, *Pricing the Priceless Child*. In addition, child mortal-
    ity was no longer taken for granted as it had been in the Middle Ages. Instead,
    greater attention was placed on the well-being and protection of children.

25 Mead, *Coming of Age in Samoa*. Empirical anthropological studies in the 1920s
    challenged the ethnocentrism embedded in the universal perspective of child-
    hood put forth by psychologists by showing how childhood was organized
    differently in other societies. In her book *Coming of Age in Samoa*, Margaret
    Mead showed that childhood experiences vary cross-culturally. For three months,
    Mead conducted ethnographic fieldwork in Samoa with Samoan families. She
    found that boys and girls at different ages had different tasks and responsibilities
    in the household. For example, the role of discipline was not relegated to adults.
    Mead writes, "The weight of the punishment usually falls upon the next oldest
    child, who learns to shout, 'Come out of the sun,' before she has fully appreci-
    ated the necessity of doing so herself" (18). Mead challenged the universality of
    childhood as a natural stage and instead showed that culture mattered. One of
    her biggest contributions to the literature of childhood was the argument that

"human character and human capacities . . . of young people depend on what they learn and on the social arrangements of the society within which they are born and reared" (xxv). Despite the nuanced provided by anthropologists like Mead, the psychological interpretation of childhood dominated Western thought in the academic and popular spheres for the first half of the twentieth century.

26 Even the sociological intervention in the 1950s was not very different from the psychological theories of childhood in terms of its natural, universal, and "forward-looking" characteristics. Corsaro, *The Sociology of Childhood*. For example, socialization theory, rather than a new sociological paradigm, was a direct "transplant" from psychological discourse. Prout and James, "A New Paradigm," 12. Socialization theory is a top-down binary model where children are regarded as "passive and conforming." Prout and James, "A New Paradigm," 13. Thus, children are not full social beings and must passively learn the rules of adult society through other adults who serve as models of socialization. There are two different models of socialization. The *deterministic model* views the child as passive but also as a threat to society "who must be controlled through careful training." Corsaro, *The Sociology of Childhood*, 9. In the *constructivist model*, on the other hand, the "child is seen as an active agent and eager learner. In this view, the child actively constructs her social world and her place in it." Corsaro, *The Sociology of Childhood*, 9.

27 Elder, *Children of the Great Depression*, 64.

28 Elder also adds that "according to cultural prescription, boys were more likely than girls to have taken economic roles." *Children of the Great Depression*, 64. Nonetheless, girls also worked inside the home while their brothers worked outside on the streets. Zelizer, *Pricing the Priceless Child*.

29 There is controversy around child stars. Many of them have become iconic movie stars who have continued to be appreciated across generations. For more on this topic, see Mason and Hood, "Exploring Issues of Children as Actors."

30 Park observed that while Korean entrepreneurs often rely on the help of their children, they do not want their children to take over the family business. Instead, the earnings from their family business provide Korean parents with the means to pay for a good education. This offers their children alternatives to working in the family business within the ethnic enclave economy. Kim, "Stepping-Stone to Intergenerational Mobility?"; Park, "Asian Immigrant Entrepreneurial Children." Rather than taking over the family business, these entrepreneurial parents encourage their children to go into "safe professions" such as law or medicine. Kim argues that the exodus of the second generation into professional positions is achieved in the context of their parents' social and human capital as well as their legal status.

31 Some scholars attribute this to Mexican immigrants' aggregate low levels of human and financial capital, which relegates them to low-wage jobs upon arrival. Kim, "Stepping-Stone to Intergenerational Mobility?"; Park, "Asian Immigrant Entrepreneurial Children." Using 2000 census data, Kaushal and colleagues found that 17 percent of immigrants from Asia entered the United States with a graduate

degree, while only 3.5 percent of immigrants from Latin America had a graduate education at the time of entry: Kaushal, Reimers, and Reimers, "Immigrants and the Economy." These educational differences translate into differences in entrepreneurial success. Kim, "Stepping-Stone to Intergenerational Mobility?" Consequently, and with the notable exception of Cubans, Latinx rates of entrepreneurship remain low and Latinx entrepreneurs receive little attention in the academic world. Valdez, "The Effect of Social Capital"; Valdez, *The New Entrepreneurs*. This does not mean, however, that Latinxs are not business owners. In their study of Mexican American entrepreneurship, Fairlie and Woodruff found that approximately 5 percent of Mexican American men and almost 3 percent of Mexican American women own businesses in the formal sector. Fairlie and Woodruff, "Mexican-American Entrepreneurship," 7. However, compared to other Latinxs, Mexican Americans are less likely to start their own business.

32 Lee, *Civility in the City*; Portes and Bach, *Latin Journey*; Kim, "Stepping-Stone to Intergenerational Mobility?"; Park, "Ensuring Upward Mobility"; Waldinger and Bozorgmehr, "The Making of a Multicultural Metropolis."

33 Lee, *Civility in the City*; Valdez, *The New Entrepreneurs*; Vallejo, *Barrios to Burbs*.

34 Loukaitou-Sideris and Ehrenfeucht, *Sidewalks*, 93.

35 Prout and James, "A New Paradigm."

36 Collins, *Black Feminist Thought*; Glenn, *Unequal Freedom*; Valdez, *The New Entrepreneurs*.

37 West and Fenstermaker, "Doing Difference."

38 Patricia Hill Collins was among the most prominent scholars to systematize intersectional theory. Her theory of a "matrix of domination" acknowledges that race, class, and gender are "interlocking systems of domination," organized and rooted in hegemonic power and exploitation. Collins, *Black Feminist Thought*; Glenn, *Unequal Freedom*, 6.

39 Espiritu, "'We Don't Sleep Around'"; Espiritu, *Asian American Women and Men*; Glenn, *Unequal Freedom*; Hondagneu-Sotelo, *Gendered Transitions*; Lopez, *Hopeful Girls*; Robert Smith, *Mexican New York*; Zinn and Dill, "Theorizing Difference."

40 Hecht, *At Home in the Street*; Zelizer, *Pricing the Priceless Child*.

41 Portes and Zhou, "The New Second Generation."

42 Alba and Nee, *Remaking the American Mainstream*; Gordon, *Assimilation in American Life*; Park, "Ensuring Upward Mobility"; Waters, "Growing Up West Indian and African American."

43 Portes and Zhou, "The New Second Generation."

44 According to this theoretical framework, the children of immigrants known as the 1.5 and second generation are experiencing multiple pathways of incorporation into the United States, which includes the traditional straight-line assimilation, or *consonant acculturation*, to the mainstream society, such as the one experience by earlier European immigrants. Children and their parents achieve consonant acculturation when both children and parents gradually learn American culture

and language. In this scenario, parents retain their authority over their children and can communicate with them in both their native language and English. In the second path, Portes and Zhou argue, some immigrants selectively acculturate by retaining aspects of their own culture while adopting others from the host society. Relying on the example of Punjabi immigrants, Portes and Zhou demonstrate that maintaining ties to their ethnic community and language can serve to buffer against downward mobility. The third and most controversial pathway is downward assimilation, or *dissonant acculturation*. According to this model, low levels of human capital, a negative context of reception, and weak co-ethnic ties lead to downward mobility into a Latinx underclass. According to Portes and Zhou, dissonant acculturation occurs when children learn American culture and language skills at a faster rate than their parents because parental authority is more likely to be undercut. Portes and Rumbaut, *Immigrant America*; Portes and Zhou, "The New Second Generation." Also see Light and Bonacich, *Immigrant Entrepreneurs*; Light and Gold, *Ethnic Economies*; and Ramirez and Hondagneu-Sotelo, "Mexican Immigrant Gardeners."

45 If we use this model to understand the experiences of Latinx street vending families, we might conclude that they are on a downward trajectory. The children in this study have definitely acculturated at a faster rate than their parents. The children speak English, they know American culture and technology, and the majority of them are U.S. citizens. I call these American generational resources (AGRs), a set of resources that are context-specific and at the root of their intersectional location (I discuss AGRs in depth in chapter 3). Moreover, the families featured in this book are growing up and working in poor neighborhoods with weak co-ethnic communities, and they work in an informal occupation that has a built-in immigrant shadow. Yet, as I explain in chapter 2, there is a silver lining, since the growing popularity of foodie culture is starting to give street vending food an "authentic" stamp of approval across diverse communities, and in these cases street vendors are developing cultural economic innovations.

46 Lareau, *Home Advantage*; Lareau, *Unequal Childhoods*.

47 Thorne, "Re-Visioning Women and Social Change"; Orellana, *Translating Childhoods*.

48 In *Kids at Work*, I highlight the voices of child street vendors and their parents to understand their day-to-day experience as street vendors in metropolitan Los Angeles, and I place their experiences in taken-for-granted social, political, economic, and cultural realities. Anthropologist Mercedes González de la Rocha reminds us that in a society where the poor have few resources, the household itself becomes one of the "resources of poverty." González de la Rocha, *The Resources of Poverty*. Moreover, power dynamics within immigrant households also shift or are renegotiated as families try to incorporate to a society that offers them limited opportunities to get ahead. Fernández-Kelly, *For We Are Sold*; Hondagneu-Sotelo, *Gendered Transitions*.

49 Capps, Fix, and Zong, *A Profile of U.S. Children*.

50 Catanzarite and Trimble, "Latinos in the United States Labor Market"; Hagan, Hernández-León, and Demonsant, *Skills of the Unskilled.*

51 Hondagneu-Sotelo, *Doméstica*; Ramirez, "Los Jardineros de Los Angeles"; Ramirez and Hondagneu-Sotelo, "Mexican Immigrant Gardeners"; Romero, *The Maid's Daughter*; Soldatenko, "Made in the USA." For a complete list, see Catanzarite and Trimble, "Latinos in the United States Labor Market"; and Wallace et al., *Immigration, Health and Work.*

52 Catanzarite and Trimble, "Latinos in the United States Labor Market"; Cross and Morales, "Introduction"; Cross and Morales, *Street Entrepreneurs*; Hondagneu-Sotelo, *Doméstica*; Kettles, "Regulating Vending"; Muñoz, "'Tamales'"; Zlolniski, *Janitors, Street Vendors, and Activists.*

53 Becerra, "Los Angeles Vendor."

54 Liu, Burns, and Flaming, "Sidewalk Stimulus."

CHAPTER 1. "IF I DON'T HELP THEM, WHO WILL?"

1 Cross and Morales, "Introduction"; Cross and Morales, *Street Entrepreneurs*; Hamilton and Chinchilla, *Seeking Community in a Global City*; Muñoz, "'Tamales.'"

2 Estrada Quiroz, "Familia y trabajo infantil y adolescente"; González de la Rocha, *The Resources of Poverty*; González de la Rocha, "Vanishing Assets."

3 Abebe and Kjørholt, "Social Actors and Victims of Exploitation"; Basu and Van, "The Economics of Child Labor"; Basu and Van, "The Economics of Child Labor: Reply"; Mortimer, *Working and Growing Up in America*; Bunster and Chaney, *Sellers and Servants*; Camacho, "Family, Child Labour and Migration"; Hecht, *At Home in the Street*; Jensen and Nielsen, "Child Labour or School Attendance?"; Ray, "Child Labor, Child Schooling"; Wahba, "The Influence of Market Wages and Parental History."

4 Edmonds and Pavcnik, "Child Labor in the Global Economy"; Elder, *Children of the Great Depression.*

5 For more on transnational parenting, see Abrego, *Sacrificing Families*; and Hondagneu-Sotelo and Avila, "'I'm Here, but I'm There.'"

6 These transnational family arrangements, in which children and parents remain separated by borders for long periods of time, are common among various immigrant families in the United States, including Central Americans (Abrego, *Sacrificing Families*), Mexicans (Hondagneu-Sotelo and Avila, "'I'm Here, but I'm There'"; Dreby, *Divided by Borders*), Caribbean people (Waters, "Growing Up West Indian and African American"), and Asians (Parreñas, *Children of Global Migration*).

7 Sociologist Mary Waters reminds us of the tensions that result when children are reunited with their parents after a long period of transnational parenting. According to Waters, children's frame of reference and desires for material goods change after immigrating to the United States. In other words, children want to have the same gadgets and clothes as their new U.S. peers. This puts more pressure on

parents who are unable to fulfill these material expectations for their kids. Waters, "Growing Up West Indian and African American."

8 For more on children and consumerism, see Pugh, *Longing and Belonging*; and Park, "Ensuring Upward Mobility."

9 Ehrenreich and Hochschild, *Global Woman*; Hochschild and Machung, *The Second Shift*; Hondagneu-Sotelo, *Gendered Transitions*; Oakley, *The Sociology of Housework*; Sarmiento, *Making Ends Meet*; Estrada Quiroz, "Familia y trabajo infantil y adolescente," 238. For example, while both boys and girls are expected to perform household chores, these chores are gendered: girls at a young age are relegated to domestic activities or *quehaceres* inside the home, while boys, on the other hand, seldom perform household chores inside the home. These household burdens on the female children seem to increase with migration. Ethnographic observations by Orellana in Central American immigrant households showed girls as young as seven doing numerous household chores (unpacking groceries, bathing and dressing a younger sibling, and cleaning), all without being asked to do so by parents. This demand for young girls to help out in the home increases not only when their mothers go to work, but also "when families are detached from the support networks of extended kin." Thorne et al., "Raising Children," 252.

10 Vallejo, "How Class Background Affects Mexican Americans' Experiences."

11 Jiménez, "Mexican Immigrant Replenishment."

12 For more on identity and belonging, see Flores-González, *Citizens but Not Americans*.

13 In 2011 the district's budget for high school summer classes was only $3 million, as compared to the $51.4 million allocated in 2008. Student enrollment during these three years dramatically dwindled from 188,500 in 2008 to 22,000 in 2011. Weldon, "Budget Cuts."

CHAPTER 2. STREET VENDING IN LOS ANGELES

1 This community was the heart of Jewish life in the 1920s; decades later, the Jewish community moved west into Hancock Park.

2 Boyle Heights is in East Los Angeles, but it is also a geopolitical space with a unique identity and clear demarcation lines.

3 Romo, *East Los Angeles*; Waldinger and Bozorgmehr, "The Making of a Multicultural Metropolis."

4 As of 2017, Los Angeles is the second-largest metropolitan city in the United States, with almost 4 million residents, 48.4 percent of whom are Hispanics or Latinxs of any race (U.S. Census). Waldinger and Bozorgmehr, "The Making of a Multicultural Metropolis."

5 Vigil, *From Indians to Chicanos*.

6 Romo, *East Los Angeles*.

7 Sánchez, "'What's Good for Boyle Heights.'"

8 Clark, "Residential Patterns."

9 Muñoz, "'Tamales.'"

10 Davis, *Magical Urbanism.*

11 Zukin, *Naked City.*

12 Kettles, "Regulating Vending."

13 Loukaitou-Sideris and Ehrenfeucht, *Sidewalks.*

14 McGahan, "Video of Elote Cart Attack."

15 Arellano, "Here's How to Help Elote Man."

16 The term *reconquista* was popularized in the 1970s by Chicano activists in the Southwest who referred to the territory that was won by the United States during the 1848 U.S.–Mexican War as the mythical land of Aztlán. The term *reconquista* has a negative connotation because it represents a threat posed by Mexicans who intend to take over the U.S. territory that previously belonged to México.

17 For more on mass deportations, see Golash-Boza, *Deported.*

18 Swanson, "LA's Moves."

19 Vendors have not remained passive. In 1987 vendors formed the Street Vendors Association of Los Angeles and later the Association of Street Vendors (Asociación de Vendedores Ambulantes). Immigrant organizations such as CARECEN and CHIRLA have supported the efforts of these vendors. In 1992 Councilman Woo submitted a proposal to the city council that created opportunities for a few street vendors to sell legally in a designated zone. In 1994 city ordinance 171913 was passed to allow the creation of vending districts; a few years later, in 1999, MacArthur Park became the first legal street vending district, where only fifteen vendors were licensed to sell. This created a "two-tier system" of licensed and illegal vendors. Hamilton and Chinchilla, *Seeking Community in a Global City.* In 2004 the number of legal vendors grew to approximately fifty. Kettles, "Regulating Vending." This legal street vending district was short-lived and was suspended in 2007.

20 Rodas, "California Gov. Jerry Brown Signs Law."

21 On the "actor-oriented perspective," see Zlolniski, *Janitors, Street Vendors, and Activists.* See also Dohan, *The Price of Poverty*; Duneier, Hasan, and Carter, *Sidewalk*; and Muñoz, "'Tamales.'"

22 Loukaitou-Sideris and Ehrenfeucht, *Sidewalks.*

23 Loukaitou-Sideris and Ehrenfeucht, *Sidewalks.*

24 Espiritu, *Asian American Women and Men*; Glenn, *Unequal Freedom*; Kim, "Stepping-Stone to Intergenerational Mobility?"

25 Loukaitou-Sideris and Ehrenfeucht, *Sidewalks.*

26 Cardoso, *Mexican Emigration.*

27 Glenn, *Unequal Freedom*, 238.

28 The Bracero Program lasted twenty years and began to dwindle in 1954, when the Immigration and Naturalization Service put into effect a deportation campaign with the derogatory name "Operation Wetback." Over a million undocumented workers were detained under this campaign. Mexican immigrant workers and Mexican Americans living in the United States for generations were socially

stigmatized and accused of stealing jobs from Americans. Mexicans were systematically excluded from jobs that offered ladders of upward mobility. Braceros, for example, were segregated and kept away from urban areas to keep them from entering other occupations. Mexican Americans who did work with White workers were paid less than their White counterparts performing the same type of unskilled labor. Gutiérrez, *Walls and Mirrors*.

29 Massey, Durand, and Malone, *Beyond Smoke and Mirrors*.

30 Kettles, "Regulating Vending"; Kettles, "Legal Responses to Sidewalk Vending." The termination of the Bracero Program coincided with the passage of the Immigration and Nationality Act of 1965, also known as the Hart Celler Act of 1965. This amendment eliminated the 1952 quotas and transformed the face of America once again with the influx of working-class immigrants of color from Latin America, Asia, and the Caribbean. Bean and Stevens, *America's Newcomers*. According to immigration scholars Bean and Stevens, "only 12.5 percent of legal immigrants came from Europe or Canada, whereas 84.4 percent were from Asian or Latin American countries" (*America's Newcomers*, 19). The braceros who qualified brought their families under the family reunification act encoded in the 1965 Immigration Act.

31 Massey, Durand, and Malone, *Beyond Smoke and Mirrors*.

32 Loukaitou-Sideris and Ehrenfeucht, *Sidewalks*.

33 Martinez, "Sidewalk Wars."

34 Hamilton and Chinchilla, *Seeking Community in a Global City*; Sirola, "Beyond Survival."

35 Hamilton and Chinchilla, *Seeking Community in a Global City*; Muñoz, "'Tamales'"; Liu, Burns, and Flaming, "Sidewalk Stimulus." Although my research focuses on Latinx street vendors, it is important to note that other ethnic groups also engage in this informal activity. See Vives, "Street Vendors on Figueroa Street." For scholarly publications, see Duneier, Hasan, and Carter, *Sidewalk*. Also see Greenberger et al., "Adolescents Who Work"; and Hsu, "More Angelenos Are Becoming Street Vendors."

36 Hsu, "More Angelenos Are Becoming Street Vendors."

37 See the Night Market website, www.626nightmarket.com.

38 Maeres, "Looking Back at Christine Sterling."

39 William D. Estrada, *Calle Olvera*, 107.

40 Kettles, "Regulating Vending"; Rosales, "Survival, Economic Mobility and Community."

41 See Los Angeles, Cal., Mun. Code § 42(b) (2004), Section 42(b) and Los Angeles, Cal., Mun. Code § 64.70.02.C.1(a)(2004); also see Kettles, "Regulating Vending"; Muñoz, "'Tamales'"; and Rosales, "Survival, Economic Mobility and Community."

42 Kettles, "Regulating Vending."

43 Alpert Reyes, "L.A. Street Vendors." According to "Graceline Shin, chief health specialist for the Department of Public Health's street vending program, vendors

can reclaim their confiscated goods if they show up at an office hearing, but they do not show up."

44 Alpert Reyes, "L.A. Street Vendors." Officers claim that receipts are not given because street vendors give the wrong address or because they flee when approached.

45 Swanson, "LA's Moves."

46 Hamilton and Chinchilla, *Seeking Community in a Global City*; Loukaitou-Sideris and Ehrenfeucht, *Sidewalks*.

47 The research for this book took place for three years, from 2008 to 2010, before SB946 was signed into law.

48 Arizpe, *Indians in the City*.

49 Muñoz, "'Tamales.'"

50 Yo era la única que no vendía quesadillas ni nada. Como iba a vender si yo iba a la secundaria? Y no! No y luego era una colonia muy pobre. Y me decían, "Tu mamá es la que vende carnitas?" porque las hacía bien ricas. [Yo contestaba,] "No, no, mi mamá está en el parque." Yo nunca decía que mi mamá vendía ahí. Y los sábados que me tocaba ayudarle, yo no le ayudaba.

51 Zukin, *Naked City*.

52 Castells and Portes, "World Underneath"; see also Alderslade, Talmage, and Freeman, "Measuring the Informal Economy"; Cross and Morales, "Introduction"; and Cross and Morales, *Street Entrepreneurs*.

53 Zukin, *Naked City*.

54 Sassen, "New York City's Informal Economy"; Benería and Roldán, *The Crossroads of Class and Gender*; Fernández-Kelly, *For We Are Sold*; Cross, "Street Vendors."

55 Abrego, *Sacrificing Families*; Hernández-León, *Metropolitan Migrants*; Hondagneu-Sotelo, *Gendered Transitions*.

56 Sassen, *The Global City*; Scott and Soja, *The City*.

57 Arizpe, *Indians in the City*; Cross, "Street Vendors"; Dyrness, "Policy on the Streets"; Hamilton and Chinchilla, *Seeking Community in a Global City*; Invernizzi, "Street-Working Children"; Muñoz, "'Tamales.'"

58 Hamilton and Chinchilla, *Seeking Community in a Global City*; Muñoz, "'Tamales.'"

59 Ehrenreich and Hochschild, *Global Woman*; Hochschild and Machung, *The Second Shift*; Romero, *The Maid's Daughter*; Stone, *Opting Out?*

60 Mi mamá se sorprendió y me dijo, "Mira a la única que nunca me ayudó fue la que vende aquí."

61 Monnet, "Espacio público."

62 Coronado, "Women and Public Policy."

63 Novo, "The 'Culture' of Exclusion."

64 Yo tenía rivalidad con las Marías. . . . Ellas decían, "Patroncita, me compra chicle?" Y yo les hacía burla. Tendría yo trece, catorce años y le dije a mi mamá, que en paz descanse, "Mamá, hazme un vestido como ese [indígena]. Y me lo hizo y

luego yo tenía mi pelo largo, y me hizo mis trenzas así. Me sentía yo Chiapaneca, pero blanca. . . . No me daba pena vender. No me daba pena estar vendiendo mis periódicos.

65 This form of internal racism in Mexico is still alive, expressed through various forms of micro and macro aggressions. Golash-Boza, *Deported*; Zamora, "Racial Remittances."

66 Supuestamente ya me iba porque salió eso de la proposición 187. Esto me hizo sentir que no querían a los ilegales y yo dije no pos ya no tengo nada que hacer aquí. Ya vámonos. No nos quieren, no nos dan papeles. No es porque no queremos trabajar. Trabajar es lo que siempre hacemos. Si no nos quieren pos vámonos. Y nos fuimos, pero como la cosa ya no estaba como antes, y antes de eso ya se había acostumbrado uno aquí. Pues ya no es lo mismo.

67 Ehrenreich and Hochschild, *Global Woman*; Hagan, Hernández-León, and Demonsant, *Skills of the Unskilled*; Hagan, Lowe, and Quingla, "Rethinking the Relationship."

68 Era un poco difícil porque al no saber como hacer los tamales los quemabamos, salían crudos, picosos. . . . Pos ya ella fue decidiendo y saboreando y ya fue como fuimos agarrando el sazón. Y en la clientela pos igual unos les gustaba y a otros no les gustaba. Hicimos de mole y no les gustó. Ahora ya hicimos tres moles que sí les gustó a los clientes.

CHAPTER 3. WORKING SIDE BY SIDE

Portions of this chapter have been published as Emir Estrada, "Changing Household Dynamics."

1 Dohan, *The Price of Poverty*.

2 Portes and Zhou, "The New Second Generation."

3 Vikki S. Katz, *Kids in the Middle*; Orellana, *Translating Childhoods*; Abel Valenzuela, "Gender Roles and Settlement Activities."

4 Orellana, *Translating Childhoods*.

5 Vikki S. Katz, "How Children of Immigrants Use Media"; Orellana, *Translating Childhoods*; Abel Valenzuela, "Gender Roles and Settlement Activities."

6 Vikki S. Katz, "How Children of Immigrants Use Media."

7 Estrada and Hondagneu-Sotelo, "Intersectional Dignities."

8 Cuando ellos empezaron a crecer, mi esposo les dijo si querían ir a ayudarles y ellos dijeron que sí. Primero lo tomaron como un juego [*risas*], pero ya ahorita sí se les hace mas pesado. Pero ellos saben, como yo les digo a ellos, de ahí sale para todo lo que ustedes vayan ocupando. Porque mis dos hijas, las dos grandes están en una escuela privada. Y pos, las pusimos en una escuela privada por . . . para tratar de sacarlas del peligro de las escuelas públicas. De ahí está saliendo para todo lo que ellas van ocupando.

9 Fernández-Kelly, *For We Are Sold*; Hondagneu-Sotelo, *Gendered Transitions*.

10 Bunster and Chaney, *Sellers and Servants*, 174; see also González de la Rocha, *The Resources of Poverty*; Sarmiento, *Making Ends Meet*.

11 Portes and Zhou, "The New Second Generation."

12 Capps, Fix, and Zong, *A Profile of U.S. Children.*

13 Portes and Rumbaut, *Immigrant America.*

14 Portes and Zhou, "The New Second Generation."

15 Portes and Zhou, "The New Second Generation."

16 Alba and Nee, *Remaking the American Mainstream.*

17 Vallejo, *Barrios to Burbs.*

18 Neckerman, Carter, and Lee, "Segmented Assimilation"; Vallejo, *Barrios to Burbs.*

19 Vallejo, *Barrios to Burbs.*

20 Vallejo, "How Class Background Affects Mexican Americans' Experiences."

21 Vallejo, *Barrios to Burbs*, 2.

22 Bunster and Chaney, *Sellers and Servants*; González de la Rocha, *The Resources of Poverty*; Sarmiento, *Making Ends Meet.*

23 Portes and Rumbaut, *Legacies*; Portes and Zhou, "The New Second Generation."

24 Dohan, *The Price of Poverty.*

25 Zukin, *Naked City.*

26 Orellana, *Translating Childhoods*; Abel Valenzuela, "Gender Roles and Settlement Activities."

27 Vikki S. Katz, "How Children of Immigrants Use Media."

28 Zukin, *Naked City.*

29 Latino USA, "No Money More Problems."

30 Capps, Fix, and Zong, *A Profile of U.S. Children.*

31 Golash-Boza, *Deported.*

32 Afrasiabi, *Show Trials*; Chang, "The Illegal Immigration Reform and Immigrant Responsibility Act"; Golash-Boza, *Deported.*

33 Rubin, "LAPD Chief."

34 Portes and Rumbaut, *Legacies.*

CHAPTER 4. MAKING A LIVING TOGETHER

1 For more on the concept of American generational resources, see chapter 3.

2 *Puesto* is a Spanish term that means street vending stand.

3 Vallejo, *Barrios to Burbs.*

4 Dawson, *Behind the Mule*; Patillo, *Black Picket Fences.*

5 Vallejo and Lee, "Brown Picket Fences."

6 According to Park, families in her study did not discuss financial issues like the amount of money they made from their sales at the restaurant. "Ensuring Upward Mobility," 43.

7 Park, "Ensuring Upward Mobility."

8 Pugh, *Longing and Belonging.*

9 O sea, sí ayudan. . . . Por ejemplo, bueno, yo tengo que picar fruta, tengo que hacer mis mermeladas y tengo que hacer harina. Entonces supongamos que le tengo que pagar a otro. Entonces, no es que te lo ahorres. Yo le digo a mi hijo, "Ten hijo cinco dolares," lo que sea. . . . El lunes se compró un iPod. Con cuanto

sacrificio lo sacó pa' comprarse un iPod. Fíjate ellos quieren darse un lujito. Entonces es una ayuda pa' nosotros y para ellos mismos.

10 A mi niña no le pago, pero me saca lo que quiere. Le digo, si me ayudas te voy a pagar el celular, si me ayudas te voy a comprar un pantalón, si me ayudas te voy a comprar esto.

11 Pugh, *Longing and Belonging*.

12 Park, "Asian Immigrant Entrepreneurial Children"; Park, "Ensuring Upward Mobility."

13 Park, "Ensuring Upward Mobility."

14 Finch and Groves, *Labour of Love*; Lewis and Meredith, *Daughters Who Care*; Ungerson, *Policy Is Personal*.

15 Atkin, *Voices from the Fields*; Guilbault, *Farmworker's Daughter*.

16 Atkin, *Voices from the Fields*, 6.

17 Guilbault, *Farmworker's Daughter*; Romero, *The Maid's Daughter*.

18 For an analysis of gender and work among immigrants in the United States, see Menjívar and Abrego, *Across Generations*.

19 Song, *Helping Out*, 47.

20 Song, *Helping Out*, 93.

21 Park, "Ensuring Upward Mobility."

CHAPTER 5. "I GET MAD AND I TELL THEM, 'GUYS COULD CLEAN, TOO!'"

A version of this paper was co-authored with Pierrette Hondagneu-Sotelo in 2013: Estrada and Hondagneu-Sotelo, "Living the Third Shift."

1 Robert Smith, *Mexican New York*.

2 González-López, *Erotic Journeys*.

3 Espiritu, "'We Don't Sleep Around.'"

4 Wolf, "There's No Place Like 'Home.'"

5 Espiritu, "'We Don't Sleep Around.'"

6 *Huarache* literally translates to sandal in Spanish, but a huarache in this context is an oval-shaped thick tortilla topped with meat, cheese, salsa, and mixed vegetables including cactus, lettuce, onion, and cilantro.

7 Pos cuando yo salgo de la escuela . . . pos yo entro a las siete y salgo como a las dos. . . . Mi hermana los cuida [a mis hermanos] cuando yo estoy en la escuela y luego yo llego de la escuela y los cuido yo. . . . Yo soy la que los cuido cuando llego a la casa.

8 Cuando [mi hermano] tenía tres o cuatro años yo lo cuidé. Pues lo cuidé, le di de comer mientras que mi mamá trabajaba. Pero ahorita ya que mi mamá ya tiene tiempo, ella lo cuida.

9 Mis hermanos nomás se paran y, bueno, trabajan, pues y yo no, yo tengo quehacer. [Yo tengo que] tender las camas, barrer, y, bueno, muchas cosas.

10 Hochschild and Machung, *The Second Shift*; Oakley, *The Sociology of Housework*; Oakley, *Becoming a Mother*, 339–46.

11 Estrada Quiroz, "Familia y trabajo infantil y adolescente."
12 Orellana, "The Work Kids Do."
13 Thorne et al., "Raising Children," 252.
14 González-López, "De Madres a Hijas"; González-López, *Erotic Journeys*; Espiritu, "'We Don't Sleep Around.'"
15 Robert Smith, *Mexican New York*.

CHAPTER 6. STREET VIOLENCE

1 Ferguson, *Bad Boys*.
2 Rios, *Punished*. *Cholo* is a Spanish term for a male who is part of a street gang.
3 Edward Orozco Flores, *God's Gangs*. According to the official website of the Los Angeles Police Department, Los Angeles is known as the "gang capital" of the nation. As of 2017, there are more than 450 active gangs in the city of Los Angeles with a combined membership of over 45,000 individuals. See also Flores and Hondagneu-Sotelo, "Chicano Gang Members in Recovery."
4 Jackson Katz, *The Macho Paradox*.
5 Ferguson, *Bad Boys*; and Lopez, *Hopeful Girls*.
6 Loukaitou-Sideris and Ehrenfeucht, *Sidewalks*. I am not suggesting that women do not experience violence on the streets. In his book *The Macho Paradox*, Jackson Katz describes how he begins his talks with a powerful question for his audience: "What steps do you take, on a daily basis, to prevent yourselves from being sexually assaulted?" The men are asked first and they are usually silent. Most agree that they do nothing because they do not think about taking action. When the women are asked the same question, though, they immediately raise their hands and provide an array of examples. Jackson Katz, *The Macho Paradox*.
7 Flores and Hondagneu-Sotelo, "Chicano Gang Members in Recovery"; Dakota Smith, "Street Vendors Fall Prey to Gangs."
8 Dakota Smith, "Street Vendors Fall Prey to Gangs."
9 Swanson, "LA's Moves."
10 Dakota Smith, "Street Vendors Fall Prey to Gangs."
11 Rios, *Punished*; Anderson, *Code of the Street*.
12 Anderson, *Code of the Street*, 32–33.
13 Canada, *Fist Stick Knife Gun*; Rios, *Punished*.
14 Canada, *Fist Stick Knife Gun*.
15 Rios, *Punished*, 54.
16 Rios, *Punished*, 144.
17 Robert Smith, *Mexican New York*.
18 Los cholos al ver dos personas no dicen nada. . . . Y muchas veces en esa zona si lo veían solo le trataban de quitar el dinero. Entonces yo vendía con mi esposa. Ella llevaba el carrito de la niña y yo llevaba el carrito de los raspados.
19 Dakota Smith, "Street Vendors Fall Prey to Gangs."
20 Me dice [el policía] mete las cosas al truck. Y yo le puché al carrito y le hice así [levantando las manos enojado y desafiándolos]. Y me dicen, "Si no las metes te

vamos a llevar arrestado." . . . Y mi papá y mi mamá me dijo así [robándome la espalda] que me callaría y que metiera las cosas. . . . Y yo así enojado. No tenía miedo. Estaba enojado. Por qué nos hacen esto si no estamos ni vendiendo droga ni haciendo nada de eso? . . . Yo lo entendí como ese dicho que dice *adding insult to injury*. Que todavía te quitan las cosas y hacen que tú las lleves y las pongas en la troca.

21 García Coll et al., "An Integrative Model."

CHAPTER 7. "MY PARENTS WANT ME TO BE SOMETHING IN LIFE, LIKE A LAWYER OR A HERO"

1 Robert Smith, *Mexican New York*; Suárez-Orozco and Suárez-Orozco, *Transformations*.

2 Park, "Ensuring Upward Mobility."

3 Kim, "Stepping-Stone to Intergenerational Mobility?"; Park, "Ensuring Upward Mobility."

4 Kim, "Stepping-Stone to Intergenerational Mobility?"

5 Beasley, "Black Professionals."

6 Glenda Marisol Flores, "Racialized Tokens."

7 Beasley, "Black Professionals."

8 Yo siempre le he dicho, como he mirado tantas injusticias de la policía aquí en mi comunidad, y en verdad que necesitamos a veces representación legal. . . . Y el primero me dijo que quería ser abogado y luego él me dijo, "No, yo no quiero ser nada más un abogado, yo quiero ser un juez."

9 Pos una ya sueña. La más chiquita es la que más sueña. No pos ella ya sueña que ella va a defender a todos los inmigrantes.

10 Porque tiene mucha comunicación con los familiares de su mamá y se da cuenta de que muchos sufren, que muchos llegan y muchos se regresan. Y muchos llegan hablando que llegaron lastimados sobre todo.

11 Una verdadera ambulante sí gana. Puede ganar hasta más que un abogado. Pero se sufre mucho porque hay veces que nos corretea la policía.

12 Pues, a mí sí me gusta que mis hijos anden conmigo, que me ayuden, que aprendan. Así como les digo a veces hay mucha gente que no sabe hacer estos trabajos . . . y como les digo, "Enséñense a vender cualquier cosa, que no les de pena." . . . Digo porque hay gente que no sabe hacer esto y a veces cuando nomás saben hacer un trabajo y de momento ya no tienen trabajo y sienten que el mundo se les cierra porque no saben hacer otra cosa.

13 Y pero si ella tiene su título, puede desempeñar las dos cosas. Luego hay cantantes que tienen tiendas. No solo se puede servir de la cantada porque luego se les va la voz. Siempre hay que llevar las dos cosas y estar bien preparadas. Ajá si usted sabe limpiar, sabe limpiar su casa, sabe hacer tamales, sabe trabajar y es abogada.

14 Kim, "Stepping-Stone to Intergenerational Mobility?"

15 Park, "Ensuring Upward Mobility."

16 Lareau, *Home Advantage*; Lareau, *Unequal Childhoods*.

17 Aries and Baldick, *Centuries of Childhood.*

18 Christensen, Allworth, and Dillon, *How Will You Measure Your Life?*

19 Más que nada para no caer donde cayó uno. . . . Ni un trabajo es malo, dice mi esposo, pero no se maten como nos matamos nosotros. Que no los miren, que por ser indocumentados, por no tener estudio lo quieren a uno pisar. . . . En cambio ustedes, pudiendo trabajar, ganando bien. . . . Ustedes con su buena cabecita. No los obligamos a trabajar. Su única obligación es que estudien.

20 Nilda no quiere que su hija termina vendiendo quesadillas. . . . Como que es un mensaje subliminal importante que [dice], "No quiero que tú sea lo mismo que yo." Como que es inculcárselo así con mucha sutileza porque muchas veces no hay las palabras . . . adecuadas para decirles . . . "Ve como yo estoy sufriendo las corretisas de la policía. Tú no caigas en eso." Ya en ellos depende si lo agarran o no.

21 Lo hacemos para que él mire que no es tan fácil tener las cosas. Las cosas, uno se las tiene que trabajar, ganar. Yo le digo, si tú no haces nada en esta vida, qué esperas de la vida?

22 Basu, "Child Labor."

23 Zhou et al., "Success Attained, Deterred, and Denied."

24 Zhou et al., "Success Attained, Deterred, and Denied."

25 Mortimer, *Working and Growing Up in America.*

26 Greenberger et al., "Adolescents Who Work"; Zhou et al., "Success Attained, Deterred, and Denied."

27 McKechnie and Hobbs, "Child Labour."

28 Steinberg and Dornbusch, "Negative Correlates."

29 Mortimer, *Working and Growing Up in America*; Newman, *No Shame in My Game.*

30 Mortimer, *Working and Growing Up in America.*

31 Basu, "Child Labor"; Basu and Van, "The Economics of Child Labor"; Basu and Van, "The Economics of Child Labor: Reply"; Mortimer, *Working and Growing Up in America.*

32 Mortimer, *Working and Growing Up in America.*

33 No, pos es un apoyo familiar. Hasta es mejor porque tanto los niños se van desenvolviendo en cosas de matemáticas. Porque hacen las cuentas, saben de los ingresos y saben como se ganan el dinero.

34 Mortimer, *Working and Growing Up in America.*

35 Vélez-Ibáñez, *Bonds of Mutual Trust.*

36 Gutierrez-Morfin, "Latino CEO José Quiñonez."

CONCLUSION

1 Aries and Baldick, *Centuries of Childhood*; Zelizer, "From Useful to Useless"; Hecht, *At Home in the Street.*

2 Nieuwenhuys, "The Paradox of Child Labor."

3 Portes and Rumbaut, *Immigrant America.*

4 National Center for Children in Poverty, "Learn." In 2016 the federal poverty threshold was as follows: $24,339 for a family of four with two children, $19,318 for a family of three with one child, $16,543 for a family of two with one child.

5 Los Angeles is the second-largest city in the United States and Los Angeles County is by far the largest county in the United States. See www.census.gov.

6 Grotberg, *200 Years of Children*; Wells, *Childhood*; Zelizer, "From Useful to Useless."

7 Prout and James, "A New Paradigm"; Wells, *Childhood*.

8 Zelizer, *Pricing the Priceless Child*.

9 González de la Rocha, "Vanishing Assets."

10 Dohan, *The Price of Poverty*; Hamilton and Chinchilla, *Seeking Community in a Global City*; Loukaitou-Sideris and Ehrenfeucht, *Sidewalks*; Muñoz, "'Tamales.'"

11 Orellana, *Translating Childhoods*; Thorne, "Re-Visioning Women and Social Change."

12 Espiritu, "'We Don't Sleep Around'"; Fernández-Kelly, *For We Are Sold*; Hondagneu-Sotelo, *Gendered Transitions*; Menjívar, *Fragmented Ties*.

13 Foner and Dreby, "Relations between the Generations"; Portes and Rumbaut, *Legacies*; Portes and Zhou, "The New Second Generation"; Romero, *The Maid's Daughter*; Robert Smith, *Mexican New York*.

14 Vikki S. Katz, *Kids in the Middle*; Orellana, *Translating Childhoods*.

15 Abrego, *Sacrificing Families*; Dreby, *Divided by Borders*.

16 Hamilton and Chinchilla, *Seeking Community in a Global City*; Muñoz, "'Tamales.'"

17 Her real name was used for this vignette. Original video was published online.

18 For an in-depth analysis of the legalization of street vending, see Hidalgo, "Black and Latina/o Street Vendors"; and Hidalgo, "Food Vendors of the Southwest."

19 Golash-Boza, *Deported*, 261.

20 Ramirez and Hondagneu-Sotelo, "Mexican Immigrant Gardeners."

21 Romero, *The Maid's Daughter*.

22 Canizales, "American Individualism."

23 Portes and Rumbaut, *Legacies*.

24 Kim, "Stepping-Stone to Intergenerational Mobility?"; Park, "Ensuring Upward Mobility."

25 *Los Angeles Times*, "Legalize L.A.'s Street Vendors."

26 To learn more about Janet Favela's story, see Martino, "Fear and Vending in L.A."

27 Angela Valenzuela, *Subtractive Schooling*.

28 Yosso, "Whose Culture Has Capital?"

29 Aliaga Linares, *Sumas y restas*.

BIBLIOGRAPHY

Abebe, Tatek, and Anne Trine Kjørholt. 2009. "Social Actors and Victims of Exploitation: Working Children in the Cash Economy of Ethiopia's South." *Childhood* 16, no. 2: 175–94.

Abrego, Leisy. 2014. *Sacrificing Families: Navigating Laws, Labor, and Love across Borders*. Redwood City, CA: Stanford University Press.

Afrasiabi, Peter. 2012. *Show Trials: How Property Gets More Legal Protection Than People in Our Failed Immigration System*. Brooklyn: Envelope Books.

Alba, Richard, and Victor Nee. 2003. *Remaking the American Mainstream: Assimilation and Contemporary Immigration*. Cambridge: Harvard University Press.

Alderslade, Jamie, John Talmage, and Yusef Freeman. 2006. "Measuring the Informal Economy—One Neighborhood at a Time." Discussion paper prepared for the Brookings Institute Metropolitan Policy Program, September.

Aliaga Linares, Lissette. 2002. *Sumas y restas: El capital social como recurso en la informalidad; Las redes sociales en el comercio ambulatorio de Independencia*. Lima: Alternativa—Fondo Editorial de la Facultad de Ciencias Sociales de la Universidad Nacional Mayor de San Marcos.

Alpert Reyes, Emily. 2015. "L.A. Street Vendors Say Police Confiscate Goods but Don't Give Receipts." *Los Angeles Times*, January 15. www.latimes.com.

Anderson, Elijah. 1999. *Code of the Street: Decency, Violence, and the Moral Life of the Inner City*. New York: Norton.

Arellano, Gustavo. 2017. "Here's How to Help Elote Man Whose Food Cart Was Violently Overturned by Loser in Viral Video." *OC Weekly*, July 25. www.ocweekly.com.

Aries, Philippe, and Robert Baldick. 1962. *Centuries of Childhood: A Social History of Family Life*. New York: Vintage.

Arizpe, Lourdes. 1975. *Indians in the City: The Case of the Marias*. México: Editorial Diana.

Atkin, S. Beth. 1993. *Voices from the Fields: Children of Migrant Farmworkers Tell Their Stories*. Boston: Little, Brown.

Basu, Kaushik. 1999. "Child Labor: Cause, Consequence, and Cure, with Remarks on International Labor Standards." *Journal of Economic Literature* 37, no. 3: 1083–119.

Basu, Kaushik, and Pham Hoang Van. 1998. "The Economics of Child Labor." *American Economic Review* 88, no. 4: 12–27.

———. 1999. "The Economics of Child Labor: Reply." *American Economic Review* 89, no. 5: 1386–88.

Bean, Frank, and Gillian Stevens. 2005. *America's Newcomers and the Dynamics of Diversity*. New York: Russell Sage.

Beasley, Maya A. 2011. "Black Professionals in Racialized and Community-Oriented Occupations: The Role of Equal Opportunity Protections and Affirmative Action in Maintaining the Status Quo." *Race/Ethnicity: Multidisciplinary Global Contexts* 4, no. 2: 285–301.

Becerra, Hector. 2009. "Los Angeles Vendor Pushes a Balky Cart through a Precarious World." *Los Angeles Times*, June 17. http://articles.latimes.com.

Benería, Lourdes, and Martha Roldán. 1987. *The Crossroads of Class and Gender: Industrial Homework, Subcontracting, and Household Dynamics in Mexico City*. Chicago: University of Chicago Press.

Bremner, Robert. 1971. *Children and Youth in America*. Vol. 1. Cambridge: Harvard University Press.

Buckingham, David. 2000. *After the Death of Childhood: Growing Up in the Age of Electronic Media*. London: Polity.

Bunster, Ximena, and Elsa M. Chaney. 1985. *Sellers and Servants: Working Women in Lima, Peru*. New York: Praeger.

Camacho, Agnes Zenaida V. 1999. "Family, Child Labour and Migration: Child Domestic Workers in Metro Manila." *Childhood* 6, no. 1: 57–73.

Canada, Geoffrey. 2010. *Fist Stick Knife Gun: A Personal History of Violence*. Rev. ed. Boston: Beacon.

Canizales, Stephanie L. 2015. "American Individualism and the Social Incorporation of Unaccompanied Guatemalan Maya Young Adults in Los Angeles." *Ethnic and Racial Studies* 38, no. 10: 1831–47.

Capps, Randy, Michael Fix, and Jie Zong. 2016. *A Profile of U.S. Children with Unauthorized Immigrant Parents*. Washington, DC: Migration Policy Institute.

Cardoso, Lawrence. 1980. *Mexican Emigration to the United States, 1897–1931*. Tucson: University of Arizona Press.

Castells, Manuel, and Alejandro Portes. 1989. "World Underneath: The Origins, Dynamics, and Effects of the Informal Economy." In *The Informal Economy: Studies in Advanced and Less Developed Countries*, edited by Bryan R. Roberts, 11–40. Baltimore: Johns Hopkins University Press.

Catanzarite, Lisa, and Lindsey Trimble. 2008. "Latinos in the United States Labor Market." In *Latinas/os in the United States: Changing the Face of America*, edited by Havidán Rodríguez, Rogelio Sáenz, and Cecilia Menjívar, 149–67. New York: Springer.

Chang, Henry J. 2009. "The Illegal Immigration Reform and Immigrant Responsibility Act of 1996." Chang & Boos' Canada-U.S. Immigration Law Center. www.american law.com.

Christensen, Clayton, James Allworth, and Karen Dillon. 2012. *How Will You Measure Your Life?* New York: HarperCollins.

Clark, William A. V. 1996. "Residential Patterns: Avoidance, Assimilation, and Succession." In *Ethnic Los Angeles*, edited by Roger Waldinger and Mehdi Bozorgmehr, 109–38. New York: Russell Sage.

Collins, Patricia Hill. 1991. *Black Feminist Thought: Knowledge, Consciousness, and the Politics of Empowerment*. New York: Routledge.

Coronado, L. 1994. "Women and Public Policy: The Social Construction of Mixtecas as a Target Population." Working Paper, Colegio de la Frontera Norte, Tijuana, México.

Corsaro, William A. 1997. *The Sociology of Childhood*. Thousand Oaks, CA: Pine Forge Press.

Cross, John. 2000. "Street Vendors, and Postmodernity: Conflict and Compromise in the Global Economy." *International Journal of Sociology and Social Policy* 20, nos. 1–2: 29–51.

Cross, John, and Alfonso Morales. 2007. "Introduction: Locating Street Markets in the Modern/Postmodern World." In *Street Entrepreneurs: People, Place and Politics in Local and Global Perspective*, edited by John Cross and Alfonso Morales, 1–21. New York: Routledge.

———, eds. 2007. *Street Entrepreneurs: People, Place and Politics in Local and Global Perspective*. New York: Routledge.

Davis, Mike. 2000. *Magical Urbanism: Latinos Reinvent the U.S. Big City*. New York: Verso.

Dawson, Michael C. 1994. *Behind the Mule: Race and Class in African-American Politics*. Princeton: Princeton University Press.

Dohan, Daniel. 2003. *The Price of Poverty: Money, Work, and Culture in the Mexican American Barrio*. Berkeley: University of California Press.

Dreby, Joanna. 2010. *Divided by Borders: Mexican Migrants and Their Children*. Berkeley: University of California Press.

Duneier, Mitchell, Hakim Hasan, and Ovie Carter. 2000. *Sidewalk*. New York: Farrar, Straus and Giroux.

Dyrness, Grace R. 2001. "Policy on the Streets: A Handbook for the Establishment of Sidewalk-Vending Programs." Ph.D. diss., University of Southern California.

Edmonds, Eric V., and Nina Pavcnik. 2005. "Child Labor in the Global Economy." *Journal of Economic Perspectives* 19, no. 1: 199–220.

Ehrenreich, Barbara, and Arlie Russell Hochschild. 2003. *Global Woman: Nannies, Maids, and Sex Workers in the New Economy*. New York: Henry Holt.

Elder, Glen H., Jr. 1999. *Children of the Great Depression: Social Change in Life Experience*. Boulder: Westview.

Enriquez, Laura, and Abigail C. Saguy. 2016. "Coming out of the Shadows: Harnessing a Cultural Schema to Advance the Undocumented Immigrant Youth Movement." *American Journal of Cultural Sociology* 4, no. 1: 107–30.

Espiritu, Yen Le. 1997. *Asian American Women and Men: Labor, Laws and Love*. Lanham, MD: Rowman and Littlefield.

———. 2001. "'We Don't Sleep Around Like White Girls Do': Family, Culture, and Gender in Filipina American Lives." *Signs* 26, no. 2: 415–40.

Estrada, Emir. 2013. "Changing Household Dynamics: Children's American Generational Resources in Street Vending Markets." *Childhood* 20, no. 1: 51–65.

Estrada, Emir, and Pierrette Hondagneu-Sotelo. 2011. "Intersectional Dignities: Latino Immigrant Street Vendor Youth in Los Angeles." *Journal of Contemporary Ethnography* 40, no. 1: 102–31.

———. 2013. "Living the Third Shift: Latina Adolescent Street Vendors in Los Angeles." In *Immigrant Women Workers in the Neoliberal Age*, edited by Nilda Flores-González, Anna Romina Guevarra, Maura Toro-Morn, and Grace Chang, 144–63. Urbana: University of Illinois Press.

Estrada, William D. 1999. *Calle Olvera de Los Angeles*. Los Angeles: Arcadia.

Estrada Quiroz, Liliana. 2000. "Familia y trabajo infantil y adolescente en México." In *Jóvenes y niños: Un enfoque sociodemográfico*, edited by Marta Mier y Terán and Cecilia Rabell, 203–47. México City: IIS-UNAM/FLACSO/Porrúa.

Fairlie, Robert, and Christopher M. Woodruff. 2010. "Mexican-American Entrepreneurship." *BE Journal of Economic Analysis and Policy* 10, no. 1.

Fass, Paula, and Mary Ann Mason. 2000. "Childhood in America: Past and Present." In *Childhood in America*, edited by Paula Fass and Mary Ann Mason, 1–7. New York: New York University Press.

Ferguson, Ann Arnett. 2001. *Bad Boys: Public Schools in the Making of Black Masculinity*. Reprint. Ann Arbor: University of Michigan Press.

Fernández-Kelly, María Patricia. 1983. *For We Are Sold, I and My People: Women and Industry in Mexico's Frontier*. Albany: State University of New York Press.

Finch, Janet V., and Dulcie Groves. 1983. *Labour of Love: Women, Work and Caring*. New York: Routledge.

Flores, Edward Orozco. 2013. *God's Gangs: Barrio Ministry, Masculinity, and Gang Recovery*. New York: New York University Press.

Flores, Edward Orozco, and Pierrette Hondagneu-Sotelo. 2013. "Chicano Gang Members in Recovery: The Public Talk of Negotiating Chicano Masculinities." *Social Problems* 60, no. 4: 476–90.

Flores, Glenda Marisol. 2011. "Racialized Tokens: Latina Teachers Negotiating, Surviving and Thriving in a White Woman's Profession." *Qualitative Sociology* 34, no. 2: 313–35.

Flores-González, Nilda. 2015. *Citizens but Not Americans: Race and Belonging among Latino Millennials*. New York: New York University Press.

Foner, Nancy, and Joanna Dreby. 2011. "Relations between the Generations in Immigrant Families." *Annual Review of Sociology* 37, no. 1: 545–64.

García Coll, Cynthia, Gontran Lamberty, Renee Jenkins, Harriet Pipes McAdoo, Keith Crnic, Barbara Hanna Wasik, and Heidie Vázquez García. 1996. "An Integrative Model for the Study of Developmental Competencies in Minority Children." *Child Development* 67, no. 5: 1891–1914.

Glenn, Evelyn Nakano. 2002. *Unequal Freedom: How Race and Gender Shaped American Citizenship and Labor*. Cambridge: Harvard University Press.

Golash-Boza, Tanya Maria. 2015. *Deported: Immigrant Policing, Disposable Labor and Global Capitalism*. New York: New York University Press.

Gonzales, Roberto G. 2015. *Lives in Limbo: Undocumented and Coming of Age in America*. Berkeley: University of California Press.

González de la Rocha, Mercedes. 1994. *The Resources of Poverty: Women and Survival in a Mexican City*. Cambridge, MA: Blackwell.

———. 2006. "Vanishing Assets: Cumulative Disadvantage among the Urban Poor." *Annals of the American Academy of Political and Social Science* 606, no. 1: 68–94.

González-López, Gloria. 2003. "De Madres a Hijas: Gendered Lessons on Virginity across Generations of Mexican Immigrant Women." In *Gender and U.S. Immigration*, edited by Pierrette Hondagneu-Sotelo, 217–40. Berkeley: University of California Press.

———. 2005. *Erotic Journeys: Mexican Immigrants and Their Sex Lives*. Berkeley: University of California Press.

Gordon, Milton M. 1964. *Assimilation in American Life: The Role of Race, Religion, and National Origins*. New York: Oxford University Press.

Greenberger, Ellen, Laurence D. Steinberg, Alan Vaux, and Sharon McAuliffe. 1980. "Adolescents Who Work: Effects of Part-Time Employment on Family and Peer Relations." *Journal of Youth and Adolescence* 9, no. 3: 189–202.

Grotberg, Edith H., ed. 1977. *200 Years of Children*. Washington, DC: Office of Child Development.

Guilbault, Rose Castillo. 2005. *Farmworker's Daughter: Growing Up Mexican in America*. Berkeley, CA: Heyday Books.

Gutiérrez, David. 1995. *Walls and Mirrors: Mexican Americans, Mexican Immigrants, and the Politics of Ethnicity*. Berkeley: University of California Press.

Gutierrez-Morfin, Noel. 2016. "Latino CEO José Quiñonez Named a 2016 MacArthur Fellow." *NBC News*, September 22. www.nbcnews.com.

Hagan, Jacqueline, Rubén Hernández-León, and Jean-Luc Demonsant. 2015. *Skills of the Unskilled: Work and Mobility among Mexican Migrants*. Berkeley: University of California Press.

Hagan, Jacqueline, Nichola Lowe, and Christian Quingla. 2011. "Rethinking the Relationship between Human Capital and Immigrant Economic Mobility." *Work and Occupations* 38, no. 2: 149–78.

Hamilton, Nora, and Norma Stoltz Chinchilla. 2001. *Seeking Community in a Global City: Guatemalans and Salvadorans in Los Angeles*. Philadelphia: Temple University Press.

Harvey, David. 1991. *The Condition of Postmodernity: An Enquiry into the Origins of Cultural Change*. Malden, MA: Wiley-Blackwell.

Hecht, Tobias. 1998. *At Home in the Street: Street Children of Northeast Brazil*. New York: Cambridge University Press.

Hernandez, D. J. 1993. "The Historical Transformation of Childhood, Children's Statistics, and Social Policy." *Childhood* 1, no. 4: 187–201.

Hernández-León, Rubén. 2008. *Metropolitan Migrants: The Migration of Urban Mexicans to the United States*. Berkeley: University of California Press.

Hidalgo, L. G. 2019. "Black and Latina/o Street Vendors of Los Angeles: Visualizing Narratives of Contested Urban Terrains." Ph.D. diss., University of California, Los Angeles.

———. Forthcoming. "Food Vendors of the Southwest: Embracing Pochteca Ancestors and Transforming Cities." *Human Organization*.

Hochschild, Arlie, and Anne Machung. 2012. *The Second Shift: Working Families and the Revolution at Home*. New York: Penguin.

Hondagneu-Sotelo, Pierrette. 1994. *Gendered Transitions: Mexican Experiences of Immigration*. Berkeley: University of California Press.

———. 2001. *Doméstica: Immigrant Workers Cleaning and Caring in the Shadows of Affluence*. Berkeley: University of California Press.

Hondagneu-Sotelo, Pierrette, and Ernestine Avila. 1997. "'I'm Here, but I'm There': The Meanings of Latina Transnational Motherhood." *Gender and Society* 11, no. 5: 548–71.

Horrell, Sara, and Jane Humphries. 1995. "The Exploitation of Little Children: Child Labor and the Family Economy in the Industrial Revolution." *Exploration in Economic History* 32: 485–516.

Hsu, Tiffany. 2014. "More Angelenos Are Becoming Street Vendors amid Weak Economy." *Los Angeles Times*, September 6. www.latimes.com.

Invernizzi, Antonella. 2003. "Street-Working Children and Adolescents in Lima: Work as an Agent of Socialization." *Childhood* 10, no. 3: 319–41.

Jenkins, Henry. 1998. "Childhood Innocence and Other Modern Myths." In *The Children's Culture Reader*, edited by Henry Jenkins, 1–37. New York: New York University Press.

Jensen, Peter, and Helena Skyt Nielsen. 1997. "Child Labour or School Attendance? Evidence from Zambia." *Journal of Population Economics* 10, no. 4: 407–24.

Jiménez, Tomás R. 2008. "Mexican Immigrant Replenishment and the Continuing Significance of Ethnicity and Race." *American Journal of Sociology* 113, no. 6: 1527–67.

Katz, Jackson. 2006. *The Macho Paradox: Why Some Men Hurt Women and How All Men Can Help*. Naperville, IL: Sourcebooks.

Katz, Vikki S. 2010. "How Children of Immigrants Use Media to Connect Their Families to the Community: The Case of Latinos in South Los Angeles." *Journal of Children and Media* 4, no. 3: 298–315.

———. 2014. *Kids in the Middle: How Children of Immigrants Negotiate Community Interactions for Their Families*. New Brunswick: Rutgers University Press.

Kaushal, Neeraj, Cordelia W. Reimers, and David M. Reimers. 2007. "Immigrants and the Economy." In *The New Americans: A Guide to Immigration since 1965*, edited by Mary C. Waters and Reed Ueda, 176–88. Cambridge: Harvard University Press.

Kettles, Gregg W. 2004. "Regulating Vending in the Sidewalk Commons." *Temple Law Review* 77, no. 1.

———. 2007. "Legal Responses to Sidewalk Vending: The Case of Los Angeles, California." In *Street Entrepreneurs: People, Place and Politics in Local and Global Perspective*, edited by John Cross and Alfonso Morales, 58–78. New York: Routledge.

Kim, Dae Young. 2006. "Stepping-Stone to Intergenerational Mobility? The Spring-board, Safety Net, or Mobility Trap Functions of Korean Immigrant Entrepreneurship for the Second Generation." *International Migration Review* 40, no. 4: 927–62.

Kwon, Hyeyoung. 2014. "The Hidden Injury of Class in Korean American Language Brokers' Lives." *Childhood* 21: 56–71.

Lareau, Annette. 2000. *Home Advantage: Social Class and Parental Intervention in Elementary Education*. Lanham, MD: Rowman and Littlefield.

———. 2003. *Unequal Childhoods: Race, Class and Family Life*. Berkeley: University of California Press.

Latino USA. 2017. "No Money More Problems: The Obstacles to Building Wealth." *NPR*, June 2. http://latinousa.org.

Lee, Jennifer. 2002. *Civility in the City: Blacks, Jews, and Koreans in Urban America*. Cambridge: Harvard University Press.

Lewis, Jane, and Barbara Meredith. 1988. *Daughters Who Care*. New York: Routledge.

Light, Ivan, and Edna Bonacich. 1991. *Immigrant Entrepreneurs: Koreans in Los Angeles, 1965–1982*. Berkeley: University of California Press.

Light, Ivan, and Steven Gold. 2000. *Ethnic Economies*. San Diego: Academic Press.

Liu, Yvonne Yen, Patrick Burns, and Daniel Flaming. 2015. "Sidewalk Stimulus: Economic and Geographic Impact of Los Angeles Street Vendors." *Economic Round Table*, June 22. https://economicrt.org.

Lopez, Nancy. 2003. *Hopeful Girls, Troubled Boys: Race and Gender Disparity in Urban Education*. New York: Routledge.

Los Angeles Times. 2013. "Legalize L.A.'s Street Vendors." November 8. www.latimes.com.

Loukaitou-Sideris, Anastasia, and Renia Ehrenfeucht. 2009. *Sidewalks: Conflict and Negotiation over Public Space*. Cambridge: MIT Press.

Maeres, Hadley. 2017. "Looking Back at Christine Sterling, the Maternalistic, Problematic 'Mother of Olvera Street.'" *L.A. Weekly*, July 11. www.laweekly.com.

Martinez, Ruben. 1991. "Sidewalk Wars: Why L.A. Street Vendors Won't Be Swept Away." *Los Angeles Weekly*, December 6–12.

Martino, Alyssa C. 2015. "Fear and Vending in L.A." *Narratively*, January 21, 2015. http://narrative.ly.

Mason, Jan, and Suzanne Hood. 2011. "Exploring Issues of Children as Actors in Social Research." *Children and Youth Services Review* 33, no. 4: 490–95.

Massey, Douglas S., Jorge Durand, and Nolan J. Malone. 2002. *Beyond Smoke and Mirrors: Mexican Immigration in an Era of Economic Integration*. New York: Russell Sage.

McGahan, James. 2017. "Video of Elote Cart Attack in Hollywood Goes Viral." *L.A. Weekly*, July 25. www.laweekly.com.

McKechnie, Jim, and Sandy Hobbs. 1999. "Child Labour: The View from the North." *Childhood* 6, no. 1: 89–100.

Mead, Margaret. 1928. *Coming of Age in Samoa*. New York: HarperCollins.

Menjívar, Cecilia. 2000. *Fragmented Ties: Salvadoran Immigrant Networks in America.* Berkeley: University of California Press.

Menjívar, Cecilia, and Leisy Abrego. 2009. *Across Generations: Immigrant Families in America*, edited by Nancy Foner, 160–89. New York: New York University Press.

Monnet, Jerome. 1996. "Espacio público, comercio y urbanidad en Francia, México y Estados Unidos." *Alteridades* 6, no. 11: 11–25.

Mortimer, Jeylan T. 2003. *Working and Growing Up in America.* Cambridge: Harvard University Press.

Muñoz, Lorena. 2008. "'Tamales . . . Elotes . . . Champurrado . . .': The Production of Latino Vending Landscapes." Ph.D. diss., University of Southern California.

National Center for Children in Poverty. 2018. "Learn: About NCCP." www.nccp.org.

Neckerman, Kathy M., Prudence Carter, and Jennifer Lee. 2010. "Segmented Assimilation and Minority Cultures of Mobility." *Ethnic and Racial Studies* 22, no. 6: 945–65.

Newman, Katharine S. 1999. *No Shame in My Game: The Working Poor in the Inner City.* New York: Russell Sage.

Nicholls, Walter J. 2013. *The DREAMers: How the Undocumented Youth Movement Transformed the Immigrant Rights Debate.* Redwood City: Stanford University Press.

Nieuwenhuys, Olga. 2003. "The Paradox of Child Labor and Anthropology." *Annual Review of Anthropology* 25, no. 1: 237–51.

Novo, Carmen M. 2003. "The 'Culture' of Exclusion: Representations of Indigenous Women Street Vendors in Tijuana, México." *Bulletin of Latin American Research* 22, no. 3: 249–68.

Oakley, Ann. 1974. *The Sociology of Housework.* London: Martin Robertson.

———. 1979. *Becoming a Mother.* Oxford: Martin Robinson.

Orellana, Marjorie Faulstich. 2001. "The Work Kids Do: Mexican and Central American Immigrant Children's Contributions to Households and Schools in California." *Harvard Educational Review* 71, no. 3: 366–90.

———. 2009. *Translating Childhoods: Immigrant Youth, Language, and Culture.* New Brunswick: Rutgers University Press.

Park, Lisa Sun-Hee. 2002. "Asian Immigrant Entrepreneurial Children: Negotiating Work, Family, and Community." In *Intersections and Divergences: Contemporary Asian Pacific American Communities*, edited by Linda Trinh Võ and Rick Bonus. Philadelphia: Temple University Press.

———. 2004. "Ensuring Upward Mobility: Obligations of Korean and Chinese American Children of Immigrant Entrepreneurs." In *Asian American Children: A Historical Handbook and Guide*, edited by Benson Tong, 123–34. Westport, CT: Greenwood.

———. 2005. *Consuming Citizenship: Children of Asian Immigrant Entrepreneurs.* Stanford: Stanford University Press.

Parreñas, Rhacel Salazar. 2005. *Children of Global Migration: Transnational Families and Gendered Woes.* Redwood City: Stanford University Press.

Patillo, Mary. 1999. *Black Picket Fences: Privilege and Peril among the Black Middle Class*. 2nd ed. Chicago: University of Chicago Press.

Pinchbeck, Ivy, and Margaret Hewitt. 1973. *Children in English Society*. Vol. 2, *From the Eighteenth Century to the Children Act 1948*. London: Routledge and Kegan Paul.

Portes, Alejandro, and Robert L. Bach. 1985. *Latin Journey: Cuban and Mexican Immigrants in the United States*. Berkeley: University of California Press.

Portes, Alejandro, and Rubén G. Rumbaut. 2001. *Legacies: The Story of the Immigrant Second Generation*. Berkeley: University of California Press.

———. 2014. *Immigrant America: A Portrait*. Rev. ed. Berkeley: University of California Press.

Portes, Alejandro, and Min Zhou. 1993. "The New Second Generation: Segmented Assimilation and Its Variants." *Annals of the American Academy of Political and Social Science* 530, no. 1: 74–96.

Prout, Alan, and Allison James. 1997. "A New Paradigm for the Sociology of Childhood? Provenance, Promise and Problems." In *Constructing and Reconstructing Childhood: Contemporary Issues in the Sociological Study of Childhood*, edited by Allison James and Alan Prout, 7–33. New York: Routledge.

Pugh, Allison J. 2009. *Longing and Belonging: Parents, Children, and Consumer Culture*. Berkeley: University of California Press.

Ramirez, Hernan. 2011. "Los Jardineros de Los Angeles: Suburban Maintenance Gardening as a Pathway to First and Second Generation Mexican Immigrant Mobility." Ph.D. diss., University of Southern California.

Ramirez, Hernan, and Pierrette Hondagneu-Sotelo. 2009. "Mexican Immigrant Gardeners: Entrepreneurs or Exploited Workers?" *Social Problems* 56, no. 1: 70–88.

Ray, Ranjan. 2000. "Child Labor, Child Schooling, and Their Interaction with Adult Labor: Empirical Evidence for Peru and Pakistan." *World Bank Economic Review* 14, no. 2: 347–67.

Rios, Victor M. 2011. *Punished: Policing the Lives of Black and Latino Boys*. New York: New York University Press.

Rodas, Clara. 2018. "California Gov. Jerry Brown Signs Law Decriminalizing Street Vending." *Daily California*, September 25. www.dailycal.org.

Romero, Mary. 2011. *The Maid's Daughter: Living inside and outside the American Dream*. New York: New York University Press.

Romo, Ricardo. 1983. *East Los Angeles: History of a Barrio*. Austin: University of Texas Press.

Rosales, Rocío. 2013. "Survival, Economic Mobility and Community among Los Angeles Fruit Vendors." *Journal of Ethnic and Migration Studies* 39, no. 5: 697–717.

Rubin, Joel. 2012. "LAPD Chief Backs Driver's Licenses for Illegal Immigrants." *L.A. NOW* (blog), *Los Angeles Times*, February 22. http://latimesblogs.latimes.com.

Sánchez, George J. 2004. "'What's Good for Boyle Heights Is Good for the Jews': Creating Multiculturalism on the Eastside during the 1950s." *American Quarterly* 56, no. 3: 633–61.

Sarmiento, Socorro Torres. 2002. *Making Ends Meet: Income-Generating Strategies among Mexican Immigrants*. New York: LFB Scholarly Publishing.

Sassen, Saskia. 1989. "New York City's Informal Economy." In *The Informal Economy: Studies in Advanced and Less Developed Countries,* edited by Alejandro Portes, Manuel Castells, and Lauren A. Benton, 60–77. Baltimore: Johns Hopkins University Press.

———. 2001. *The Global City: New York, London, Tokyo.* 2nd ed. Princeton: Princeton University Press.

Scott, Allen, and Edward W. Soja. 1998. *The City: Los Angeles and Urban Theory at the End of the Twentieth Century.* Berkeley: University of California Press.

Sirola, Paula. 1992. "Beyond Survival: Latino Immigrant Street Vendors in the Los Angeles Informal Sector." Paper presented at the 17th International Congress of the Latin American Studies Association, Los Angeles, California.

Smith, Dakota. 2015. "Street Vendors Fall Prey to Gangs, Will L.A.'s Move to Legalize Them Help?" *Daily News,* January 22. www.dailynews.com.

Smith, Robert. 2005. *Mexican New York: Transnational Lives of New Immigrants.* Berkeley: University of California Press.

Soldatenko, Maria Angelina. 1999. "Made in the USA: Latinas/os?, Garment Work and Ethnic Conflict in Los Angeles' Sweat Shops." *Cultural Studies* 13, no. 2: 319–34.

Song, Miri. 1999. *Helping Out: Children's Labor in Ethnic Business*. Philadelphia: Temple University Press.

Steinberg, Laurence, and Sanford M. Dornbusch. 1991. "Negative Correlates of Part-Time Employment during Adolescence: Replication and Elaboration." *Developmental Psychology* 27, no. 2: 304.

Stone, Pamela. 2008. *Opting Out? Why Women Really Quit Careers and Head Home.* Berkeley: University of California Press.

Suárez-Orozco, Carola, and Marcelo M. Suárez-Orozco. 1995. *Transformations: Immigration, Family Life, and Achievement Motivation among Latino Adolescents.* Redwood City: Stanford University Press.

Swanson, Abbie Fentress. 2017. "L.A.'s Moves to Protect Immigrant Street-Food Vendors Come with a Catch." *NPR,* February 26. www.npr.org.

Thorne, Barrie. 1987. "Re-Visioning Women and Social Change: Where Are the Children?" *Gender and Society* 1, no. 1: 85–109.

———. 2004. "The Crisis of Care." In *Work-Family Challenges for Low-Income Parents and Their Children,* edited by Ann C. Crouter and Alan Booth, 165–78. Mahwah, NJ: Lawrence Erlbaum.

Thorne, Barrie, Marjorie Faulstich Orellana, Wan Shun Eva Lam, and Anna Chee. 2003. "Raising Children, and Growing Up, across National Borders." In *Gender and U.S. Immigration,* edited by Pierrette Hondagneu-Sotelo, 241–62. Berkeley: University of California Press.

Ungerson, Clare. 1987. *Policy Is Personal: Sex, Gender and Informal Care.* New York: Routledge.

Valdez, Zulema. 2008. "The Effect of Social Capital on White, Korean, Mexican and Black Business Owners' Earnings in the U.S." *Journal of Ethnic and Migration Studies* 34, no. 6: 955–73.

———. 2011. *The New Entrepreneurs: How Race, Class, and Gender Shape American Enterprise*. Redwood City: Stanford University Press.

Valenzuela, Abel. 1999. "Gender Roles and Settlement Activities among Children and Their Immigrant Families." *American Behavioral Scientist* 42, no. 4: 720–42.

Valenzuela, Angela. 1999. *Subtractive Schooling: U.S.-Mexican Youth and the Politics of Caring*. Albany: State University of New York Press.

Vallejo, Jody Agius. 2012. *Barrios to Burbs: The Making of the Mexican American Middle Class*. Redwood City: Stanford University Press.

———. 2015. "How Class Background Affects Mexican Americans' Experiences of Subtle Racism in the White-Collar Workplace." *Latino Studies* 13, no. 1: 69–87.

Vallejo, Jody Agius, and Jennifer Lee. 2009. "Brown Picket Fences: The Immigrant Narrative and 'Giving Back' among the Mexican-Origin Middle Class." *Ethnicities* 9, no. 1: 5–31.

Vélez-Ibáñez, Carlos G. 1983. *Bonds of Mutual Trust: The Culture Systems of Rotating Credit Associations among Urban Mexicans and Chicanos*. New Brunswick: Rutgers University Press.

Venkatesh, Sudhir. 2006. *Off the Books: The Underground Economy of the Urban Poor*. Cambridge: Harvard University Press.

Vigil, James Diego. 1998. *From Indians to Chicanos: The Dynamics of Mexican-American Culture*. Long Grove, IL: Waveland.

Vives, Ruben. 2016. "Street Vendors on Figueroa Street: An Entrepreneurial Spirit Rises from the Depths of Poverty." *Los Angeles Times*, April 14. https://workingwomanreport.com.

Wahba, Jackline. 2006. "The Influence of Market Wages and Parental History on Child Labour and Schooling in Egypt." *Journal of Population Economics* 19, no. 4: 823–52.

Waldinger, Roger, and Mehdi Bozorgmehr. 1996. "The Making of a Multicultural Metropolis." In *Ethnic Los Angeles*, edited by Roger Waldinger and Mehdi Bozorgmehr, 3–38. New York: Russell Sage.

Wallace, Steven P., Xóchitl Castañeda, Sylvia Guendelman, Imelda Padilla-Frausto, and Emily Felt. 2008. *Immigration, Health and Work: The Facts behind the Myths*. Oakland: California Center for Population Research.

Waters, Mary C. 2001. "Growing Up West Indian and African American." In *Islands in the City: West Indian Migration to New York*, edited by Nancy Foner, 193–215. Berkeley: University of California Press.

Weldon, Tim. 2011. "Budget Cuts Forced California Schools to Slash Summer Programs." Council of State Governments. http://knowledgecenter.csg.org.

Wells, Karen. 2009. *Childhood: In a Global Perspective*. Cambridge: Polity.

West, Candace, and Sarah Fenstermaker. 1995. "Doing Difference." *Gender and Society* 9, no. 1: 8–37.

Wolf, Diane L. 2002. "There's No Place like 'Home': Emotional Transnationalism and the Struggles of Second-Generation Filipinos." In *The Changing Face of Home: The Transnational Lives of the Second Generation*, edited by Peggy Levitt and Mary C. Waters, 255–94. New York: Russell Sage.

Yosso, Tara J. 2005. "Whose Culture Has Capital? A Critical Race Theory Discussion of Community Cultural Wealth." *Race Ethnicity and Education* 8, no. 1: 69–91.

Zamora, Silvia. 2016. "Racial Remittances: The Effect of Migration on Racial Ideologies in Mexico and the United States." *Sociology of Race and Ethnicity* 2, no. 4: 466–81.

Zelizer, Viviana A. 1985. *Pricing the Priceless Child: The Changing Social Value of Children*. Princeton: Princeton University Press.

———. 1998. "From Useful to Useless: Moral Conflict over Child Labor." In *The Children's Culture Reader*, edited by Henry Jenkins, 81–94. New York: New York University Press.

Zhou, Min, Jennifer Lee, Jody Agius Vallejo, Rosaura Tafoya-Estrada, and Yang Sao Xiong. 2008. "Success Attained, Deterred, and Denied: Divergent Pathways to Social Mobility in Los Angeles's New Second Generation." *Annals of the American Academy of Political and Social Science* 620, no. 1: 37–61.

Zinn, Maxine Baca, and Bonnie Thornton Dill. 1996. "Theorizing Difference from Multiracial Feminism." *Feminist Studies* 22, no. 2: 321–31.

Zlolniski, Christian. 2006. *Janitors, Street Vendors, and Activists: The Lives of Mexican Immigrants in Silicon Valley*. Berkeley: University of California Press.

Zukin, Sharon. 2011. *Naked City: The Death and Life of Authentic Urban Places*. New York: Oxford University Press.

academic aspirations and achievements: Asian immigrant parents on, 129–30, 136, 168n30; immigrant bargain framework and, 20, 129–34, 138, 156; of new Latinx immigrants, 168n31; of nonworking and working children, differences, 133–34, 139; prejudice and discrimination impact on, 130; self-motivated, 133–34; street vending as "scare" factor for, 20, 137–40; of street vending children, 121, 131–34, 156; street vending parent resources to support, 141–42; street vending parents, for children, 61, 65, 67, 131–39, 141; street vending parents motivation tactics for, 20, 137–40

acculturation models: consonant, 169n44; dissonant, 19, 69–70, 149, 155, 169n44; immigrant children AGRs impact on family, 64–65, 155; parent-child relations and, 15, 19, 69–70, 169n44; for street vending children, 69–70, 170n45

adoptions, 167n24

African Americans, 85; turning to street vending, 50; working with their family, 158–59

age: housework responsibility relation to, 50, 102, 103, 167n25, 172n9; of research participants, 5, 5, 6–7; street vending responsibility relation to, 105

agency: collective, 3, 18; of street vending children, 28–31, 41, 72, 153. See also economic agency and role

AGRs. See American generational resources

Alcaraz, Lalo, 46

Allworth, James, 136

American generational resources (AGRs): acculturation impacted by, 64–65, 155; citizenship status as, 18, 72, 78–81; defining, 18, 69, 155; English language skills as, 18, 72–76, 75, 170n45; parent-child relations impacted by, 18–19, 64, 70–72, 156; as protection for undocumented parents, 78–81; of street vending children, significance of, 19, 64, 71–81, 155–56; technology and popular culture knowledge as, 65, 71, 76–78, 170n45

Anderson, Elijah, 118

Aries, Philippe, 166n16

arrests. See criminalization; police

artwork, 7, 165n9

Asian immigrants: academic/career expectations for children of, 129–30, 136, 168n30; discrimination in U.S. historically, 49; entrepreneurship and family work of, 12, 87, 89–90, 97, 98, 129–30, 136, 168n30; Latinx immigrants entrepreneurship compared with, 12, 87, 97, 98; night markets, 50

assimilation. See acculturation models; classical assimilation theory; segmented assimilation theory

Atkin, S. Beth, 90

authenticity, 44; customers desire for, 18, 43, 45, 46, 55, 57, 77, 155; gentrification contrasted with, 45

Aztlán, 173n16

baby strollers, 58
Baldick, Robert, 166n16
Beasley, Maya, 130
Becerra, Hector, 17
blogs. *See* social media
border crossings, 26, 49–50, 62
Boyle Heights, Los Angeles, 43–45, 149, 172nn1–2
boys. *See* gender roles; sons/boys
Bracero Program, 49, 173n28, 174n30
Brazil, 11, 14
Bush administration (2001–2009), 79

Canada, Geoffrey, 119
capital femenino, 99
career goals/expectations: of Asian immigrant parents, 129–30, 136, 168n30; criminalization of street vending impacts on, 144–45; criminal justice as, 121, 131–33, 135, 136; for empowerment, 131, 138; of ethnic minority parents for children contrasted, 129–31, 136; gender role in immigrant, 58; immigrant bargain framework and, 20, 129–34, 138, 156; immigration justice motivating, 80–81, 133; street vending aiding in, 114–15, 134–36, 143–45, 157; of street vending children, 121, 131–34, 156; street vending parents, for children, 61, 65, 67, 131–39, 141; street violence influencing, 132–33
celebrities, 11–12, 168n29
Central American immigrants: housework responsibilities for children of, 50, 172n9; in street vendor ratio, 50. *See also* Latinx immigrants; Latinx youth
Centuries of Childhood (Aries and Baldick), 166n16
Chiapas, México, 60
Chicago School, 14
childcare work: daughters responsibilities for, 36–37, 102–3; street vending relation to, 38–39

childhood: in agrarian societies historically, 165n15; debates/scholarship on concepts of, 10–11, 13, 147, 150, 165n15, 166n16, 166n20, 167n25, 168n26; in Middle Ages, 166n16; nurturing, global differences on, 11, 14; psychological interpretation of, 167n25, 168n26; as socially and culturally constructed, 13, 20–21, 147–48; sociological paradigm of, 168n26; street vending children reflections on, 83, 96–97, 150
child labor: celebrity, 11–12, 168n29; as exploitation, 166n20; industrialization relation to, 150, 167n24; legislation, 150; in México, 26; scholarship on "developing countries," 26; for undocumented immigrants, 16, 26. *See also* street vending children
Children of the Great Depression (Elder), 11
child stars, 11–12, 168n29
child work/labor. *See specific topics*
Chinchilla, Norma, 51
Chinese immigrants: academic/career expectations for children of, 129–30, 136; discrimination in U.S. historically, 49; entrepreneurship compared with Latinx immigrants, 12, 87, 97, 98
cholo, 179n2
Christensen, Clayton, 136
church, involvement with, 148–49
citizenship status, 5; as AGRs, 18, 72, 78–81; deportations regardless of, 80; "foreignness" treatment despite, 31–32, 98; immigrant families with mixed, 70, 78–81, 154; impacts of, 70, 72; for street vending children, 72, 78–81
city ordinances. *See* legislation/laws
classical assimilation theory, 14–15
class status/structure, 69, 70–71, 136, 169n44
"code of the street," 118, 120
collective agency/action, 3, 18. *See also* social activism

collectivist immigrant bargain, 20, 129–34, 138, 156
Collins, Patricia Hill, 169n38
Coming of Age in Samoa (Mead), 167n25
communal family obligation code, 84–90, 97, 98, 155
concerted cultivation, 136
Consuming Citizenship (Park), 87
credit scores, 145
criminalization: job applications impacted by, 144–45; of street vending, 47–48, 52–54, *54*, 80, 118, 144–45, 152–54
criminal justice career, 121, 131–33, 135, 136
Cuban immigrants, 12
culinary skills, 27–28, 33–34, 57
cultural capital, 15
cultural commodification, 51–52
cultural economic innovation, vii, 18, 43, 56, 59, 61, 63, 155, 170
cultural factors: in childhood construction, 13, 20–21, 147–48; behind street vending, 18, 26, 33, 41–42, 48, 55–56, 62–63
cultural inheritance, 62–63
cultural transplant, 56
cundinas/tandas/lending circles, 145
customers: authenticity as motivation for, 18, 43, 45, 46, 55, 57, 77, 155; diversity and views of, 44–45; English language skills influence for, 73–76, *75*; gendered views and responses of, 108–13

daughters/girls: childcare responsibilities of, 36–37, 102–3; flirting for, 112–13, 124; food preparation responsibility of, 101, 103–4; gang threat for, 124–26; on gender inequality, 105–6, 107; housework responsibilities of, 30, 99–104, 172n9; hygiene beliefs about, 108–11; protection and mobility restriction of, 20, 99, 107–8, *111*, 113, 123–25; sexual assault protection awareness of, 179n6; street vending responsibilities/role of, 19–20,

101–15, *110*, *111*, 117; street violence neutralized by, 125–28; virginity of, views on, 99, 108
Davis, Mike, 44
decision-making processes, 18–19, 67, 68–69, 86
demographics, research participants, 5, *5*, 6–7, 16–17
Department of Homeland Security, 79
Department of Labor, U.S., 150
deportation, 46–47, 79–80, 154, 173n28
Deported (Golash-Boza), 80, 154
Dillon, Karen, 136
disadvantaged and marginalized populations: intersectionality theory on, 13–14, 169n38; scholarship on, 13–14, 70–71, 169n38; street vending significance for, 41
discrimination. *See* prejudice and discrimination; racism
dissonant acculturation, 19, 69–70, 149, 155, 169n44
Doméstica (Hondagneu-Sotelo), 7
domestic work. *See* housecleaning employment; housework
downward assimilation. *See* dissonant acculturation
driver's license, 81
DVDs and CDs, vending of, 77–78, 123

East Los Angeles Community Corporation (ELACC), 156–57
economic agency and role: of Great Depression youth, 11; of street vending children, 2–3, 7, 8, 15–16, 28–29, 64, 67–68, 72, 81–82, 151
economic empathy: material motivations relation to, 90–91; nonworking children lack of, 90, 93–97; for street vending children, 19, 27, 33, 82, 90–93, 155
economic innovation: of street vending, 18, 42, 48, 56, 60–63, 155–56, 170n45; street vending as, historical view of, 18

economic mobility: dissonant acculturation relation to, 69, 169n44; of ethnic minorities, differences in, 12, 15, 156; for Mexican immigrants, 71–72, 173n28; research approach to, 71–72, 156; street vending children contribution to, 71–72, 81

education. See academic aspirations and achievements; school

Ehrenfeucht, Renia, 12–13, 44–45

ELACC. See East Los Angeles Community Corporation

Elder, Glen H., Jr., 11, 168n28

embarrassment: with housecleaning employment, 9; of parents, 95; for street vending adults in México, 59; for street vending children, 32, 65, 143

empathy: economic, 19, 27, 33, 82, 90–97, 155; physical, 68, 84, 91, 92

empowerment: career aspirations for, 131, 138; with English language skills, 69, 80; in street vending for children, 20, 87, 115

English language skills, 3, 8, 64; as AGRs, 18, 72–76, 75, 170n45; customers influenced by, 73–76, 75; empowerment with, 69, 80; police relations impacted by, 72–73; stereotypes challenged with, 74; of street vending children, 71–76, 75, 170n45

entertainment business, 11–12, 168n29

entrepreneurship: economic mobility in ethnic, 12, 15, 156; ethnic minority, comparisons of, 12, 87, 89–90, 97, 98, 129–30, 136, 168n30; Mexican immigrant, 12, 87, 89–90, 168n31

Espiritu, Yen Le, 99, 152

Estrada, Emir, 6, 6

Estrada, William D., 51

ethnic minorities: career expectations for children contrasted, 129–31, 136; economic mobility differences among, 12, 15, 156; entrepreneurship for, differences in, 12, 87, 89–90, 97, 98, 129–30, 136, 168n30; school curricula on culture of, 157–58; street vending historically for, 18, 48–51. See also specific ethnicities

Eurocentrism, 14–15

exploitation, 149–50, 166n20, 167n24

Fair Labor Standards Act (1938), 150

family. See immigrant families; parent-child relations

family bartering, 86–87

family-owned businesses. See entrepreneurship; street vending

family work, 2, 4, 4, 45, 53; in agrarian societies historically, 165n15; AGRs of children in, 19, 64, 71–81; of Asian immigrants, 12, 87, 89–90, 97, 98, 129–30, 136, 168n30; awareness, importance of, 158–59; as buffer to "troubled" path, 92, 149; children rejection of, 94–97; communal family obligation code with, 84–90, 97, 98, 155; dynamics and relations, understanding, 13, 21, 67–69, 151–55; empathy of children in, 19, 27, 33, 68, 82, 84, 90–93, 155; in Great Depression, 11; moral judgments and debates on, 12–13, 147, 149, 167n24; mutual support and protection with, 13–17, 88–89, 148–51; non-immigrant youth experience in, 8–9; parent-child relations impacted by, 16, 18–19, 91–93, 155; relationship strength and intimacy with, 91–93, 155; remuneration with, 86–88; research motivation from personal experience of, 7; self-supportive work compared to, 9–10; structural forces behind, 26–29, 41–42, 48. See also street vending; specific topics

farm work, 3, 8, 90, 155

Favela, Janet, 156–57

feminist scholarship, 14, 19–20, 30, 100, 103

Ferguson, Ann Arnett, 117

Fernández-Kelly, María Patricia, 152
fieldwork: direct participation in, 1–2, 6, 6, 47, 165n1; sites and situations, 5–6, 153, 165n8
Filipino immigrants, 99, 108
flirting, 112–13, 124
Flores, Edward, 116
Flores, Glenda, 130
"foodie" culture, 43, 46, 50, 57, 77, 155, 170n45
food preparation. *See* culinary skills; preparation, street vending
formal sectors/economies: Latinx immigrants exclusion from, 3, 26, 42; street vending income compared with, 62, 79–80

gangs: career goals influenced by experience with, 132–33; daughters/girls threat from, 124–26; family work influence on joining, 92; in Los Angeles, 116, 179n3; police response to threat from, 119; sons/boys threat and violence from, 118–22; street vendors fear of reporting, 118
gardening work, 3, 155
garment industry, 3, 58, 61, 155
gender, research participants, 5
gender roles: adoptions and, 167n24; customers response to, 108–13; for Great Depression children, 168n28; in housework responsibilities, 30, 99–107, 172n9; in immigrant families, 67–68, 72, 99–104, 106, 152, 172n9; in immigrant job opportunities, 58; justifications for beliefs about, 108–12; male privilege paradox and, 20, 105–6, 118–22, 128; patriarchal order impact on, 68–69, 72, 106; scholarship on immigration and, 152; for street vending children, 19–20, 24, 101–15, *110*, *111*, 117; of street vending parents, 58, 68–69; street violence relation to, 20, 117,

121–28, 179n6; unemployment and, 11. *See also* daughters/girls; sons/boys
gentrification, 45
girls. *See* daughters/girls; gender roles
Golash-Boza, Tanya Maria, 80, 154
Gold Rush (1849), 43
González de la Rocha, Mercedes, 151, 170n48
González-López, Gloria, 99
Great Depression, 11, 168n28
Gutierrez, Marco, 46–47

Hakas, Carlos, 45–46
Hart Celler Act. *See* Immigration and Nationality Act (1965)
healthcare legislation/laws, 61–62
health department inspections, 51, 53–54
Hecht, Tobias, 11, 14
home environment: childcare in, 36–39, 102–3; merchandise in, 37; preparation for street vending in, 1, 2, 6, 27–28, 33–34, 39, 101, 103–4
homework assistance: older children responsibility for, 37–38; parents resources for, 141–42, 152
Hondagneu-Sotelo, Pierrette, 7, 152
housecleaning employment, 3, 7, 9, 155
housework, 155; age relation to responsibility for, 50, 102, 103, 167n25, 172n9; daughters responsibilities for, 30, 99–104, 172n9; feminist scholarship on, 103; gender roles in, 30, 99–107, 172n9; sons/boys role in, 102, 103, 104, 107, 172n9; street vending work relation to, 30, 31, 36–39
Hsu, Tiffany, 50
human capital, 130, 141, 168nn30–31, 169n44
hygiene practices, 108–11

Illegal Immigrant Reform and Immigrant Responsibility Act (IIRIRA), 80
illness, 25, 83–84

immigrant bargain framework, 20, 129–34, 138, 156

immigrant children/youth: citizenship for, with undocumented parents, 78–81, 154; collective agency of, 3; communal family obligation code for, 84–90; as language brokers, 3, 8, 64, 69, 71, 74; as media brokers, 65, 71, 76–78; popular culture knowledge of, significance in, 65, 71, 76–78, 170n45. See also American generational resources; Latinx youth; street vending children

immigrant families: church involvement of, 148–49; communal family obligation code for, 84–90; economic role and agency of street vending children within, 2–3, 7, 8, 15–16, 28–29, 64, 67–68, 72, 81–82, 151; Eurocentric view of, 14–15; gender roles in, 67–68, 72, 99–104, 106, 152, 172n9; immigrant narrative played out for, 84–85, 91; language brokers for, immigrant children as, 3, 8, 64, 69, 71, 74; mixed-citizenship, 70, 78–81, 154; mutual nurturing within, 17–18; mutual support within, 13–17, 88–89, 148–51; poverty statistics for, 150; segmented assimilation theory on, 14–15, 18–19, 69–71; sociology of, 67–68; transnational family dynamics for, 27, 154, 171nn6–7. See also American generational resources; specific topics

immigrant narrative, 84–85, 91

immigrant shadow, 31–32, 98, 170n45

Immigration and Nationality Act (1965), 174n30

Immigration and Naturalization Service (INS), 50, 173n28

immigration justice, 80–81, 133

immigration legislation/laws, 50, 56, 61–62, 80, 173n28, 174n30

Immigration Reform and Control Act (IRCA), 50

income, street vending, 62, 67, 79–80

industrialization, 44, 51, 58, 150, 167n24

informal sectors/economies: for Latinx immigrants, 3, 7, 17, 25, 42, 89–90, 95–96, 155; secrecy with, 97, 157; for undocumented immigrants, 17, 25, 42, 95–96. See also street vending

INS. See Immigration and Naturalization Service

intergenerational family dynamics, 18, 21, 64, 147, 155, 158

Internet. See social media

intersectionality theory, 13–14, 169n38

Invernizzi, Antonella, 10–11

invisibility: of street vending children, 2–3, 97–88, 145, 152; of women immigrants, 152

invisible labor/invisible subjects, 3, 20, 143, 145–46, 152, 157

IRCA. See Immigration Reform and Control Act

Jewish community, 43, 172n1

Jiménez, Tomás R., 31–32

job applications, 144–45

Katz, Jackson, 179n6

Katz, Vikki, 64–65

Kettles, Greg, 44, 49

Kim, Dae Young, 130

Korean immigrants, 12, 87, 98, 129–30, 168n30, 177n6

language brokers, 3, 8, 64, 69, 71, 74

Lara, Ricardo, 48, 152

Lareau, Annette, 136

Latinos for Trump, 46

Latinx immigrants: academic achievements of new, 168n31; Asian immigrant entrepreneurship compared with, 12, 87, 97, 98; collective group lending circles for, 145; daughters of, mobility restrictions for, 20, 99,

107–8, *111*, 113, 123–25; in East Los Angeles, 43–44; formal sectors/economies exclusion for, 3, 26, 42; gender roles for children of, 99–104, 172n9; informal sectors/economies for, 3, 7, 17, 25, 42, 89–90, 95–96, 155; in Los Angeles, population statistics for, 44, 172n4; respect for women among, 126; stereotypes of, 31–34, 64; as Trump supporters, 46–47; unemployment rates for, 17

Latinx youth: deportation of parents for, implications of, 154; informal sectors/economies for, 3, 7, 89–90, 155; material expectations, impact of, 171n7; work ethic of, 32–33, 41. *See also* street vending children

lawyer. *See* criminal justice career

legalization efforts, street vending, 157, 173n19; Trump election impact on street vending, 47–48; 2018 victory in, 54

legislation/laws: child labor, 150; on healthcare for undocumented immigrants, 61–62; immigration, 50, 56, 61–62, 80, 173n28, 174n30; for native-born infants, 70; street vending, 47–48, 49, 51, 54, 152, 173n19, 175n47

lending circles/*cundinas*/*tandas*, 145

Linares, Lissette Aliaga, 158

Lopez, Nancy, 117

Los Angeles: Boyle Heights, 43–45, 149, 172nn1–2; gangs in, 116, 179n3; Latinx immigrant population in, 43–44, 172n4; Mexican population historically in, 43–44; Olvera Street street vending in, 51–52, 57; population statistics for, 44, 172n4, 182n5; street vending activism in, 156–57, 173n19; street vending historically in, 18, 49–51; street vending ordinances/legislation in, 47–48, 49, 51, 54, 152, 173n19, 175n47; street vending statistics in, 50; Trump election impact on street vending in,

47–48; University of California, 7, 157, 158–59

Loukaitou-Sideris, Anastasia, 12–13, 44–45

The Macho Paradox (Katz, J.), 179n6

MAF. *See* Mission Asset Fund

marginalized populations. *See* disadvantaged and marginalized populations

las Marías, 55, 59–60

material motivations, 171n7; communal family obligation code and, 88–89; economic empathy relation to, 90–91; for street vending children, 28, 31, 34, 41, 66–67, 68

math skills, 142

maturity, 27, 34–35, 41, 97, 146, 155

Mead, Margaret, 167n25

media brokers, 65, 71, 76–78

Menjívar, Cecilia, 152

merchandise: DVDs and CDs as, 77–78, 123; in home environment, 37

Mexican immigrants: academic achievements of new, 168n31; border crossings for, 26, 62; daughters of, mobility restrictions for, 20, 99, 107–8, *111*, 113, 123–25; economic mobility for, 71–72, 173n28; entrepreneurship for, 12, 87, 89–90, 168n31; in Los Angeles historically, 43–44; mutual support within families of, 13–17, 88–89, 148–51; stereotypes of, 31–34; Trump election impact for, 46–48; U.S. treatment historically of, 49–51, 173n28. *See also* Latinx immigrants; Latinx youth

México: Bracero Program between U.S. and, 49, 173n28, 174n30; child labor in, 26; internal racism in, 60, 176n65; *las Marías* street vendors in, 55, 59–60; remittances to U.S. from, 59; street vending historically in, 18, 26, 42, 54–55, 59–60; street vending stigma in, 59–60; street violence rehabilitation in, 119–20. *See also* U.S.-Mexican War

Middle Ages, childhood in, 166n16
Mission Asset Fund (MAF), 145
moral judgments, 12–13, 99, 147, 149, 167n24
Mortimer, Jeylan, 139, 143–44
motivations: behind research, 7–13; for street vending children, 26–31, 33, 41, 66–67, 68; for street vending parents, 24–25, 40–41, 56, 57–58, 62, 63, 79. *See also* academic aspirations and achievements; material motivations
mutual support and protection, 13–18, 88–89, 148–51. *See also* communal family obligation code

National Center for Children in Poverty (NCCP), 150
nationality, research participants, 5
NCCP. *See* National Center for Children in Poverty
The New Entrepreneurs (Valdez), 12, 156
New York, 18, 48
nurturing: childhood, national differences on, 11, 14; mutual, within families, 17–18

Obama administration, 79, 80
obligation. *See* communal family obligation code
occupations. *See* career goals/expectations; formal sectors/economies; informal sectors/economies
Olvera Street, Los Angeles, 51–52, 57
Orellana, Marjorie Faulstich, 8, 15, 103

parent-child relations: acculturation model and, 15, 19, 69–70, 169n44; AGRs impact in, 18–19, 64, 70–72, 156; economic empathy impacting, 19, 27, 33, 82, 90–93, 155; family work impact on, 16, 18–19, 91–93, 155; for mixed-citizenship families, 78–81, 154; respect in, 19, 27, 87–88; strength and intimacy in street vending families, 91–93, 155

parents. *See* street vending parents
Park, Lisa Sun-Hee, 87, 89, 129–30, 168n30, 177n6
patriarchal order, 68–69, 72, 106
peer relations, 32–34, 65–66, 93, 113
personality types, 29–30
Peru, 10–11, 158
police: career goals of joining, 131–32; enforcement and harassment, 52–54, 54, 80, 118, 120, 123, 127, 134, 152–54, 174n43, 175n44; English language skills impacting relations with, 72–73; gang threat response from, 119
popular culture knowledge, 65, 71, 76–78, 170n45
Portes, Alejandro, 15, 81, 169n44
poverty: "resources" of, 42, 151, 170n48; statistics, 150, 182n4
prejudice and discrimination: academic trajectory and, 130; of Chinese immigrants historically in U.S., 49; of ethnic minorities, differences in, 12; with street vending, 14, 18, 31–34, 44–45, 59–60, 144, 157; U.S. climate of immigrant, 151
preparation, street vending: clothing considerations in, 2; culinary skills in, 27–28, 33–34; daughters responsibility for, 101, 103–4; at home, 1, 2, 6, 27–28, 33–34, 39, 101, 103–4; peers experience of, 33–34
Pricing the Priceless Child (Zelizer), 165n15, 167n24
pride, 27–28, 66–67, 89–90, 143, 158
Proposition 187, 61–62
Pugh, Allison, 89

Quiñonez, José, 145
Quiroz, Liliana Estrada, 103

racial remittances, 60
racism: career choices for protection against, 130, 134; in México, 60,

176n65; segmented assimilation theory and U.S., 14–15. *See also* prejudice and discrimination

Ramirez, Benjamin, 45–46

reconquista, 46, 173n16

remittances, 27; from México to U.S., 59; racial, 60

remuneration, 86–88

research methods and sources: direct participation fieldwork as, 1–2, 6, *6*, *47*, 165n1; on economic mobility, 71–72, 156; fieldwork sites and situations for, 5–6, 153, 165n8; goals and inquiry focus for, 16; motivations behind, 7–13; time period for, 3–4, 6–7, 165n1, 175n47

research participants, 1–2, 165n12; ages of, 5, *5*, 6–7; demographics of, 5, *5*, 6–7, 16–17; recruitment methods for, 4–5; trust gained with, 4, 52

resources of poverty, 42, 151, 170n48. *See also* González de la Rocha, Mercedes

respect: in parent-child relations, 19, 27, 87–88; for women in Latinx culture, 126

résumés, 144–45

Reyes, Emily Alpert, 53–54

Rios, Victor, 118–19

Romo, Ricardo, 43

Rumbaut, Rubén, 81

safe professions, 130

Samoa, 167n25

SB 946 legislation, 48, 54, 175n47

schedules, street vending. *See* work schedules and patterns, street vending

scholarship: on childhood standards and theories, 10–11, 13, 147, 150, 165n15, 166n16, 166n20, 167n25, 168n26; on child labor in "developing countries," 26; on disadvantaged and marginalized populations, 13–14, 169n38; feminist, 14, 19–20, 30, 100, 103; on

gendered analysis of immigration, 152; segmented assimilation theory, 14–15, 18–19, 69–71

school: ethnic culture brought to, 157–58; farm work impacting, 90; homework assistance, older children responsibility for, 37–38; street vending balanced with, 38, 138–42; street vending funding, 65, 67, 98, 116, 129, 143, 145–46; summer, budgets, 36, 172n13; summer vacation work schedule, 35–36; teasing at, 32; for undocumented immigrants, 61; vending at, 23–24, 39; work schedules in relation to, 35–36, 39–41. *See also* academic aspirations and achievements

segmented assimilation theory, 14–15, 18–19, 69–71

sexual danger, 99, 125, 179n6

Smith, Dakota, 118, 124, 127

Smith, Robert, 99, 119

social activism, 3, 18, 156–57, 173n16, 173n19

social capital, 14, 20, 144, 168n31

social media: immigrant children as resource for, 76–77; street vending support through, 46, 57; as street vending tool, 76–77, 83

social skills, 29–30, 157

Song, Miri, 97

sons/boys: gang threat and street violence for, 118–22; housework for, 102, 103, 104, 107, 172n9; hygiene beliefs about, 108–11; street vending responsibilities/role of, 19–20, 24, 104–7

stereotypes: English language skills challenging, 74; of Latinx immigrants, 31–34, 64; of street vending, 31–34, 64, 97

Sterling, Christine, 51

stigma, 173n28; with street vending, 14, 18, 31–34, 44–45, 59–60, 144, 157; with street vending in México, 59–60 street vending, *4, 24, 25, 45, 53*; as academic "scare" tactic, 20, 137–40; age relation to responsibility in, 105; authenticity appeal for customers of, 18, 43, 45, 46, 55, 57, 77, 155; awards for, 57; career goals aided by, 114–15, 134–36, 143–45, 157; carts construction for, 165n2; childcare work relation to, 38–39; children rejection of, 94–97; criminalization of, 47–48, 52–54, *54*, 80, 118, 144–45, 152–54; culinary skills in, 27–28, 33–34, 57; cultural factors behind, 18, 26, 33, 41–42, 48, 55–56, 62–63; customer diversity in views on, 44–45; daughters/girls responsibilities and role in, 19–20, 101–15, *110, 111*, 117; for disadvantaged and marginalized populations, significance of, 41; discrimination and stigma with, 14, 18, 31–34, 44–45, 59–60, 144, 157; DVDs and CDs as products for, 77–78, 123; economic innovation of, 18, 42, 48, 56, 60–63, 155–56, 170n45; fieldwork, direct participation in, 1–2, 6, *6, 47,* 165n1; "foodie" culture impact on, 43, 46, 50, 57, 77, 155, 170n45; gang threats with, 118–22; health department inspections of, 51, 53–54; housework relation to, 30, 31, 36–39; hygiene practices, 108–11; income potential with, 62, 67, 79–80; as learned compared to culturally adopted, 62–63; legalization efforts for, 47–48, 54, 157, 173n19; legislation/laws, 47–48, 49, 51, 54, 152, 173n19, 175n47; in México historically, 18, 26, 42, 54–55, 59–60; "otherness" enforced with, 31–32, 98; parent-child relation strength and intimacy with, 91–93, 155; patriarchal order differences in U.S., 68–69; physical challenges of, 2, 28, 34, 40, 84, 91, 92; police interactions and

threat with, 52–54, *54*, 80, 118, 120, 123, 127, 134, 152–54, 174n43, 175n44; product diversity of, 43; racism experienced in, 32–33; research sites and situations, 5–6, 153, 165n8; at school, 23–24, 39; school funded by, 65, 67, 98, 116, 129, 143, 145–46; secrecy with, 97, 98; skills and opportunities gained with, 20, 29–30, 142–45, 157; social activism supporting, 156–57, 173n19; social media and online support for, 46, 47; social media as tool for, 76–77, 83; sons/boys responsibilities and role in, 19–20, 24, 104–7; stereotypes of, 31–34, 64, 97; street violence protection strategies with, 122–24; stress from, 84, 134, 138; structural forces behind, 26–29, 41–42, 48, 59; technology use in, 77–78, 83; Trump election impact on, 47–48; for undocumented immigrants, significance of, 17, 25, 28, 42, 79, 151; urban revival with, 44–45; in U.S. historically, 18, 48–51; violence with, 45–46, 116–28; work roles, overview of, 27–28; work schedules for, 17, 30, 31, *35,* 35–41

street vending children: academic/career aspirations of, 121, 131–34, 156; acculturation for, 69–70, 170n45; agency of, 28–31, 41, 72, 153; AGRs, significance of, 19, 64, 71–81, 155–56; on benefits of work, 113–15; childhood debates and, 147; childhood reflections of, 83, 96–97, 150; circumstances/motivations of, 26–31, 33, 41, 66–67, 68; citizenship status for, 72, 78–81; communal family obligation code for, 84–90; decision-making contributions of, 18–19, 67, 68–69, 86; driver's license significance, 81; economic agency and role of, 2–3, 7, 8, 15–16, 28–29, 64, 67–68, 72, 81–82, 151; economic empathy for, 19, 27, 33, 82, 90–93, 155; economic mobility contributions of, 71–72, 81; embarrassment for, 32, 65, 143; English language skills of, 71–76, *75*, 170n45; on exploitation perception, 149–50; gender roles for, 19–20, *24*, 101–15, *110*, *111*, 117; invisibility of, 2–3, 97–98, 145, 152; job application tactics for, 144–45; material motivations for, 28, 31, 34, 41, 66–67, 68; maturity of, 27, 34–35, 41, 97, 146, 155; on nonworking relatives, 93–94, 149; peer relations for, 32–34, 65–66, 93, 113; peer tensions for, 65–66; physical empathy of, 68, 84, 91, 92; pride of, 27–28, 66–67, 89–90, 143, 158; remuneration expectations for, 86–88; school-work balance for, 38, 138–42; social life complaints of, 96–97; technology and popular culture knowledge of, 65, 71, 76–78, 170n45; work ethic for, 32–33, 41, 87–88, 135, 145–46

street vending parents: academic/career expectations for children, 61, 65, 67, 131–39, 141; academic resources from, 141–42; academic "scare" tactics of, 20, 137–40; children embarrassment of, 95; circumstances/motivations of, 24–25, 40–41, 56, 57–58, 62, 63, 79; gender roles of, 68–69; relationship strength and intimacy with children, 91–93, 155; work ethic instilled by, 40–41, 135; work schedule for, 38, 39–40

street violence: career goals influenced by, 132–33; female presence neutralizing, 125–28; gender roles relation to, 20, 117, 121–28, 179n6; México as site for rehabilitation from, 119–20; protection strategies, 122–24; street vending and, 45–46, 116–28. *See also* gangs

stress: children empathy for parents, 68, 84; school-work balance, 140–41; from street vending, 84, 134, 138

structural forces, 26–29, 41–42, 48, 59

summer school, 36, 172n13

summer vacations, 35–36

tandas/cundinas/lending circles, 145

Taylor, Tamara, 158

technology: immigrant children knowledge of, 65, 71, 76–78, 170n45; street vending use of, 77–78, 83. *See also* social media

theft, 120, 121, 122

Thorne, Barrie, 15

translations, about, 7

transnational family dynamics, 27, 154, 171nn6–7

Trump, Donald: deportation fears under, 79, 154; Latinx immigrants supporting, 46–47; Mexican immigrants impacted by election of, 46–48

trust, 4, 52

UCLA. *See* University of California, Los Angeles

undocumented immigrants, 5; AGRs as protection for, 78–81; border crossing costs for, 26, 62; child labor significance for, 16, 26; citizenship for children of, 78–81; deportation statistics in 2011 for, 79; driver's license prohibited for, 81; healthcare legislation/laws for, 61–62; informal economies for, 17, 25, 42, 95–96; Latinx immigrants supporting deportation of, 46–47; school for, 61; street vending significance for, 17, 25, 28, 42, 79, 151; U.S. treatment historically of, 49–50, 173n28

unemployment: gender and, 11; Latinx immigrant rates of, 17; street vending as response to, 59, 155

United States (U.S.): Bracero Program between México and, 49, 173n28, 174n30; Chinese immigrants treatment historically in, 49;

United States (*cont.*)
    Department of Labor on family
    work for children, 150; family work
    in history of, 11; immigrant prejudice
    climate in, 151; immigration histori-
    cally in, 43–44; Mexican immigrants
    treatment historically in, 49–51,
    173n28; remittances from México to,
    59; segmented assimilation theory and
    racism in, 14–15; street vending his-
    torically in, 18, 48–51; undocumented
    immigrants treatment historically in,
    49–50, 173n28
University of California, Los Angeles
    (UCLA), 7, 157, 158–59
U.S. *See* United States
U.S.-Mexican War (1848), 43, 46, 173n16

vacation work schedules, 35–36
Valdez, Zulema, 12, 156
Vallejo, Jody Agius, 31, 70, 71, 84–85
violence. *See* gangs; sexual danger; street
    violence
virginity, 99, 108
Voices from the Fields (Atkin), 90

West Coast Vendy Award, 57
White Anglo Saxon Protestant, 70
women: immigrant job opportunities, 58;
    invisibility of immigrant, 152; respect
    in Latinx culture for, 126. *See also*
    gender roles
work ethic: of Latinx youth, 32–33, 41;
    parents teaching, 40–41, 135; for street
    vending children, 32–33, 41, 87–88, 135,
    145–46
work roles, overview of, 27–28
work schedules and patterns, street vend-
    ing: examples of children's self-made,
    35, *35*, 36, *36*; housework relation to,
    30, 31, 36–39; for parents, 38, 39–40;
    school nights and weekends, 39–41;
    school schedule relation to, 35–36,
    39–41; types of, 17; vacation, 35–36;
    weekend only, 36–39
World War II, 44, 49

Zamora, Sylvia, 60
Zelizer, Viviana, 10, 14, 150, 165n15, 167n24
Zhou, Min, 15, 169n44
Zukin, Sharon, 44

ABOUT THE AUTHOR

Emir Estrada is Assistant Professor of Sociology in the School of Human Evolution and Social Change at Arizona State University.